The GENE AUTRY BOOK

by
DAVID ROTHEL

Empire Publishing Company, Inc.
Route 3, Box 83
Madison, NC 27025
1988

Also by David Rothel

Who Was That Masked Man?: The Story of The Lone Ranger
The Singing Cowboys
The Great Show Business Animals
Those Great Cowboy Sidekicks
The Roy Rogers Book

Author
Casa Vaquero
7254 Bridle Path Way
Sarasota, Florida 34241

ISBN 0-944019-02-1 hardcover
ISBN 0-944019-03-X softcover
Library of Congress Catalog Card Number 87-82382

Manufactured in the United States

1 2 3 4 5 6 7 8 9 10

CONTENTS

ACKNOWLEDGMENTS

In a sense I've been preparing this book for over forty years. I started my research one Saturday afternoon at the Lincoln Theatre in Elyria, Ohio, when I was about eight years old. I've been working on it—off and on—ever since. It has been only recently, relatively speaking, that I've had help, and for that help I am deeply grateful.

I'm grateful for Gene Autry's generous cooperation when I was preparing *The Singing Cowboys.* My personal interview with him at that time had the benefit of providing additional material for this volume. Moreover, I am most appreciative of Mr. Autry's comments regarding the first edition of this book. My hope is that he will also be pleased with this revised edition.

I'm deeply indebted to Jimmy Glover, my extraordinary Gene Autry authority and collector, who provided many photos (especially for the memorabilia chapter), suggested and contacted people to serve on the film rating panel, answered my obscure questions regarding Gene Autry or pointed me in the direction of someone who could answer the questions, provided some Autry materials that I didn't even realize existed, and was, in addition, a friend I could always rely on for straight-arrow advice as the book progressed. Thank you, Jimmy.

The film rating panel is credited within the text of the book, but on this acknowledgment page I wish to thank them for their gracious and time-consuming efforts and for allowing me to utilize their Autry expertise to make this a more useful and meaningful reference book. Thank you, Truman Evitt, Jimmy Glover, Gary Parmenter, Charlie Rhine, Sr., Jesse Rush, and Jon Guyot Smith. My additional thanks to Gary Parmenter and Jon Guyot Smith for their discography materials. The television log is a result of the contributions of Jon Guyot Smith and Truman Evitt—many thanks, gentlemen.

The memorabilia chapter could not have been accomplished without the input of Bill Lane, John Stone, and Art Thomas—all of whom are mentioned in more detail within the chapter. Thank you, Stanley Martin, for your information and photos; thanks to C.A. Fuller of the *Daily Ardmoreite* in Ardmore, Oklahoma. The photos and column on Gene Autry, Oklahoma, are much appreciated. Thanks to Clint Brown for arranging interviews and serving as a guide during my Hollywood visit. Thank you, Ron and Linda Downey (The World of Yesterday), for publishing the first edition of this book and for being so helpful on this revised edition. Thanks to Aaron Grimsley for the generous loan of many fan magazines. Great appreciation goes to Rhonda Lemons of Empire Publishing for overseeing the production of this book. And many thanks to my good friend Ken Taylor for photos and other materials.

The Gene Autry On Tour chapter is a result of the generous cooperation of Gail Davis, Bert Dodson, Dick Jones, Jock Mahoney, Fred Martin, and Alex Gordon. A special thank you to Alex for allowing me to reprint portions of articles he has written and for the "on tour" photos which add so much to the chapter.

Many thanks to Joanne D. Hale, executive director of the Gene Autry Western Heritage Museum, for providing background information on the development of the museum.

And, finally, thanks to my best friend and wife, Nancy. I had mentioned to her during the early stages of the book that I was looking for something different that I could use to help catch the spirit and aura that was and is Gene Autry. A few evenings later she handed me the first of three poems that she would subsequently write for the book. I feel these poems express the essence of Gene Autry, of the American cowboy, and of us, the audience that remains eternally fascinated by them.

A FEW WORDS BEFORE SADDLING UP. . .

This is a book for fans of Gene Autry. I think I can safely assume that you qualify. Chances are you haven't bought the book, borrowed it, or taken it out of the library if your pulse does not quicken at the remembrance of Gene saving the heroine in the runaway buckboard or bringing the outlaws to justice in the final reel of the film just before the ride-into-the-sunset closing song. Starting with the assumption that you are a Gene Autry enthusiast, I have compiled a volume that should refresh your memory on many things and, hopefully, provide additional information on Gene Autry that you never knew.

Regarding the trivia sections, they are not designed with the idea that you are likely to answer the questions from memory. The sections are not so much a game as they are informational material in the form of questions and answers. Utilizing the Q & A format, basic Gene Autry career and personal information is provided. In addition, some little-known, unusual, and behind-the-scenes information is presented that you are likely to find intriguing.

The discography and the movie and television filmographies are as complete and as accurate as my research could provide. Probably no reference book is without error, and I'm sure this book is not an exception. However, I have checked my sources repeatedly and, to the best of my knowledge, the information is accurate. (One of the greatest fears a writer has is that he will discover a glaring error upon first perusal of his published book.)

Above all else, this book is meant to be an affectionate tribute to Gene Autry. I hope you like it, Mr. Autry.

David Rothel
Casa Vaquero
Sarasota, Florida
December 1987

DEDICATED

to

America's Favorite Cowboy,

GENE AUTRY

GENE AUTRY

His horse was a flashy chestnut laced with chrome
Soft eyed, soft mouthed,
Straight legs, broad chest,
A trot you could sit the while the miles slipped by,
A lope you could ease down into and relax.
At a flat out run you could turn and aim to shoot.
A cowboy's horse: quick to react, power in check,
Quiet, patient, thinking with his rider—told in ears;
Trusting and willing, following a silent aid secure,
But watchful lest his judgment be required;
So rode the man.

The man was a country boy, a small town lad
Gentle manners, quiet voice,
Easy smile, ambling gait,
Taught that the world had a right to expect from men
A certain sense of right and wrong and pride;
Taught to treat a woman with respect,
But to stand up for what was right when that was right;
A man whose word you knew that you could trust—told in eyes.
A lilting voice and a winsome way brought friends
And encouragement to share his gift of song,
And made a star.

The star was a singing cowboy, hat and spurs
Fast gun, hard fists,
Quick smile, ready tune,
A rancher or neighbor always there to prove
There are people who'll help no matter what the cost;
A Ranger or sheriff or lawman whose role made clear
That humanity's laws apply to every man.
His hopes and his joy in life rang clear—told in song.
His native charm and his hero's roles brought fans
Who flocked to see and touch and share the dream;
A hero was born.

A legend's lessons from this hero grew
Helping hand, kind heart,
Loyal friend, fearless foe,
Taught us that we should respect ourselves and those
Who lived by codes of honesty and care.
Showed us that right did triumph over wrong,
And helping others was its own reward.
Children copied lessons that he taught—told in play.
He was a man, a star, a hero to admire,
The champion on Champion whose name we spoke with pride,
The man they call Gene Autry.

NR

"He was a champion on Champion."

—Johnny Cash

GENE AUTRY'S

Cowboy Code

1. *The cowboy must never shoot first, hit a smaller man, or take unfair advantage.*
2. *He must never go back on his word or a trust confided in him.*
3. *He must always tell the truth.*
4. *He must be gentle with children, the elderly, and animals.*
5. *He must not advocate or possess racially or religiously intolerant ideas.*
6. *He must help people in distress.*
7. *He must be a good worker.*
8. *He must keep himself clean in thought, speech, action, and personal habits.*
9. *He must respect women, parents, and his nation's laws.*
10. *The cowboy is a patriot.*

CHAPTER 1
"AND HERE'S THE BOSS MAN HIMSELF, GENE AUTRY!"

That's the way Gene was introduced each week for many years on his "Melody Ranch" radio show for the Wrigley Company and CBS. You knew that, of course, and you are more than just aware of the many films made for Republic and Columbia Pictures, the television series, his many hit phonograph recordings, his razor-sharp business acumen, and that he owns the California Angels baseball team. All of these things and probably a lot more are known to you, and yet here you are (like me) seeking more information on this singing cowboy.

You and I are not alone, my friend. We who were the children of the thirties, forties, and fifties grew up with Gene Autry as our hero, and there are a lot of us who are still undeniably fascinated by "America's Favorite Cowboy." The evidence is all around. Check the phenomenal sales registered on re-releases of Gene's recordings from thirty, forty, and even fifty years ago; notice the sky-rocketing prices on *any* Gene Autry memorabilia. If one is lucky enough to find a collector who will part with a 16mm print of a "Gene Autry Show" television episode, he must be prepared to dig deep into his jeans for plenty of green. Videotapes of Gene's films are fast sellers, too, as are audio recordings of his old "Melody Ranch" radio series. If Gene makes a public appearance or comment of even the slightest "news" value, one can count on the press services to pick it up and carry it across the country. Amazingly, Gene Autry's popularity with his generations of fans continues though he has not actively performed for almost thirty years.

This phenomenon of popularity does not just happen. There has to be something special about a man whose presence touches so many people in such a meaningful way for so many years.

Gene Autry has never been one to talk a great deal about himself. So to better understand our subject, we shall have to turn detective and psychologist as we examine the evidence of Gene's life. Perhaps then we shall better understand him and our fascination.

There must have been a "specialness" about Gene that began to emerge even as he was growing up along the Texas-Oklahoma border during the early part of this century. He had a high school diploma going for himself in the way of formal education, but there can be little doubt that he specialized in the "horse sense" of the country folks with whom he grew up. His father was a horse trader and cattle dealer, and Gene, like his father, was destined to do a lot of "horse trading" in later years for radio and television stations; hotels; cattle ranches; a baseball team; and motion picture, radio and television contracts--just to name a few deals. Gene learned early on that the best business contract was the one where *all* parties involved were happy with the finally agreed upon deal. This became the credo he always followed in his business dealings.

The young Autry didn't have friends in high places to help him with his dream of a show business career, but somewhere along the line this relatively shy boy gradually acquired the "knack," if you will, for quickly making friends and gaining their trust and loyalty. His own trust of and loyalty to friends, business associates, and employees have always been a hallmark of his career. Gene's philosophy through the years regarding co-workers has been to find the best people available for the job at hand, to pay them a very good salary, and then to leave them alone to do the job. This philosophy has resulted in a staff that has remained remarkably intact throughout Gene's career. Two good examples are Carl Cotner and Armand "Mandy" Schaefer. Carl Cotner, Gene's musical director, was with him from 1935 until his death in 1987. Their whole association was based on a handshake. Gene met Mandy Schaefer when he first arrived for work at Mascot Pictures in 1934. Soon Mandy became Gene's personal supervisor for film production and remained in that capacity until the last film rolled through an Autry camera.

During his youth our would-be troubadour discovered the pleasures of strumming his Sears guitar and singing for the applause of the folks around his little community. Gene's grandfather, a Baptist minister, helped the boy with his vocalizing and gave him additional experience by letting him sing in the church choir. But this was small-time, to say the most, and Gene undoubtedly realized that his longed-for professional singing career was an extremely remote possibility. After all, this dusty Texas-Oklahoma border country was the equivalent of a show business Siberia. But here again is where a certain "specialness" within Gene helped to equalize the odds which seemed so much against him. Gene has always had a tenacity within him that is truly remarkable, that his later good friend John Wayne would call "grit."

Gene somehow—either as an innate personal characteristic or through an instilling process which took place during his formative years—acquired an insatiable desire to succeed in his chosen career fields—to succeed and to do it with grace. Gene has never walked over the bodies of others to make his way in show business or the business world in general. He has achieved and prevailed by doing his homework and by working harder than most others around him. Gene would probably attribute his successes to simply following the old-fashioned American work ethic.

Part of that Autry work ethic can be gleaned by examining the way in which Gene often piggybacked his various business activities. While on personal appearance tours, he would make innumerable contacts with the personnel of local radio stations that played his records. He would seek out and chat with the movie exhibitors who ran his films. He got to know these people on a first name basis and, as might be expected, they liked the cowboy movie star who wasn't too big for his britches, who would take time to stop by and "shoot the breeze" with them. Wise to the value of good press relations, Gene was always quick to respond to reporters' requests for interviews and photo sessions. He also knew what made a good story—like flying Champion across the country to make a rodeo date. *Nobody* had ever done *that* before! And then there were the fans. Gene always had time to shake hands with clamoring youngsters (of all ages, as they say) and to sign autographs seemingly by the thousands while on personal appearance tours. His style was always courteous and friendly, yet business-like. He never forgot that his business was the business of "show," and he looked after it. By the time his career began to flourish, he had already established a coterie of "friends" all over the country—radio record spinners, press reporters and feature writers, film exhibitors, business connections of all kinds, and a multitude of fans—who cared about him as a person who was "like one of the family" as well as a show business personality.

All of this attention to details, of course, required a tremendous amount of effort, time, and stamina. Over the years Gene's friend and film sidekick Pat Buttram frequently cautioned him that he was working too hard, pushing himself too much. Gene's response was always, "If it were easy, everyone would be doing it."

But it isn't just Gene's hard work and unbridled tenacity to succeed that have caused us to keep coming back to the man's films, records, radio and television programs, and to remain fascinated with him personally despite the passing of so many years. In the preparation of this book I had the pleasure of corresponding with Autry authority Jon Guyot Smith, who teaches a music course entitled "Gene Autry and The Singing Cowboys" at Mercy College in New York. In one of Jon's letters to me I felt he captured this final hard-to-put-your-fingers-on "specialness" that *is* the Gene Autry we still cling to. As Jon wrote:

> *Perhaps part of his genius lies in his ability to come across as "unremarkable"—comfortable (and comforting) and as more of a "friend" than a super-hero. On records he did not dazzle us with the spectacular or the unattainable. We sensed, even as children, that the man was very* ***real.*** *You met him, David, and I'm sure you will agree that* **sincerity** is *one quality Gene possesses in abundance.*

Art Satherley, the man who signed Gene to his first record contract, perceived this quality in Gene, too. As he commented, "The clear element was the sincerity which the people weren't accustomed to. Gene's singing was done in a manner that the public would accept in all its sincerity."

And so, it would seem, the "horse sense," the "knack" for making friends and gaining their trust and loyalty, the "tenacity" to succeed in all areas of endeavor, and the embracing of the public—all of these qualities of "specialness" are permeated by the most important quality of all—sincerity. It all seems so simple, so down-home American, so—what shall we say?—so Gene Autry.

CHAPTER 2
ONE MAN'S LIFE — ANOTHER MAN'S TRIVIA

If you can answer most of the questions which follow, you certainly qualify as a Gene Autry authority. The questions are designed not so much to test knowledge of Gene Autry as they are to provide a reference source of interesting Autry information. So, as Dr. Parker (Gabby Hayes), the proprietor and barker for the traveling medicine show in TUMBLING TUMBLEWEEDS, might have touted the local yokels:

What follows, friends and neighbors, is a giant comprehensive compendium of a multitudinous array of questions (and answers)—ranging from the picayune to provocative—covering the grand and glorious, Texas to Tinseltown, life and career of America's favorite singing cowboy.

If you find the queries too boggling for your brain cells, I have an amazing elixir here, first discovered by the Indians centuries ago and guaranteed to rejuvenate tired, overworked brain cells. Yes, my friends, just one American dollar, one Washington greenback is all that's required to purchase a giant bottle of my world famous Dr. Parker's Magic Rejuvenating Elixir. But first, friends and neighbors, go ahead, test your knowledge. I'll be waiting in the wagon with a fresh supply of my elixir just in case.

* * *

Q - When and where was Gene born?
A - September 29, 1907, in Tioga, Texas.

* * *

Q - What is Gene's real name?
A - Orvon Gene Autry.

* * *

Q - What were the names of Gene's mother and father?
A - Elnora Ozmont and Delbert Autry.

Q- Gene, the oldest child in the family, had three siblings. Can you identify them.?
A - Vida and Wilma were Gene's sisters; his brother was named Dudley. Dudley later changed his name to Doug when he tried his luck in show business.

* * *

Q - How old was Gene when he got his first guitar?
A - Twelve years old.

* * *

Q - Where did Gene buy his first guitar?
A- He bought the guitar from a Sears-Roebuck catalogue.

* * *

Q - How much did Gene pay for that first guitar?
A - Eight dollars cash.

* * *

Q - Who gave Gene vocal lessons, and how old was Gene at the time?
A - Gene was only five years old when his grandfather, a Baptist preacher, taught him to sing. Gene's grandfather needed singers in his church choir.

* * *

Q - What was the name of the medicine show Gene joined one summer when he was still a teen-ager with dreams of becoming a cowboy singing star?
A - The Fields Brothers Marvelous Medicine Show.

* * *

Q - How much did Gene earn as a member of the Fields Brothers Marvelous Medicine Show?
A - Gene earned $15.00 a week for the three months he stayed with the show.

* * *

Q - When young Gene couldn't find work in show business, he finally took a job in what line of work?
A - He became a telegraph operator for the Frisco Line in Chelsea, Oklahoma.

Q - What famous entertainer dropped by the telegraph office, overheard Gene idly singing, and encouraged the young telegrapher to seek a career in show business?
A - Late one night Will Rogers stopped by the telegraph office to send his newspaper column to his syndicate. He listened to the guitar strumming troubadour for several minutes and, as he was leaving, he told Gene, "You know, young fella', you ought to get yourself a job on radio." It wasn't long before Gene followed that advice.

* * *

Q - Gene's first radio work was for what station?
A - KVOO in Tulsa, Oklahoma.

* * *

Q - What was Gene's pay at KVOO?
A - Nothing!

* * *

Q - Gene became known by what title while he was singing at KVOO?
A - "The Oklahoma Yodeling Cowboy."

* * *

Q - When did Gene make his first commercial recording?
A - October 9, 1929.

* * *

Q - What two well-known brothers provided backup guitar for Gene at his first recording session?
A - Frankie and Johnny Marvin.

* * *

Q - What songs were recorded by "The Oklahoma Yodeling Cowboy" at his first recording session?
A - "My Dreaming of You" and "My Alabama Home." Jimmy Long wrote "My Alabama Home."

* * *

Q - For what company did Gene record these songs?
A - The Victor Company.

* * *

Q - Who was the person who first signed Gene to a recording contract?
A - Art Satherley, the head artists and repertoire man at American Record Company. "Uncle" Art Satherley would later become a legendary figure in the country-Western recording business.

Q - When Gene started to get recognition for his singing, he had the opportunity to sign his first record contract with either Victor, a top recording company, or a much smaller company, American Record Corporation. Why did Gene decide to sign with the smaller company?
A - "Uncle" Art Satherley was the new top executive at AMC in 1930. He advised Gene, "I'm just starting with American Record and if you'll sign with me, I'll do everything in the world I can to promote you. You'd be my first artist. Victor is a big company and they have several big artists that they have to concentrate on. I don't think you'll get the promotion from Victor that I can give you." Satherley's logic seemed right to Gene, so he signed with American Record Company.

* * *

Q - What was Gene's first hit record?
A - "That Silver-haired Daddy of Mine."

* * *

Q - Who wrote "That Silver-haired Daddy of Mine"?
A - Gene and his friend and fellow telegrapher Jimmy Long.

* * *

Q - How did it happen that Gene later became related to his friend and collaborator, Jimmy Long?
A - Gene married Jimmy's niece, Ina Mae Spivey, on April 1, 1932.

* * *

Q - Who sang with Gene on his hit recording of "That Silver-haired Daddy of Mine?"
A - Jimmy Long.

* * *

Q - What was on the flip side of the original recording of "That Silver-haired Daddy of Mine"?
A - "Mississippi Valley Blues."

* * *

Q - What was a major commercial outlet for the American Record Company during Gene's first years with them?
A - The Sears-Roebuck stores and catalogue.

* * *

Q - How much of a cash advance did Gene get for each recording he cut for American Record Company?
A - Fifty dollars a side for each record.

A GENE AUTRY SCRAPBOOK CLIPPING

THE VETERAN of the Melody Ranch group is Frankie Marvin, the quiet little fellow with the comical grin, who stands on the fringe of the group playing his electric steel guitar. Frankie doesn't take up a stance on the outskirts because he feels exclusive or has been banished from the inner circle, but because the acoustical requirements of his electrically controlled instrument necessitate his being a distance from the microphone. So often has Frankie had to explain his seeming separation from his companions, that now the other boys tease him by calling him "The Shadow," "Old Untouchable" and "Who Dat?"

Marvin takes this ribbing with superb good nature and, shifting his perpetual wad of chewing gum, can usually top his pals' remarks with a snappy if succinct comeback.

There is a great deal of sentimentality attached to Frankie Marvin's long association with Gene Autry. Years ago, when Gene was just starting his fabulous career, in the days when he was known as Oklahoma's Yodeling Cowboy, Frankie and Johnnie Marvin had already arrived as Big Time entertainers. The Marvin Brothers were Oklahoma born and raised, and it was only natural to them that they lend a helping hand to boost a boy from home, particularly anyone as ambitious and serious-minded as young Gene Autry. They permitted the newcomer to sing a few Western ballads as part of their act.

Autry never forgot this friendly gesture, and when he made good he sent for Frankie and Johnnie Marvin and prevailed upon them to join his outfit.

Johnnie became associated with Gene in a business capacity, but Frankie went into the deal as a musician with his trusty guitar. During the war, while Johnnie Marvin was entertaining troops in the South Pacific, he contracted a tropical malady that resulted in his death. Johnnie's passing was a blow to Frankie, but he found much comfort in the friendship with Gene that he and his brother had cherished over the years. An Autry show or picture would be incomplete without Frankie Marvin somewhere in sight, and although he is not noted for his loquacity, he is an integral part of any Gene Autry entertainment.

In his own right, Frankie Marvin, who plays by ear and admits that he never took a music lesson, is acknowledged one of the country's foremost exponents of the electric steel guitar. His interpretation of "Steel Guitar Blues" has been hailed as outstanding. He has composed and recorded dozens of novelty tunes, notably "Popcorn Papa," a juke-box favorite.

FRANKIE MARVIN

★ ★ ★ ★ ★ ★ ★ ★ ★ ★

Frankie at home is a solid, substantial citizen of Burbank, California, with a pretty wife and a just-as-pretty teen-age daughter. He has recently built a new house with which he has not yet had time to get acquainted. These days, when he's not plucking his steel guitar he is making plans for an old-fashioned housewarming as soon as he returns from his present tour.

(Publicity release from *Gene Autry Souvenir Program*, 1949.)

Introducing . . . .
MRS. GENE AUTRY

The Autrys at Home.

MRS. GENE AUTRY

WE'D like to introduce you, now, to the woman behind Gene Autry—Mrs. Ina Autry, his one and only wife for the past 20 years. She remains in the background of Gene's career, but nevertheless is an important part of it, a fact to which Gene is only too willing to attest. Not a career woman in the " Business World " sense of the word, Ina possesses a strong feminine intuition that has often helped Gene to reach a decision on a business problem.

One instance of this resulted in Gene recording what turned out to be his biggest-selling record hit. He had been asked to record this song but didn't think it was his type. Ina read the lyrics, liked them and persuaded Gene to record the song. It was " Rudolph, the Red-Nosed Reindeer " which has sold almost 5,000,000 records.

Ina accompanies Gene on most of his trips, eschewing the one-night stands though, since they are a pretty rugged venture even for a man. She keeps herself busy in their beautiful home nestled in the hills of Laurel Canyon in North Hollywood. She also watches over Gene's mammoth wardrobe, keeping his more than 300 shirts and trousers in repair, seeing that his pure white Stetsons are clean. And when Gene recently built a 22-office building and sound stage in the heart of Hollywood to house his various television and radio interests, he left the job of decorating the interior completely in the hands of his Missus.

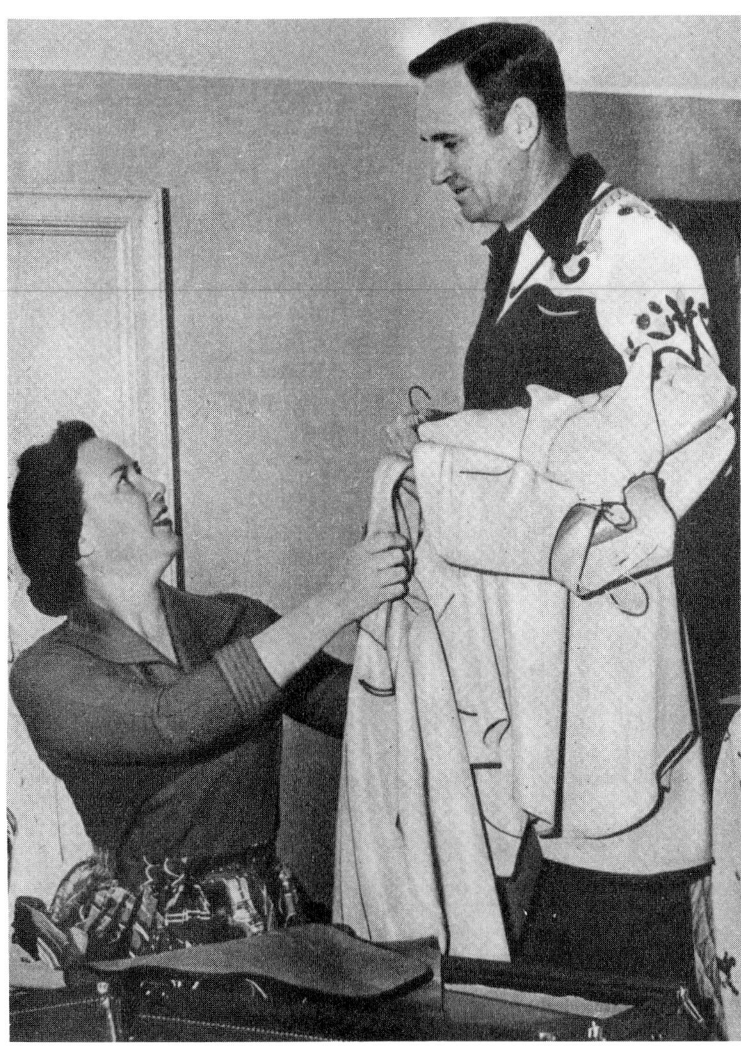

Gene and Ina were married on April 1, 1932. Ina Mae, as he always calls her, is the niece of a former railroad buddy, Jimmy Long. She was going to teachers' college in Springfield, Mo., and boarding with the Longs when Gene met her. Theirs was a long distance courtship. At the beginning Gene was touring the personal appearance circuit in the mid-West. Later, when he got a steady job on the radio in Chicago, he would let her know he was thinking of her by dedicating a tune to her. He finally proposed to her in a restaurant just after they had ordered their meal. They never did finish that meal.

She's pretty, brunette, vivacious and completely wholesome . . . a perfect partner for Gene.

The Autrys leave their car to attend a Hollywood function.

(The preceding publicity release originally appeared in *The Western Film Annual* by F. Maurice Speed, MacDonald & Co., London, 1953.)

Q - Gene's first regular national radio exposure (1931-1934) was on what program?
A - "WLS Barn Dance" from WLS in Chicago.

* * *

Q - What did the call letters of WLS stand for?
A - World's Largest Store. The station was owned by Sears.

* * *

Q - Gene's recording success started the tradition of celebrating a million record sales with a gold record. Gene was the first to receive a gold record. What was the song that won him the gold record?
A - "That Silver-haired Daddy of Mine."

* * *

Q - Who was the movie producer responsible for bringing Gene to Hollywood and getting him started in films?
A - Nat Levine. Levine produced Gene's first sixteen movies.

* * *

Q - Gene started his film career in 1934. What was the first film in which he appeared?
A - IN OLD SANTA FE.

* * *

Q - Who was the star of the film IN OLD SANTA FE?
A - Ken Maynard.

Gene is seen here in the early 1930s with the personal appearance cast from the WLS "National Barn Dance" radio program. (Notice numbers.) Number 3 is Patsy Montana; 4 is Smiley Burnette. That is Max Terhune on Smiley's right.

A very young Gene posed for this portrait which was to be used for publicity and for the cover of sheet music.

* * *

Q - Gene only sang a few songs in his first film. What was the *first* song that Gene ever sang in films?
A - "The Wyoming Waltz."

* * *

Q - How much was Gene paid for performing in IN OLD SANTA FE?
A - $500.

* * *

Q - Gene received a film offer from what other motion picture company prior to signing a contact with producer Nat Levine of Mascot/Republic Pictures?
A - Monogram Pictures. This offer from Monogram spurred Levine to quickly sign Gene to a contract.

* * *

Q - What was Gene's first starring film?
A - PHANTOM EMPIRE, a twelve-chapter serial released by Mascot Pictures.

Q - PHANTOM EMPIRE was a successful mating of what two film genres?
A - The Western and science fiction.

* * *

Q - What was the inspiration for the subject matter of PHANTOM EMPIRE?
A - As Gene related to your author in an interview, "The idea for the serial came up when a writer named Wally MacDonald went to have some teeth pulled. They put him under the gas, and somehow or another during the time he was under he dreamed up this idea of the PHANTOM EMPIRE."

* * *

Q - What was the name of the underground city in Gene's serial PHANTOM EMPIRE?
A - Murania.

* * *

Q - What was the title of Gene's first starring *feature* film?
A - TUMBLING TUMBLEWEEDS (1935).

* * *

Q - What was the first film in which Smiley Burnette appeared with Gene?
A - IN OLD SANTA FE. Smiley came out to Hollywood with Gene.

* * *

Q - What was the name of the character Smiley played in Gene's Republic films?
A - Frog Millhouse.

* * *

Q - What was the name of the character Gene played in all of his starring films except one?
A - Gene Autry. Gene started the trend of cowboy stars using their own names in their starring films.

* * *

Q - In what starring film did Gene play a character other than himself?
A - SHOOTING HIGH (1940) for Twentieth Century-Fox.

* * *

Q - What was the name of the character Gene played in SHOOTING HIGH?
A - Will Carson.

* * *

Q - Why did Gene play Gene Autry in films rather than some fictional character?

A - According to Gene, "It was not my idea. When I first came to Hollywood they wanted to take advantage of the fact that at that time I was a big record seller and they wanted to take advantage of the big publicity that I had built up in radio and my records. They started out doing that because I was a household name like Bing Crosby. Everybody knew Bing. I think by using my name in those pictures it was a big help for me to start with. But later on it was a sort of detriment, because to make a different type of a Western picture you'd have to take a name. I couldn't hit someone smaller than I was. I couldn't walk into a bar like a cowboy would and have a drink. If I did something like that, they'd say, 'Oh, no, Gene Autry wouldn't do that; he has too many mothers and grandmothers that knew Gene Autry as the good guy. You can't do it.' If I made a picture in those days like Clint Eastwood makes today, they would have drummed me out of Hollywood."

* * *

Q - John Wayne and Gene made the first two films under the newly formed Republic Pictures banner. What were the titles of the two pictures?

A - WESTWARD HO (Wayne) and TUMBLING TUMBLEWEEDS (Autry). Both pictures were made in 1935.

* * *

Q - Famed cowboy sidekick and character actor George "Gabby" Hayes appeared with Gene in only four films. Can you name them?

A - IN OLD SANTA FE (1934), TUMBLING TUMBLEWEEDS (1935), IN OLD MONTEREY (1939), and MELODY RANCH (1940).

* * *

Q - Who does Gene feel was the best horseman of all the cowboy stars?

A - Ken Maynard.

* * *

Q - In what film did Gene play his only dual role?

A - THE BIG SHOW (1936). Gene played movie cowboy star Tom Ford and his stuntman Gene Autry. (Gene played his "father" in a flashback scene in RIM OF THE CANYON [1949], but it would not really be considered a dual role.)

* * *

Q - THE BIG SHOW script was developed to encompass what special event that was taking place at that same time in 1936?

A - The Texas Centennial.

* * *

Q - Gene's first film contract with Nat Levine called for what weekly salary?

A - $150.

* * *

Q - What was Gene's main reason for wearing gloves in his early films?

A - Like many inexperienced actors, Gene didn't know what to do with his hands while emoting in front of the camera. Gloves gave him something to do—tug on them—thus covering his uneasiness about those things hanging on the ends of his arms.

* * *

Q - Which of Gene's films was based on a story written by Johnston McCulley, the creator of Zorro?

A - ROOTIN' TOOTIN' RHYTHM (1937). Jack Natteford did the screenplay.

* * *

Q - In which of Gene's films does the future Wild Bill Elliott (then known as Gordon Elliott) play a villain?

A - BOOTS AND SADDLES (1937).

* * *

Q - Why is ROUNDUP TIME IN TEXAS an incongruous title for this film Gene made in 1937?

A - Most of the film takes place in Africa.

* * *

Q - Pert Kelton, who played an important featured role in Gene's picture RHYTHM OF THE SADDLE (1938), created a role on television many years later which brought her and two other actresses much fame. What role did she create?

A - Alice Kramden of "The Honeymooners" with Jackie Gleason.

* * *

Q - Former silent screen star William Farnum appeared in featured roles with Gene in six films. Can you name the films?

A - GIT ALONG, LITTLE DOGIES (1937), PUBLIC COWBOY NO. 1 (1937), MEXICALI ROSE (1939), COLORADO SUNSET (1939), ROVIN' TUMBLEWEEDS (1939), SOUTH OF THE BORDER (1939).

Q - Who does Gene consider the greatest stunt man of all time?
A - Yakima Canutt.

* * *

Q - What was Gene's first merchandising item and what company produced it?
A - The Official Gene Autry Guitar was offered by Sears-Roebuck in the early 1930s.

* * *

Q - What early Hollywood occurrence convinced Gene that he should always wear cowboy garb?
A - He was disillusioned when he first met one of his cowboy screen heroes, Hoot Gibson, and discovered he was dressed in tacky two-toned shoes and a loud sports coat. Gene resolved to never let his fans down by maintaining the Western image they expected of him because of his movie appearances.

* * *

Q - Two actors who had previously played Tarzan in films appeared together in featured roles with Gene in COLORADO SUNSET (1939). Name the two Tarzans.
A - Elmo Lincoln, the first screen Tarzan in TARZAN OF THE APES (1918), and Buster Crabbe, who played the jungle swinger in TARZAN THE FEARLESS in 1933.

* * *

Q - When Gene threatened to strike Republic Pictures in the late 1930s for more money, Republic countered by threatening to replace him with a new singing cowboy they had under contract. Who was this Western warbler in the wings?
A - Leonard Slye alias Dick Weston alias Roy Rogers.

* * *

Q - When Gene finally settled his contract dispute with Republic Pictures after striking the studio, what were the financial terms of Gene's new contract?
A - He was to earn $12,500 per film with six to eight films to be made each year.

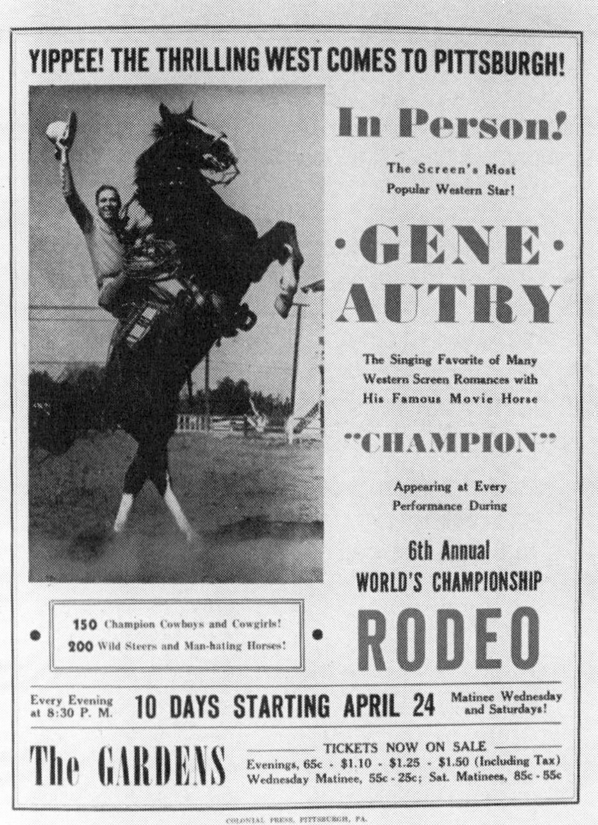

For many years Gene toured with his "World's Championship Rodeo" throughout the United States. The highlight of Gene's rodeo tour each year was his appearance at New York's Madison Square Garden.

Gene's triumphant parade in Dublin, Ireland. An estimated crowd of 750,000 people jammed the streets to see him. It was the largest single crowd ever assembled in Ireland.

Q - In what year did Gene make his first rodeo appearance in Madison Square Garden?

A - 1939.

* * *

Q - What was the most emotionally moving experience of Gene's career in show business?

A - Gene's 1939 tour of the British Isles, especially his reception in Dublin. Half a million fans came out to see his parade. His show in Dublin's Theater Royal was packed for all performances. After each show the adoring fans would jam the alley behind the theater and chant, "We want Gene." He would go out on the fire escape and sing them songs and talk with them. The last night was the most moving of all. The fans packed the alley, and, as Gene fondly recalled in his interview with the author, "I never heard anything like it. They sang 'Come Back to Erin,' and weaved back and forth, and it was a very heart-touching scene."

* * *

Q - One of Gene's biggest hit records was "South of the Border." What is the rather surprising fact about the two composers of the song?

A - The composers, Michael Carr and Jimmy Kennedy, are Englishmen who had never been to Mexico or the United States prior to writing the song. They wrote the song with Gene in mind, even though they had never met the singing cowboy before offering the song to him during his 1939 British Isles tour.

* * *

Q - How much did Republic Pictures pay for the film rights to the song "South of the Border"?

A - $1,000.

Q - When Gene was first introduced to Ronald Reagan in the 1930s, what advice did he give to Mr. Reagan?

A - He suggested that the future actor and President should stay in radio as a baseball announcer because he got to see all of the games free and got to hang around the players.

* * *

Q - In 1940 Gene ranked fourth among all Hollywood money-making stars at the box office. Who were the three stars who ranked higher?

A - Mickey Rooney, Spencer Tracy, and Clark Gable.

* * *

Q - Gene's horse Champion holds what aviation distinction?

A - He was the first horse to fly from California to New York. In 1940 Gene had to be in New York for a rodeo appearance two days after he finished a film in Hollywood. TWA agreed to fly the horse to New York so that he and Gene could make it to the rodeo on time. It was also a great publicity stunt!

* * *

Q - In Gene's film MELODY RANCH (1940) what product is the sponsor of his radio program?

A - Nose Posse, a head cold remedy.

* * *

Q - Who plays the commercial announcer on the radio program in Gene's film MELODY RANCH?

A - Fittingly, Jimmy Durante plays the touter of the sponsor's product, Nose Posse.

* * *

Q - What was the title of Gene's Sunday Newspaper comic Strip?

A - It was called GENE AUTRY RIDES!

* * *

Q - Gene's Sunday newspaper comic strip was written by what screenwriter who wrote many of Gene's films?

A - Gerald Geraghty.

Q - Who was the artist who drew the Autry Sunday paper comic strip?
A - Till Goodan. Goodan was a cowboy who turned to cartoon art. Reportedly, he was better at drawing horses and saddles than he was at drawing people. What do you think?

* * *

Q - When did Gene's "Melody Ranch" radio series go on the air?
A - January 7, 1940, on CBS.

* * *

Q - The "Melody Ranch" radio series was sponsored by what company during all of its years on the air?
A - The Wrigley Gum Company.

* * *

Q - Which of their products did the Wrigley Company promote on "Melody Ranch"?
A - Doublemint Gum was Gene's main sponsor, but occasionally he would also tout Wrigley's Spearmint Gum. Gene would generally finish a Doublemint commercial by saying, "I like it!"

* * *

Q - What was Gene's beginning salary for the "Melody Ranch" weekly radio program?
A - $1,500 each week. Eventually his salary was to rise to $5,000 for his weekly radio get-togethers.

* * *

Q - Here's an easy question. Gene's theme on the "Melody Ranch" program was what song?
A - "Back in the Saddle Again," of course.

* * *

Q - Lou Crosby was Gene's announcer for several years on the "Melody Ranch" radio program. He would generally open each show with what line to describe Melody Ranch?
A - "Where the pavement ends and the West begins."

* * *

Q - When Charlie Lyon was announcer for the "Melody Ranch" program, how did he usually introduce Gene?
A - "Now, here's the boss man himself, America's favorite cowboy, Gene Autry."

Q - Pat Buttram, the regular comic on "Melody Ranch" for many years, always called Gene by what name?
A - "Mister Artery."

* * *

Q - In addition to Pat Buttram, who was on the "Melody Ranch" program for many years to provide comedy and (unlike Pat) was asked to sing occasionally?
A - Johnny Bond.

* * *

Q - Who conducted the "Melody Ranch" orchestra?
A - Carl Cotner, who played the fiddle. (See Scrapbook Clipping on page 33.)

* * *

Q - What musical trio were regulars on the "Melody Ranch" program for many years?
A - The Cass County Boys. (See Scrapbook Clipping on page 34.)

* * *

Q - The last song that Gene sang on each "Melody Ranch" program was referred to in what way?
A - It was called the "Cowboy Classic."

* * *

Q - Did Gene name his own home Melody Ranch after the radio program?
A - Yes. Gene built the ranch back in 1940, the same year the radio series began. At that time the location was considered remote—way out in the San Fernando Valley. (See Scrapbook Clippings starting on page 30.)

* * *

Q - What was the name of the juvenile actor who looked like a young version of Smiley Burnette and appeared in several of Gene's films of the early 1940s?
A - Joe Strauch, Jr.

* * *

Q - Smiley played Frog in Gene's Republic series. What was the name of the character that young look-alike Joe Strauch, Jr. played?
A - Tadpole, of course.

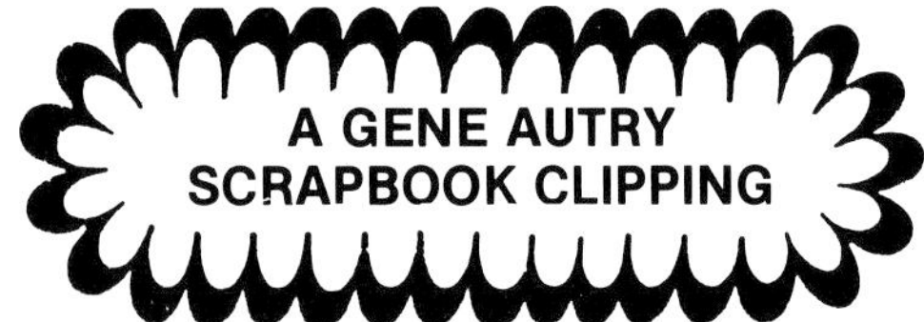

GENE'S RANCH:

bunkhouse, stables, corral — his 290-acre spread has all the trimmin's

■ There's a de luxe Autry "town house" out in Laurel Canyon, and there are a couple of other places in Texas and Arizona where Gene might hang his hat occasionally, but the place he and Ina Autry call home is Melody Ranch. Gene's dream-come-true spread 'way out in the San Fernando Valley. Back in 1940 (when he built it and named it for his brand new Wrigley-CBS radio show), engineers told Gene he'd be loco to set a house down in that spot. Streams pouring from the high mountain ridges above would ruin it in no time. The cowboy himself rigged the special foundation and piping system which have kept it snug and sturdy. His own ideas, too, were the design of the unique two-story high indoor training ring and the air conditioned 22-stall stable located so he can step right from his own parlor into Champ's, without setting foot outside. Inside, the house is all pine-panelled and loaded with Western-iana. There are built-in banks in the den

Gene, John Agee, trainer of all the Autry horses, chat in the ranch's tack room.

Gene and Ina Mae take Little Champ out for his daily exercise.

and a tooled leather-covered chair whose backrest is made of horns from half a dozen long-horned steers; one parlor wall is glassed-in, diorama corral scene, complete with hand carved cowboy figurines; a big bed upstairs boasts head and footboard fashioned from wheel and bow of an ancient oxcart. But Melody Ranch isn't just a show place. It's a real working spread—and the workingest folks on it are the boss man and his lady. Ina's always busy tending her flowers and plants; preserving, canning, baking, in the big streamlined kitchen. Gene does enough chores for three hands. When he's not training the horses, he's out mending a fence or repairing one of his 62 saddles, or there's always some picking or pruning to be done. Twenty-year-wed Gene and Ina have no young 'uns of their own, but there are always lots of kids around the place. The Autrys being the kind of genuine Westerners they are, the latchstring's always out at Melody Ranch.

Melody Ranch, the place Gene calls home, nestles in the heart of the San Fernando Valley.

(The preceding publicity release originally appeared in *Who's Who in Western Stars*, Volume 1, No. 1 1952.)

Gene poses here for a publicity photo for his CBS radio series, "Melody Ranch."

Carl Cotner

★In the Gene Autry show, the nearest approach to a "long-haired" musician is a young man who, to all appearances seems the least likely to be such. He is Carl Cotner, violinist (though he prefers to be called a fiddler) upon whom rests the responsibility for the music and musical backgrounds of the Gene Autry weekly coast-to-coast broadcasts and the Gene Autry Rodeos and personal appearances.

Carl began his musical career some years ago with every intention of becoming a serious violinist whose goal was membership in a symphony orchestra, or, possibly a recital in Carnegie Hall. He was sidetracked somewhere along the line by a depression and the fact that musicians have to eat.

Despite the fact that he had studied violin technique, harmony and all the nuances of musicianship at Cincinnati College, Cotner found that he could bend his fiddle to an old-time hoedown as adeptly as any backwoods Kreisler, and get paid for it, too.

Much to his surprise, Carl won a national country fiddler's contest, so he decided to forego such classics as the "Meditation from 'Thais' " and stick to "Turkey in the Straw," and a wise decision it was, for, before long Cotner was filling professional engagements at dances and gatherings all around the country wherever a "fiddlin' fool" was a prerequisite.

Gene Autry, who also was barnstorming at the time, came across Carl Cotner in his travels. Gene felt that he needed a good all-around fiddler, and asked Carl to join his group. It was as simple as that, and Cotner has been with the Autry organization for more than a decade.

At first, Carl merely played the violin as one of the Melody Ranch Boys. When the war came, and his boss went into the Air Corps, Carl enlisted in the Infantry. Because he was a professional musician he was immediately placed in charge of an infantry band, promoted to sergeant and shipped to the South Pacific, where he spent a long time making jungle-weary troops as music-conscious as they were battle-conscious.

With the end of the war, Carl resumed his work with the Melody Ranch Boys, but was almost immediately made director of music for the Autry broadcasts. In this capacity Carl conducts the studio orchestra and composes the "bridges" or incidental background music heard during the dramatic portions of the show. When the rustlers are up to their dirty work, Carl's right there with sinister sounding music, and when Gene Autry speaks softly to the pretty girl from the neighboring ranch, Carl endeavors to get the audience into a hearts-and-flowers frame of mind with some sweet melody. This jumping from one mood to another in a half hour's time is, Carl admits, somewhat disconcerting, but since Cotner has a corner on light-heartedness and good humor, it doesn't seem to bother him. He is the practical joker of the Melody Ranch hands. He never tires of devising elaborate shenanigans with which to bedevil his companions, all of whom arrive at every rehearsal and performance fully prepared for the Cotner cut-ups.

During the war, Carl married a pretty professional pianist named Georgia. She and her favorite fiddler live in a comfortable North Hollywood home, with a garden, a puppy and a brand new automobile, all of which, Carl says, he acquired by "being able to play 'Listen to the Mocking Bird' almost as good as any amateur fiddler."

(Publicity release from *Gene Autry Souvenir Program*, 1949.)

A GENE AUTRY SCRAPBOOK CLIPPING

THE CASS COUNTY BOYS

The Cass County Boys, as a unit, started with Fred Martin, accordionist, because it was he, then a staff musician for Radio Station WFAA, Dallas, Texas, who was drafted to fill a ten-minute interval of air time between programs. Fred had no formal musical pattern to follow, so he "ad libbed" with his accordion and a few songs. Jerry Scoggins, a fun-loving fellow with a guitar, who was also a staff musician, joined Fred just for a gag. Then, Bert Dodson, who slapped a mean bull fiddle, got into the act. The three boys blended very well and began to make arrangements, and before they knew it they found themselves booked for local shows. They named themselves The Cass County Boys, because Martin was born in Cass County, Texas.

Fred is a lanky six foot plus, soft spoken and friendly. He has a fine musical education, and nearly became a teacher of music. He plays other instruments, but the accordion is his specialty and he can squeeze anything out of it from Brahms to Boogie. He married a Texas girl, who sometimes travels with him on his many tours. Last summer the Martins became the parents of a baby girl, and between the new daughter and a lot of new ideas for his hobby of amateur photography, Fred can hardly wait to get back to his North Hollywood home.

FRED MARTIN

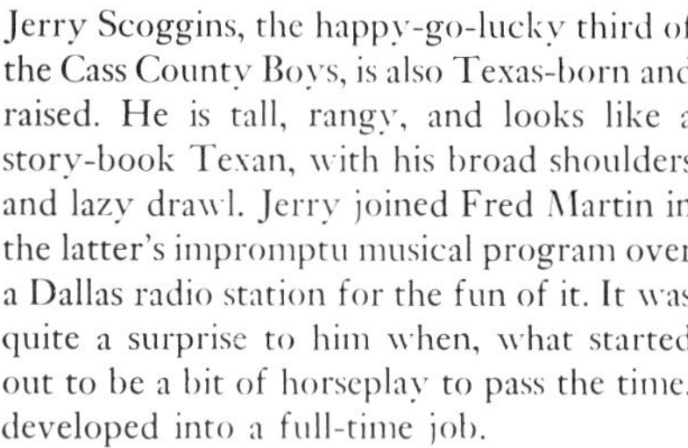

Jerry Scoggins, the happy-go-lucky third of the Cass County Boys, is also Texas-born and raised. He is tall, rangy, and looks like a story-book Texan, with his broad shoulders and lazy drawl. Jerry joined Fred Martin in the latter's impromptu musical program over a Dallas radio station for the fun of it. It was quite a surprise to him when, what started out to be a bit of horseplay to pass the time, developed into a full-time job.

Jerry is one of the best guitar players in the business, and has the kind of a baritone voice that makes bobby-soxers squeal with delight. Though he laughs a lot, and doles out charm in big portions, Jerry, nevertheless, is a serious musician intent on the career that chance flung into his path. Like Fred and Bert, Jerry is married to a Texas girl and lives in North Hollywood. He has a six-year-old daughter.

JERRY SCOGGINS

Bert Dodson joined Fred and Jerry and brought along his overgrown fiddle to the trio. Bert is the erstwhile chubby one of the three, but last year, as he was singing the Too Fat Polka, he suddenly realized that the words struck close to home. He went on a rigid diet, and now is a svelte happy medium in size between his two partners. Bert's great trial is getting in and out of taxicabs with his outsized music-maker. He has never tried toting it on horseback. Sometimes taxi drivers hurry down side streets when they see Bert coming. Despite such problems, Dodson is a cheerful, uncomplaining fellow who carries his burden philosophically.

Gene Autry hired the Cass County Boys while he was in the Army Air Force and heard them playing a USO hospital engagement. Just as the boys were about to sign on the dotted line, Bert went into the Marine Corps. Autry was so keen about the trio that he promised to hold a place for the boys when the war ended. True to his word, as soon as Gene returned to civilian life he sent for the Cass County Boys. By that time Bert was no longer a Leatherneck, and had rejoined his buddies. The three went with Autry and have been with him ever since on all his radio, rodeo, and personal appearance programs. Bert is married, the father of a small son, and, like his companions, lives in North Hollywood.

9

BERT DODSON

(Publicity release from *Gene Autry Souvenir Program, 1949.*)

Q - The fathers of Smiley Burnette and Pat Buttram had what in common (in addition to sons who were cowboy sidekicks)?
A - They were both ministers.

* * *

Q - Where did Pat Buttram and Gene first meet?
A - At the "National Barn Dance" radio program on which they were both appearing during the 1930s.

* * *

Q - When Gene guest starred in the Twentieth Century-Fox film SHOOTIN' HIGH (1940), what was his salary for the picture?
A - $25,000.

Q - Who was Gene's co-star in SHOOTIN' HIGH?
A - Jane Withers, who had a tremendous real-life crush on Gene at the time.

* * *

Q - What community in the United States changed its name to honor Gene?
A - Berwyn, Oklahoma, population 227, officially changed its name to Gene Autry, Oklahoma, on November 4, 1941. The idea was the creation of a Berwyn citizen named Cecil Crosby. Crosby got the needed signatures on a petition, got the U.S. Postal Department to approve it, and soon there was a Gene Autry, Oklahoma.

This picture was taken on Sunday, November 16, 1941, the day Berwyn celebrated the changing of its name to Gene Autry, OK. Gene was there to broadcast his "Melody Ranch" program live from the town. The actual date for the name change was November 4th, but Gene couldn't be there that day. No, the horse is not Champ.

Gene Autry remembered

By C.A. Lawrence
Lifestyles Editor

GENE AUTRY-It was Nov. 16, 1941—just 21 days before America was thrust into a second world war, but the only thing the people in this usually sleepy little town had on their minds was the biggest Oklahoma celebration since the Land Rush.

The folks here were celebrating the renaming of their town that day from Berwyn to Gene Autry. It wasn't much to get excited about except for the fact The Singing Cowboy himself was going to be in town and was going to broadcast his live radio show nationwide — right from the heart of Gene Autry, Okla., population 227.

At the time, Gene Autry the singer and actor was the hottest box office attraction Hollywood had latched onto. Oh, there were others like Clark Cable, Mickey Rooney and Spencer Tracy who everyone adored and Hollywood raved about. But, it was Gene Autry and his horse, Champion, who were pulling in all the dollars from the common folks at movie houses across the nation.

Gene Autry was everything a young man could dream of being. He was handsome; had a smile a mile wide. He could sing. He could ride. He always wore a white hat. And, yes, he ALWAYS got the girl in the end.

So, why not name a town after a guy like that? That's exactly what most of the people here wanted to do, especially after Autry bought a 1,200 ranch just two miles west of town and moved his rodeo stock here.

Shortly after Autry made the purchase, a petition bearing the names of most everyone in town was filed with the county requesting the name change. About a month later — Nov. 4, 1941 - Berwyn officially became Gene Autry when the chairman of the board of county commissioners signed the resolution at the Carter County Courthouse.

In less than two weeks, the people here had planned one of the biggest celebrations Oklahomans had ever witnessed.

It is estimated 35,000 people came to see Gene Autry in person that day. The town's present postmaster, Effie Hutchins, and Allene Haney, who owned the local store 35 years, were at the celebration and remember it well. They both have autographed pictures of the man who's "still the greatest."

"People were so thick you couldn't have the parade," Haney said. "It couldn't even get through town. They had it all lined up and when it got started there were so many people in the streets, they just had to stop it."

"Gene roped the old Berwyn post office sign and pulled it down," Hutchins said. "All the men had been arguing over who was going to get it and a little boy from Ada grabbed it as soon as it fell and ran off with it."

Everyone got into the spirit when word arrived that Autry would attend the event. A four-hour program including the parade that never really happened and a stage show were planned.

Gov. Leon C. Phillips announced he would be on hand. Noted national newspapermen made plans to be here and Life magazine said it would send two photographers.

The Daily Ardmoreite ran a special 24-page section saluting Autry's ranch and rodeo.

The Jordon Bus Co. offered roundtrip bus service from Ardmore to Gene Autry for 50 cents that day. The bus company also ran a special bus from the Ardmore Airport to accommodate all those who flew in for the celebration. Santa Fe Railroad, which still runs right through the middle of town, announced that at 2 p.m. the Berwyn sign at the depot would be replaced by a Gene Autry sign. All tickets and timetables thereafter would bear the new name.

Residents had cleared away weeds and leveled nearby fields to accommodate the thousands of cars they expected. People started arriving into town several days before the big event took place.

When the day finally arrived—an 83-degree Sunday—people rushed into town like floodwater. They came by car, train, horseback and wagon and they call came for one reason only—to get a glimpse of Gene Autry, the western star who had set the Hollywood record for the most fan mail in a given week—over 50,000 pieces.

Juanita Hutson, captain of the Berwyn girls basketball team, presented Autry with a scroll bearing all the names of Gene Autry's citizens.

Hutson, now Mrs. Juanita Motsinger, 60, of Grand Prairie, Texas, remembers the day well.

"The high school had voted me to be the one to give him the scroll because I was captain of the basketball team," she said. "I was on the stage with him during the program, but before it got started all of us who were going to be on the stage had been sitting in a train car together. They had all these train car sidetracked back behind the stage so we'd all be there for the event.

Motsinger said there were so many people in town, had they not been waiting in the train car, they never would have gotten through the crowd to get on the stage.

She said Autry talked to her while the group sat in the train car and she remembers him as being "very nice and polite. He just went along with everything and did what they asked him to do."

"I think I was 16 years old. It wasn't a real thrill for me because I was so scared," she said. "I said I'd much rather been home milking cows. I was real bashful. But, I'd love to get to talk to him now."

Motsinger, whose grandfather owned land next to Autry's Flying A Ranch west of town, said one of the greatest things about the entire celebration was all the free spearmint gum the Wrigley Company handed out that day.

"That was a real treat for some of the children because of the hard times," she said.

Motsinger said one of the nicest things she knows Autry did for the town was to purchase new suits for the Berwyn basketball team. "We really needed them," she said. "It was during the war."

Aside from Autry's appearance on stage which included a few songs and a speech for the crowd, the biggest event of the day was when his 5:30 radio show got underway and the nation was tuned in and turned on to Gene Autry, Okla.

For three short weeks, the tiny community relished in the limelight, and talked about the big day Autry came to Town. But, on Dec. 7 the Japanese bombed Pearl Harbor and America went to war. So did Gene Autry and his plans for the gigantic Flying A Ranch Stock and Rodeo Show went astray.

The ranch was sold and Autry only returned here a few times afterward. His movie and singing career slowed, but his name has continued to live on, especially in the hearts of Gene Autry fans all over the world.

The postmaster here said self-addressed cards and letters still come in from people everywhere requesting a Gene Autry postmark. Many people have attempted to write the famous actor by sending their letters to Mr. Gene Autry, Gene Autry, Okla., but unfortunately, they never reached the singing cowboy.

"I get a lot of mail for Gene," said the postmaster. "But, I just return to sender."

"You know, back when we changed the name of the town, Gene Autry was number one," she said. "Of course, we all thought so. Still do."

***(The Daily Ardmoreite, Ardmore,* Oklahoma, Sunday, June 23, 1985.)**

Q - When Gene broadcast his "Melody Ranch" radio program from the newly named Gene Autry, Oklahoma, on November 16, 1941, it was also a special day for the state of Oklahoma. What made that Sunday special for the citizens of the state?

A - It was the 34th anniversary of Oklahoma's statehood.

* * *

Q - What is the only Autry film in which future singing cowboy star Jimmy Wakely appeared?

A - HEART OF THE RIO GRANDE (1942). The Jimmy Wakely Trio sang in the film.

The sign on the General Store in Gene Autry, Oklahoma, proclaims the 1987 population to be 200, the elevation 729 feet. Business appears to be a little on the slow side this day. (Photo by C. A. Fuller)

We are looking south down the tracks of the old Santa Fe in Gene Autry, Oklahoma. (Photo by C. A. Fuller)

A wedding was held July 4, 1985, during the Gene Autry Days Red Bean and Chili Cook-off. The bride was driven into town in a horse-drawn buggy, and the couple was married on a platform set up for the band which entertained all day. The building in the background is the Gene Autry, Oklahoma, Post Office. (Photo by Joyce Franks)

In a sense, Gene was simply following his "Cowboy Code" when he enlisted in the service. As he wrote, "The cowboy is a patriot."

Q - What was the original title intended for Gene's film HEART OF THE RIO GRANDE?
A - DEEP IN THE HEART OF TEXAS. The studio had to revert to the other title when they discovered that Universal Pictures had the rights to the song.

* * *

Q - What was Gene doing when he heard the news of Pearl Harbor on December 7, 1941?
A - Getting ready to do his weekly radio show, "Melody Ranch."

* * *

Q - Was Gene drafted or did he volunteer for service in World War II?
A - He volunteered (much to the dismay of Republic Pictures).

* * *

Q - What was Gene's last film before he entered the service?
A - BELLS OF CAPISTRANO (1942).

Gene continued to do his "Melody Ranch" radio show during the War while he was assigned to Special Services. Because he made appearances all over the country, many of the broadcasts were done on the road. Here he is seen doing the program from KNX in Los Angeles.

Q - What was unusual about the way in which Gene was sworn into the service for World War II?

A - He was sworn in during a broadcast of the "Melody Ranch" radio program.

* * *

Q - What was Gene's duty during the War?

A - At first he was put to use recruiting, entertaining the troops, and selling war bonds. But Gene wanted a more direct role in the war effort when he enlisted. After earning his pilot's wings on his own time, Gene was finally placed in the Air Ferry Command co-piloting huge cargo planes of men and materials from such far outposts as North Africa, India, China, and Burma.

During the years Gene was in the service, Republic re-released many of his films so that their investment (Gene) would not be forgotten by his fans.

A GENE AUTRY SCRAPBOOK CLIPPING

Hi Buckaroo

The Army told him he'd done his job, but there was still a war on, wasn't there, and still plenty of homesick G.I.'s. . .

By PAT MURPHY

Coming home Gene found everything at Melody Ranch just as he'd left it, including best girl, Ina Mae Spivy, whom he wed 13 years ago.

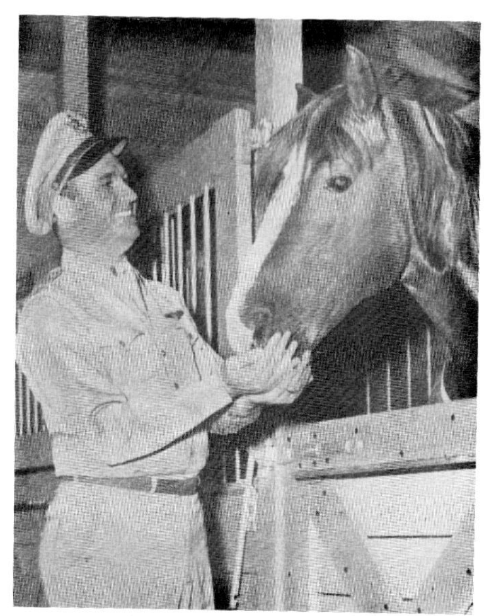

Champion's put on weight, "but, heck," says Gene, "so have I." Horse won't go overseas. Lacks the transportation.

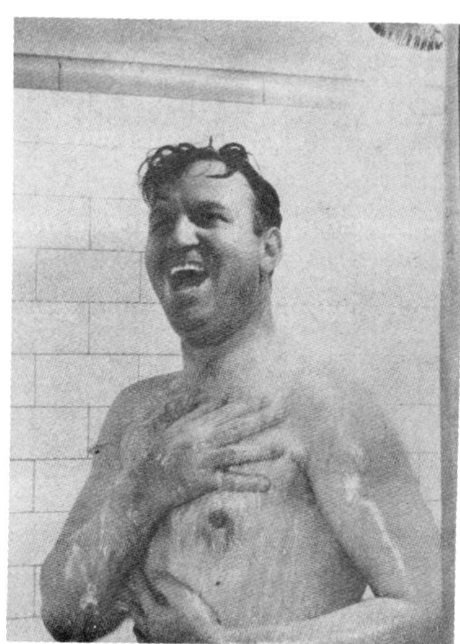

The rumple-haired guy in the big bed stirred drowsily, then sat bolt upright blinking his eyes sleepily. The sun slanted warmly through the window across the room. Golly, it must be late! He reached for his watch on the night table beside him. Ten o'clock! It *was* late! The C.O.'d be sore as the dickens. . . .His flight. . . .Why hadn't someone . . .

And then, "Hold on pardner," he told himself as his eyes took in the familiar pine-paneled walls, the comfortable, sturdy furniture, his boots over there by the dresser and on the chair beside it; neatly hung, his bright blue pants and matching butterfly-embroidered shirt. The aroma of freshly percolating coffee filled his nostrils. Ina! He sank back on the pillow grinning happily. The boss of Melody Ranch was home.

Gene Autry has been honorably discharged by the Army Air Forces after three years of service. His branch, the Air Transport Command was blessed with an excess number of pilots. Men who were qualified for other types of jobs within the service were transferred, others discharged. Gene was scheduled to go back into Special Services, where he began his army career in July, 1942, but there a problem arose.

Obviously the job for which Gene Autry was best qualified was that of entertaining troops, but there's a rule that says officers do not entertain enlisted men. Put Flight Officer Autry behind a desk? Preposterous! Now if he weren't in uniform — Uncle Sam decided Gene could do the rest of his war job best as a civilian.

Sure was swell to be home. Gene stayed all of two

Hi Buckaroo

Rumor has Gene in all sorts of picture deals with everyone from brother Dudley to L.B. Mayer. Truth is plans must await outcome of Republic suit.

Took him a week to get used to his embroidered shirts, bright trousers, after three years in khaki. His *At Mail Call* disc is juke box topper.

weeks! That was just long enough to round up a troup of fine western entertainers, get himself back in uniform—this time the USO olive drab—and then he was off to the Pacific. He didn't even need to wait for all the anti-disease shots customarily given for such trips, since the Army sees to it you have those regularly and Gene's were still plenty fresh.

The cowboy's galloping off to entertain overseas as soon as he was out of the Army is the first instance in which a veteran has immediately volunteered for another type of service. Gene happens to feel that just because the Army can no longer use him is no sign he can't do a piece more toward helping win the war. He knows how badly the boys at bases far from home need an occasional bit of cheering up and the sight of a friendly, familiar face to remind them the folks back home haven't forgotten. Gene knows all about that because he was there—in Tunis, Arabia, Iran, India. Then his job was co-piloting the ATC's giant cargo planes carrying men and supplies to the far-flung China, Burma, India bases, but many's the time, red-eyed with fatigue, tense and grimy from a tough trip, he'd be approached

CONTINUED

by the Special Services officer at a field with an apologetic.

"Say, I know you've had a rough trip, but could you possibly stop off in the day room and give the boys a song or two. It's been a long time since they've seen anyone from home." Gene would douse a little cold water over his face to stave off sleep and over he'd go where there was always a boy who had a harmonica or sometimes even a guitar and maybe if the guys at the base had been lucky there was a piano and they had a three or four-piece combo who knew how to bang out. *Mexicali Rose* and *El Rancho Grande* and Gene forgot all about being tired and the O.D. looked right past the clock that said it was time for "Lights Out."

Gene is just the ticket for a bunch of guys far from home and gripping like crazy to hang onto their sense of just *being* American. There's nothing in the world more American than an American cowboy. He symbolizes our great open spaces, our vast, rich lands, our wonderful freedom to come and go and do as we please. To those boys the name of Gene Autry means American cowboy and there is about his looks the sandy hair, the clear blue eyes, the wholesome open face—and about his person—the aura of the great American dream. Work hard, be honest, deal squarely and fairly and you'll get there. Gene meant home come to them.

Like most men who go overseas, he himself was fascinated by the strange places he visited, went sight-seeing for all he was worth, found most of the souvenirs far too expensive and was mighty glad to get back to the U.S.

In Egypt he rode a camel. Not only do the beasts not smell like Chanel No. 5, but comparing the comfort of their floating power to Champion's is like comparing a jeep to a Lincoln Zephyr. He saw the pyramids and the sphinx; in Tunis he stayed at the hotel that has been Nazi General Rommel's headquarters just a few months before, and he found his fans are all shapes and colors and sizes, and all over the globe. Everywhere he went great crowds of kids gathered and he found the custom of getting autographs is universal. He'd known his pictures were shown in far corners, but to meet fans face to face in Saudi Arabia, and Jerusalem and have them recognize him and follow him about the streets just as they do at home—well, it did something to him that made him mighty proud.

The China-India-Burma route is one of the ATC's toughest. Because of the great variety of weather the pilots encounter, a great deal of the flying must be done with instrument and that takes extra special handling which will give you an idea of how the Army rated Gene.

On his return from the CBI he was stationed at Love Field flying cargo across the country to the Eastern seaboard. He and Ina kept an apartment in nearby Dallas and it wasn't long before the friendly Autrys were a happy part of the easy social life of the field. When Gene could be home of an evening they'd have another flyer and his wife in for a game of bridge—the cowboy plays a sharp hand, too—or on an occasional gala evening they'd form a party of six or eight and treat themselves to dinner at one of the Texas city's fine hotels or restaurants. Most of the nights were early ones, for Gene had to rise and shine by four to be at the field, get his weather reports and check out by six.

At rodeo time in New York, when the big show came into Madison Square Garden, the show of which Gene's part owner, he and his chief pilot would swap trips with a couple of other boys and come in to see the show. Captain Hal—he and Gene called each other "Sahib"—is a native Texan who loves rodeos almost as much as Gene does. Sometimes during the show's long run they'd get to make it a couple of times.

One morning they arrived planning to stay for the night and see the show, only to find a change of orders awaiting them. They were to leave early that evening and the word had been passed along from their C.O. not to foul up his schedules by swapping off with anyone on the Eastern end of the trip—or else. They took off on the dot—and in the middle of New York's now historic hurricane, with a tail wind that practically blew them from New York to Dallas without benefit of horsepower.

"Yes, sir, that was a rough trip," chuckles Gene, "and I was plenty scared, but not half so scared as the first time I ever went up."

That was some nine years ago. He was playing a personal appearance engagement in Dallas when he received an invitation to appear on Rudy Vallee's radio show in Hollywood. The only way he could make it would be for him to fly. Gene wasn't sure he ought to. Planes, he figured, were pretty risky and definitely not here to stay. Once talked into it, he admits he fretted all the way to the Coast. But when he arrived in seven hours refreshed and unrumpled from the trip that takes two days by train, he decided there must be something to this flying after all. It was for him. As a civilian he was one of the top mileage passengers of American Airlines, and, of course, Champion was the first horse to fly across country when Gene brought him East for the 1940 rodeo. In the Air Forces Gene chalked up some 1800 flying hours of his own.

Mucho okay is what Gene has to say about the Army—and he's not kidding. He liked it; the friends he made, the experiences, fun and not such fun—but experiences, the wonderful opportunity to fly the very finest aircraft in the world—what more could a guy ask of anything. No, he wouldn't swap those three years for the million bucks and all the star lustre that might have been his had he stayed behind.

In choosing the Pacific, Gene picked the toughest section of the Purple Heart Circuit for his first USO tour. Unless you're 100 percent physically, you can't even make the grade to get there, much less withstand the heat, the dampness, the lack of even the most meagre living conveniences. But that's where he's needed most, so that's it.

"One good thing about it," he grins, "I guess I won't have to worry about my settin' up exercises to take off this extra fifteen pounds the Army grub put on me!"

Could be you won't see much of Gene 'til post-V.J. He expects to be mighty busy entertaining the boys 'til then. If he can sandwich it in, he figures he might do his radio show in the Fall and he might even make a couple of rodeo dates, but it will be some time before he returns to picture making. For one thing, there's that dispute with Republic Studios. That is still hung up in the courts. Gene will be making recordings right along, though. Last January, with the permission of the War Department, he resumed waxing for Columbia, with whom he's just signed a big new deal. The only other recording star with anything remotely resembling the plush terms of his new pact is the Old Groaner. That's right, too, because when you get into the western department Gene's absolute juke box and disc selling king.

The afternoon after his session at the separation center at Santa Ana, Gene came trudging up the steps of Melody Ranch loaded down with heavy army gear. Under one arm, conspicuous for its bright green wrappings, was a rather thick oblong package.

"Whatever have you there?" Ina asked after the greetings were over and Gene got his things together to unpack.

The cowboy blushed. "Er—neckties."

Ina laughed incredulously. "Neckties, why whatever for, Gene, when all you ever wear are kerchiefs?"

"I know," the cowboy was abashed, "but gosh, Ina, they looked so darn purty in the store—all yellow and red and bright blue—I just went in and got 'em without thinkin', I guess."

Ina tried to look severe. "Why Gene, for goodness sake, how many?"

"'Bout twenty, I reckon," numbled Public Cowboy Number One, beating a hasty retreat into his bunkroom. . . .

Just ex-G.I. Joe with the universal hankering to assert his khaki independence.

(The preceding publicity release originally appeared in *Movie Stars Parade*, September, 1945.)

Q - How many screen Champions did Gene use in his career?

A - There were three "official" Champions for films, but there were Champion doubles galore. The first Champion was a dark sorrel with a blaze face and three white stockings on its legs. The right front leg did not have a stocking. The original movie Champion died in 1947. When Gene returned to films after World War II, he introduced Champion, Jr., who was a lighter sorrel, had four white stockings, and a narrow white blaze on his face. The third Champion was used in the "Gene Autry Show" television series, the feature films of the fifties, and "The Adventures of Champion" television series. The third horse was also a light sorrel with four white stockings, but he had a wide white blaze face. There was also a pony named Little Champ which appeared in several of the feature films and made personal appearances with the "personal appearance" Champion.

The original movie Champion gives us an over-the-shoulder glance during snack time at Melody Ranch. You could always identify the original Champion by the distinctive blaze on his face and the three white stockings on all but the right front leg.

This is the second Champion, called Champion, Jr., who appeared in Gene's films from after World War Ii until about 1950.

This is the third Champion. He was used in the television series and the Columbia feature films of the 1950s.

Q - Is it true that Gene used Tom Mix's horse Tony for personal appearances?

A - Well, yes and no. As Gene told the author in an interview, "When Tom Mix quit making films, he went on tour with the circus. A fellow named Johnny Agee, who had been the top horse trainer for Ringling Brothers-Barnum and Bailey Circus for many, many years, had this horse that he had trained—what we called 'high schooled'—to do tricks. He called the horse Lindy because he was born on the day Lindbergh flew the Atlantic. He looked exactly like Mix's original Tony. When Tom Mix went on tour with the circus, he made a deal with Johnny. He hired him and leased the horse Lindy to ride in the circus. They called the horse Tony, Jr. After Mix retired, Agee came over to me—that was about '36 or '37—and had a talk. He said he'd like for me to use his horse Lindy when I did any stage appearances because the horse was trained for the stage and for rodeos. So we made a deal and Johnny went to work for me taking care of all my horses. He worked the original Champion, too." After the War Gene used a personal appearance Champion, Jr., not to be confused with the film Champion, Jr.

* * *

Q - In the Motion Picture Herald poll of exhibitors Gene placed first among "Top Money-making Western Stars for which years?

A - 1937, 1938, 1939, 1940, 1941, and 1942. When Gene returned to films after the War, he ranked second only to Roy Rogers from 1947 to 1954, the last year the poll was taken.

* * *

Q - What was Gene's first film after the War?

A - SIOUX CITY SUE (1946) for Republic Pictures.

* * *

Q - What was the basis for the squabble Gene had with Republic Pictures after his return from World War II?

A - Republic wanted to hold Gene to his contract signed before the War, including the extension for the years he had been away. Gene maintained that the contract should be considered in force during the War and that he should not be forced to remain in "servitude" beyond the original concluding date. Gene also wished to become his own boss by producing his films.

This is the "personal appearance" Champion, Jr. and Little Champ.

Gene's trainer, Johnny Agee, is pictured here with the Champion, Jr. which Gene used primarily for personal appearances.

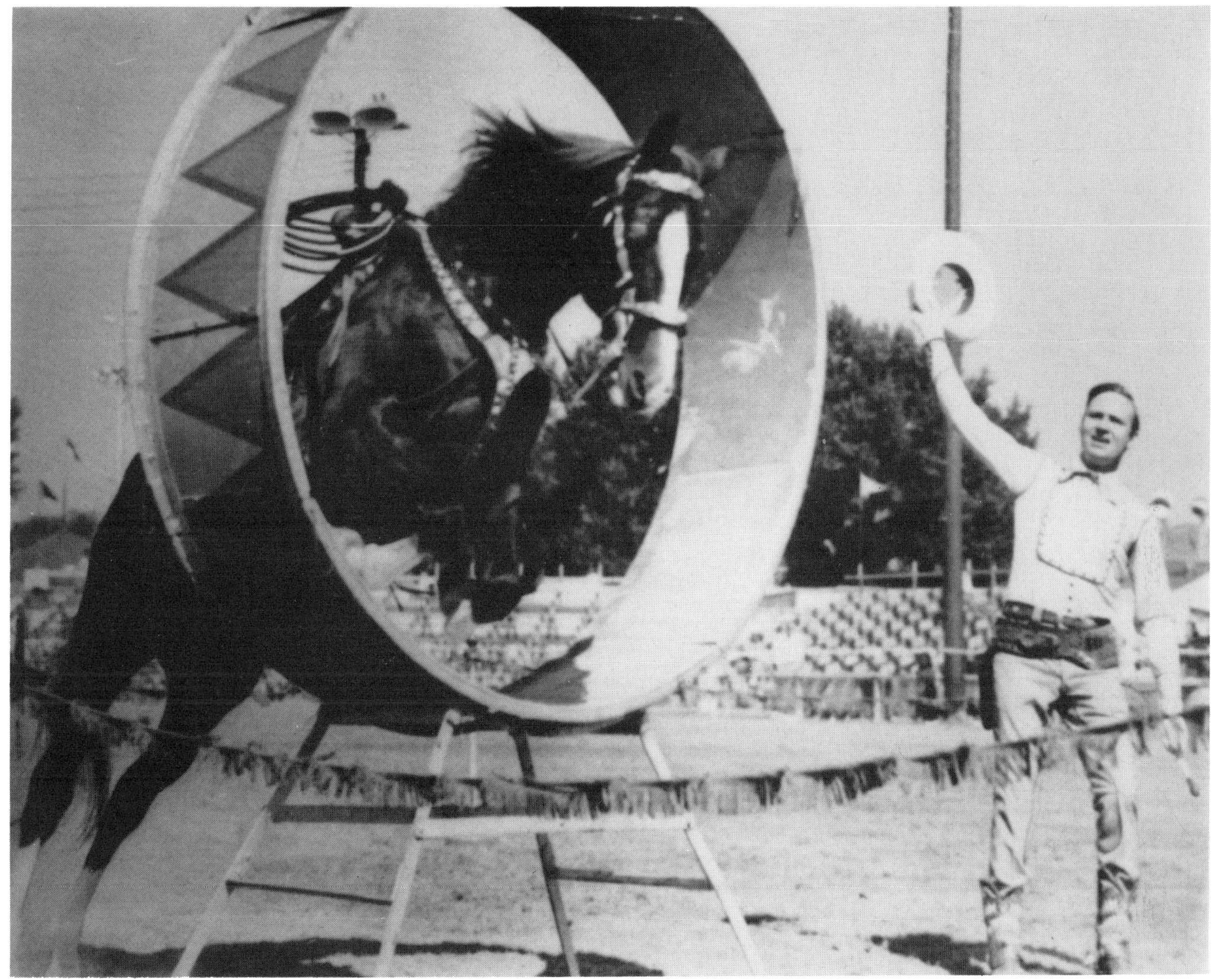

Gene is putting the "Lindy" Champion through his paces in this photo from the late 1930s. The horse can be seen performing this same stunt in Gene's film entitled YODELIN' KID FROM PINE RIDGE (1937).

Q - How was the dispute with Republic Pictures resolved?

A - Gene won his lawsuit against Republic but during the appeals by Republic, he struck a deal with Herbert Yates, the head of the studio. Gene agreed to make five features for Republic for a percentage of the profits. If Republic won the appeal, Gene would return; if they lost, Gene was a free agent. Gene won.

* * *

Q - What were the basic terms of Gene's contract with Columbia Pictures?

A - Gene had complete control over the films and kept half of the profits. As *Variety* reported the story:

Gene Autry's new Columbia deal will have him heading an indie production unit with a 50-50 profit split on four pictures a year. Pact, under which Col will supply all film-making facilities, takes effect April 1, 1947, and will have Gene Autry Productions releasing through Col for two years with openings for extension at the end of that period.

. . . Films will be budgeted at between $300,000 and $350,000 each by Col, which will also build lot facilities on their Valley Ranch property. . . .Film budgets at Col will be higher than at Rep. where cost was pegged at around $200,000.

WIN A TRIP TO HOLLYWOOD

Help Gene Autry solve his problem and be his guest for a full week in filmdom! Or win any of ten super prizes. Here's how!

Gene Autry has a problem. Throughout his screen career as Public Cowboy Number One his famous mount Champion has shared the spotlight with him. Now Champ is fifteen years old and Gene, returning to pictures after three years in the Army can't quite decide what to do about him. He's putting the dilemma up to his fans: Should Gene keep Champ in his forthcoming Republic movies? Should he train a new horse to ride the range with him? Gene and MOVIE STARS PARADE will award ten super prizes for the ten best answers to his problem.

FIRST PRIZE: A week in Hollywood as Gene Autry's guest with all expenses paid by him PLUS a complete fall outfit consisting of suit and selected accessories.
SECOND PRIZE: A fall outfit chosen by MSP's fashion editor.
THIRD PRIZE: An Elgin wristwatch.
FOURTH PRIZE: Deluxe Sheaffer's fountain pen and pencil set.
FIFTH TO TENTH PRIZES: Sheaffer's fountain pen and pencil sets.

In submitting your letter please observe the following rules:

1. Fill in the coupon below and attach it to your letter of fifty words or less explaining why you think Gene Autry should keep Champion. Or, if you think he should get a new horse, explain why.

2. All letters should be addressed to Gene Autry, MOVIE STARS PARADE, 295 Madison Avenue, New York 17, N. Y.

3. All letters must be postmarked no later than July 20th, 1946.

4. Anyone may enter the contest except employees of Bilbara Publishing Company or affiliated companies.

5. Decision of the judges will be final and all lettets become property of Bilbara Publishing Co. and none can be returned. The judges will be W. M. Cotton, MSP's publisher, Muriel Babcock, Editorial Director, and MSP's editorial staff.

6. In case of duplicate entries the one postmarked first receives the prize.

Dear Gene:

I think you should keep Champion. ☐
I think you should have a new horse. ☐

I attach my letter to this official contest entry blank.

My name is..............................

I live at..............................

City...... Zone.... State.... My age....

This "Win a Trip to Hollywood" contest appeared in *Movie Stars Parade* in the Spring of 1946.

GENE'S HORSES:

champ and little champ do everything but talk

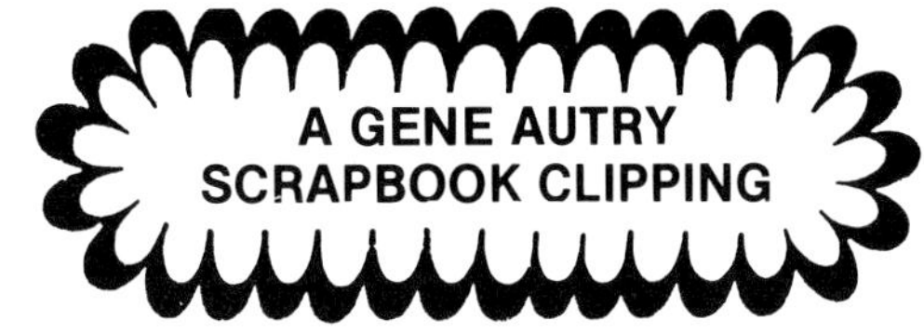

■Take the word of his trainer, John Agee, whose experience dates through Ringling's Circus 'way back to Tom Mix and Tony, Champion has the world's largest repertory of tricks. He dances to any rhythm, kneels, marches, bows, unties knots with his teeth, laughs, kisses, and "signs" his name—all on cue. That's far from all. He has two show specialties many trainers will tell you no horse can perform. One is a jump through a hoop of flame; the other, a crashing leap through a paper poster bearing his and Gene's likeness on the reverse side. Horses are as skittish of fire as people, and if you thought you were about to crash through a solid wall (the paper seems just that to a horse) could anyone teach you to do it? Champ's smart, but it's his confidence in Gene that counts. Even a horse knows he can trust a man who names him beneficiary of a $25,000 life insurance policy.

Couple of years ago, Gene decided Little Champion was ready to go to work. He and Johnny taught the youngster some simple tricks like walking a plank and jumping through a low hoop. Out home at Melody Ranch he performs like a veteran. Before an audience he's all hambone. Stumbling, hesitating, balking, he conveys the idea his stint is really tough and he's such an innocent-looking little critter he makes the customers eat it up, all but stealing the old man's thunder. Champ doesn't worry though. After all, he's the immortal whose hoofprints are in Grauman's cement; who wrote equine history flying Coast to Coast (in 1940); the star who gets 1,000 fan letters per month; and can draw a crowd of thousands, even without Gene.

(The above publicity release orginally appeared in *Who's Who in Western Stars*, Volume 1, No. 1, 1952.)

In this picture from the Grauman's Chinese Theatre ceremony, Gene is riding the Champion, Jr. that he used for most of his personal appearances.

Q - In what year were Gene's boot and Champion's hoof prints immortalized in cement in the courtyard of Grauman's Chinese Theatre?

A - 1949.

* * *

Q - What was Gene's own personal favorite from the long list of films that he made?

A - Gene's answer might change depending on his mood when asked, but his frequent response over the years has been THE LAST ROUNDUP (1947). It was his first picture for Columbia under his own banner, Gene Autry Productions, Inc.

* * *

Q - Although Gene had many comic characters in his feature films, he really only had two regular comic sidekicks throughout his career. Who were they?

A - Smiley Burnette appeared with Gene in 58 features plus two serials (MYSTERY MOUNTAIN starring Key Maynard and PHANTOM EMPIRE) and their first film roles supporting Ken Maynard in IN OLD SANTA FE. Pat Buttram appeared with Gene in 17 features and most of the 91 "Gene Autry Show" television episodes. (See Scrapbook Clippings on pages 56 and 57.)

* * *

Q - What was the only Autry film in which the then juvenile actor Robert "Bobby" Blake appeared?

A - THE LAST ROUNDUP.

* * *

Q - How many feature films did Gene make in color?

A - Two: THE STRAWBERRY ROAN (1948) and THE BIG SOMBRERO (1949). Many of his Columbia features were released in a sepia tone, but that would not qualify as color in the generally accepted meaning.

* * *

Q - What color process did Gene use for his two color features?

A - Cinecolor.

* * *

Q - Gene utilized the talents of many former cowboy film stars in feature roles in his films. How many can you name?

A - Those actors included Bob Steele, Robert Livingston, Jack Holt, Russ Hayden, Tom Keene, and Kirby Grant.

Q - In THE STRAWBERRY ROAN Gene rode a pinto horse through much of the film that was to become the star horse for another cowboy hero. What future star horse did Gene ride?

A - The horse was the beautiful pinto ridden by the Cisco Kid (Duncan Renaldo) in 156 television episodes. Cisco called the horse Diablo.

* * *

Q - In which of his films did Gene sing his hit song, "Here Comes Santa Claus"?

A - THE COWBOY AND THE INDIANS (1949).

* * *

Q - Juvenile actor Frankie Darro, who was featured with Gene in PHANTOM EMPIRE, returned to play a role in another Autry film years later. What was the film?

A - SONS OF NEW MEXICO (1950).

* * *

Q - What was Gene's biggest selling record?

A - "Rudolph the Red-nosed Reindeer." As of 1977 the record had sold over ten million copies. Gene's wife Ina talked him into recording the song after Gene dismissed it as just another novelty song. Ina was touched by the story of the song which reminded her of the Ugly Duckling story. Remember, the other reindeer "laughed and called him names" until he saved Christmas eve. Gene has a platinum record for "Rudolph," which stands for the five-millionth copy sold.

GENE'S BUDDIES:

"out where a friend is a friend"—

PAT BUTTRAM knows that Gene's the kind of man who sticks by his friends—in good times or bad, no matter what.

gene's loyal as they come

FRANKIE MARVIN and CARL COTNER are among Gene's oldest friends, with him all the time.

■ Look down the list of any cast headed by Gene Autry and you'll see a brace of familiar names again and again . . . Smiley Burnette, Johnny Bond, Pat Buttram, Carl Cotner, Frankie Marvin, The Cass County Boys. Glance behind scenes at the production-business end of Autry Enterprises, and year after year you'll find the same folks. It's the biggest family act in show business, yet no two are related by blood, only by their affection and loyalty to Gene, and vice versa. Gene and Smiley were saddle pals back in Chicago radio, went West together, made sixty-three films before war, contract commitments broke it up. They're back together now on p.a. tours, in the movie **Whirlwind.** Only one performer's photo hangs on the wall in Gene's big office on Sunset Blvd. It's simply but eloquently inscribed, "To Gene, Thanks For Everything, Smiley." Pat Buttram, funnyman with Gene on radio, TV and movies, didn't have to worry about the bills during recent hospitalization. Gene quietly picked up the tabs and held Pat's show spots for him 'til he was well. The Cass County Boys met up with the cowboy while they were appearing on the same recruiting show during the early part of the last war. Gene liked the way they played, told them they had a job with him come peace and resumption of his air activities. It was almost five years later and one of the fellows Bert Dodson was in service, when Gene long distanced them and then left his offer open until Bert could rejoin them. Frankie Marvin, electric guitarist, daring horseman, comedian and all around Mr. Talent (he's the chap who makes Rudolph, The Rednosed Reindeer prance during the Autry p.a. song presentation) is one of the oldest Autry cohorts. Frankie and his brother Johnnie were in New York vaudeville when Gene made his first trip East and they helped him get his first recording audition. Johnnie died during the war, but you'll never see—or hear, an Autry production without Frankie in it somewhere. Don't get the idea that any of Gene's gang are simply hangers-on. Each one is a talented performer in his own right. Gene's loyalty is based in part on his appreciation of their ability, and he's humbly grateful for their faith in sticking with him. It's easy to see that "Out where a friend is a friend" isn't just part of a song to Gene, it's a way of life.

JOHNNY BOND lends his melody to Gene's shows and in return gets that well-known Autry loyalty.

THE CASS COUNTY BOYS and Gene. Fred Martin, and Jerry Scoggins.

1937: SMILEY BURNETTE and Gene in an early picture.

1951: SMILEY and Gene, still pals, after nearly 15 years.

(The preceding publicity release originally appeared in *Who's Who in Western Stars*, Volume 1, No. 1 1952.)

Q - What date did the "Gene Autry Show" television series go on the air?
A - July 23, 1950, on CBS.

* * *

Q - What was the name of Gene's television production company?
A - Flying A Productions.

* * *

Q - Composer Stan Jones had a bit part in an Autry film which bore the title of one of Jones' songs. What was the film/song title?
A - WHIRLWIND (1951). Jones also wrote another song which became the title of an Autry feature film—RIDERS IN THE SKY (1949).

* * *

Q - What silent movie star (who played Messala in the original BEN HUR of 1926) rounded out his career playing a featured role in a Gene Autry Western?
A - Francis X. Bushman in APACHE COUNTRY (1952).

* * *

Q - Many talented young performers, future stars, got their start or early training in Gene's films. How many such performers can you name?
A - The list would include Dick Weston (Roy Rogers) and The Sons of the Pioneers, Ann Rutherford, Max Terhune, Jock Mahoney, Dick Jones, Gail Davis, Clayton Moore, Jay Silverheels, Hugh O'Brian, Alan Hale, Jr., Russell Arms (later a singer in television's "Your Hit Parade"), Jim Davis (Jock Ewing on "Dallas"), Denver Pyle ("Dukes of Hazzard"), and others.

* * *

Q - How many movies did Gene star in during his film career?
A - Gene *starred* in 89 feature films and 1 serial. This does not include, of course, several guest appearances and bit parts in two Ken Maynard films.

* * *

Q - What happy occurrence probably made the last six feature films for Columbia especially memorable and nostalgic for Gene?
A - He was rejoined by his first and most frequent sidekick of his career, Smiley Burnette.

Q - Is is true that Gene fell off Champion during an opening night performance at Madison Square Garden in New York?
A - Yes. As Gene explained it in an interview, "I guess I was probably the first cowboy star to fall off a horse before 18,000 people at Madison Square Garden. I had on a pair of new white cotton gloves, and when I went to swing off Champion and take a bow, my hand slipped and I fell flat on my face in the dirt. I went to the microphone, brushing off my clothes, and said, 'I get off that way all the time!' Everyone howled."

* * *

Q - When Pat Buttram seriously hurt himself during the filming of the "Gene Autry Show" television series, what three comic actors took over as Gene's sidekick until Pat could return?
A - Chill Wills, Alan Hale, Jr., and Fuzzy Knight. When Pat was hurt by a miniature cannon that exploded during the making of an episode called *The Peacemaker,* Chill took over and they refilmed the episode.

* * *

Q - When Gene made his last feature film for Columbia, it signaled the close of an era—the B Westerns were coming to the end of the trail. The title of Gene's last film was especially fitting for this period of time. What was the title?
A - LAST OF THE PONY RIDERS (1953).

* * *

Q - The Melody Ranch Movie Location used by Gene for filming the many television series he produced was formerly owned by what studio?
A - Monogram Pictures.

* * *

Q - Gene and John Wayne only appeared once together professionally in their careers. What was the occasion?
A - In June of 1958 they appeared together on an NBC-TV "Wide, Wide World" program segment entitled *The Western.* The live 90-minute show was partly broadcast from Gene's Melody Ranch Movie Location in Newhall, California. It featured such Western film and TV stars as James Garner,

James Arness, Gabby Hayes, Gary Cooper, Walter Brennan, and director John Ford. Wayne appeared in the Ford segment of the program. Gene was the on-location host for the program along with Dave Garroway, the in-studio host from New York.

The type of white cotton gloves which caused Gene to fall off Champion at Madison Square Garden is very visible in this photo taken at the Boston Garden in October of 1946.

Q - Whatever happened to the Melody Ranch Movie Location?
A - It burned in a fire storm that devastated much of that area around the San Gabriel Mountains. The fire occurred in 1962.

* * *

Q - What was the last time Gene performed at the Melody Ranch Movie Location?
A - In the June of 1958 "Wide, Wide World" television program.

* * *

Q - In what film did Gene first kiss the heroine, and who was she?
A - THE SINGING VAGABOND (1935). He kissed Ann Rutherford.

* * *

Q - Who were Gene's most frequent heroines in his movie career?
A - Gail Davis, 14 films; June Storey, 10 films; Fay McKenzie, 5 films, Ann Rutherford and Lynne Roberts, 4 films each.

Q - The "Melody Ranch" radio series went off the air in what year?
A - 1956.

* * *

Q - Why did Gene not appear on the last "Melody Ranch" radio program?
A - According to Gene, Pat Buttram and the rest of the cast wanted to prepare a tribute to Gene as a farewell performance.

* * *

Q - During the years following World War II, Gene put together a broadcasting empire of radio and television stations in various cities. What did he call his broadcasting company?
A - Golden West Broadcasting.

* * *

Q - Gene once owned as many as five hotels. Which is the only one he still operates?
A - The Gene Autry Hotel in Palm Springs, California.

This is the front gate of the Melody Ranch Movie Location as it appears today.

Gail Davis was Gene's most frequent leading lady, appearing in fourteen features before starring in eighty-one episodes of "Annie Oakley" on television for Gene's Flying A Productions. Gail also appeared with Gene in many of his own television episodes.

June Storey was Gene's leading lady in ten features between 1939 (HOME ON THE PRAIRIE) and 1940 (RIDE, TENDERFOOT, RIDE).

Fay McKenzie appeared as Gene's leading lady in five successive films beginning with DOWN MEXICO WAY (1941) and concluding with HOME IN WYOMIN' (1942).

Lynne Roberts was particularly adept at portraying the professional woman who inadvertently becomes involved in both a business sense and romantically with the singing cowboy. Lynne appeared in SIOUX CITY SUE (1946), SADDLE PALS (1947), ROBIN HOOD OF TEXAS (1947), and THE BLAZING SUN (1950).

Beautiful Ann Rutherford was Gene's heroine in four features and had the distinction of giving him his first screen kiss. The features were MELODY TRAIL (1935), SINGING VAGABOND (1935), COMIN' ROUND THE MOUNTAIN (1936), and PUBLIC COWBOY No. 1 (1937).

Pretty, perky, and precocious Mary Lee specialized in the kid sister role in many films. Although never appearing old enough to play the leading lady, Mary nevertheless charmed, sang, and danced her way through nine of Gene's films between 1939 (SOUTH OF THE BORDER) and 1941 (THE SINGING HILL).

Q - Did Gene and Roy Rogers ever feud as was reported many times over the years?

A - As Gene has commented: "That was just a publicity thing. The Republic publicity department thought it would be a good idea for Roy and me. But there was no personal feud whatsoever." As if to prove that this was the case, Roy and Gene went on a golfing date in the spring of 1950 that was covered in depth by *Movie Life.*

A GENE AUTRY SCRAPBOOK CLIPPING

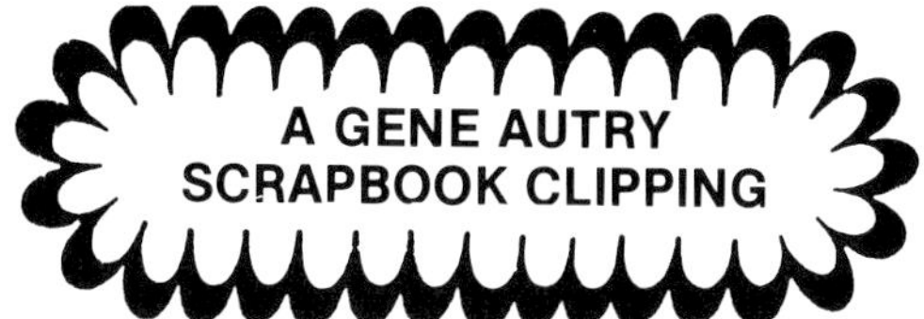

Movie Life
APRIL
25c

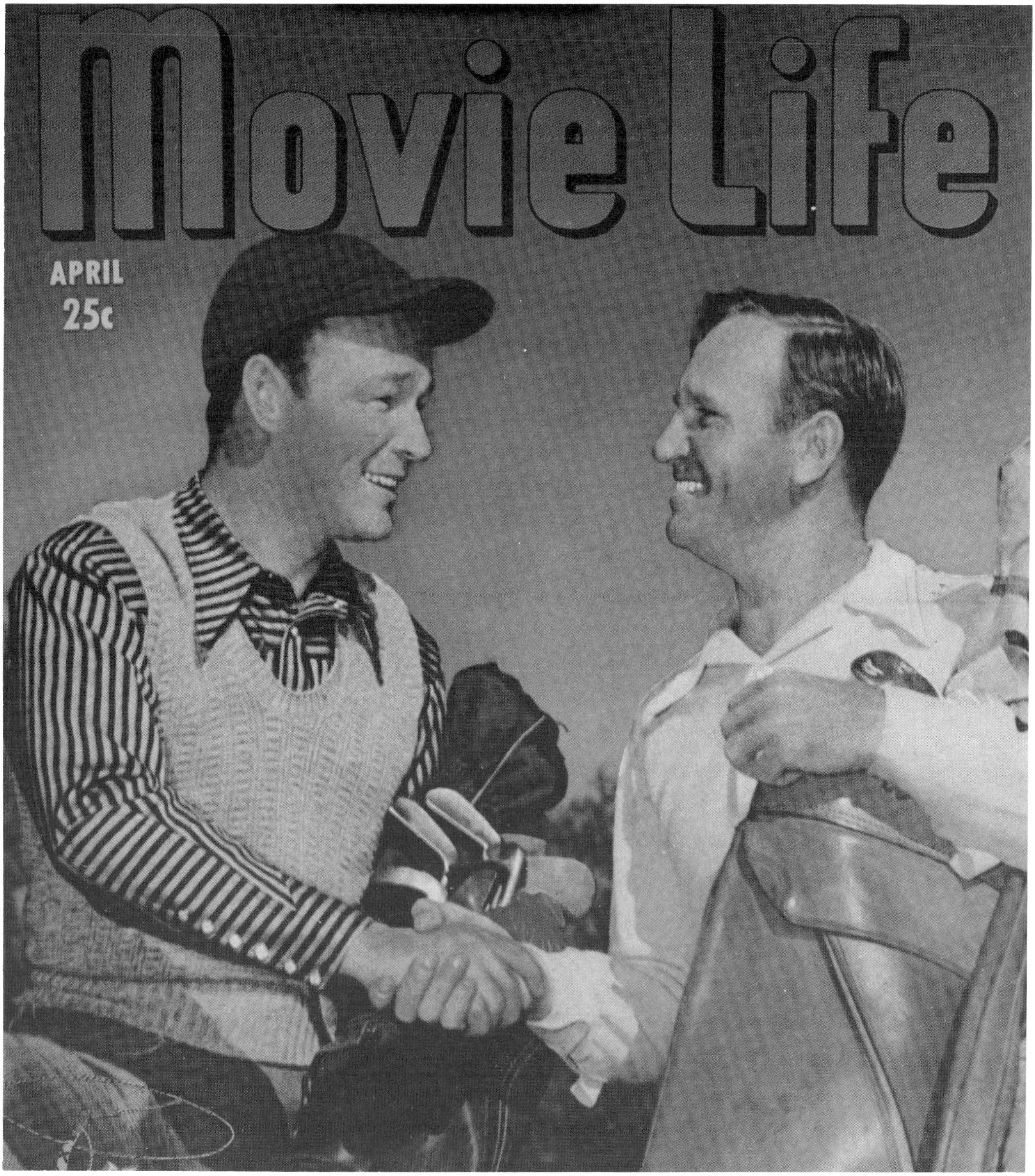

roy and gene play golf!

BOTH MEMBERS OF Lakeside Country Club, Gene and Roy spend so much between-pictures time off on rodeo tours, other P.A. jaunts, that they'd never managed to make a golf date before. Soon as they did, MOVIE LIFE went into action to grab cover photo, scoop pictures of pair pal-ing around the greens.

We Follow the Cowboy Kings along the Fairway to Get Exclusive Pictures of the First Autry-Rogers Match

MEETING at the club, Roy and Gene park cars side by side (Roy's at left). Autry has a phone in his Cadillac; part of its equipment may be seen just inside the opened trunk, next to spare tire.

FANCY BAGS on display in locker room look mighty dudish. Roy had just returned from hunting trip in High Sierras; Gene had flown in from Chicago, where he presented National 4-H Club awards.

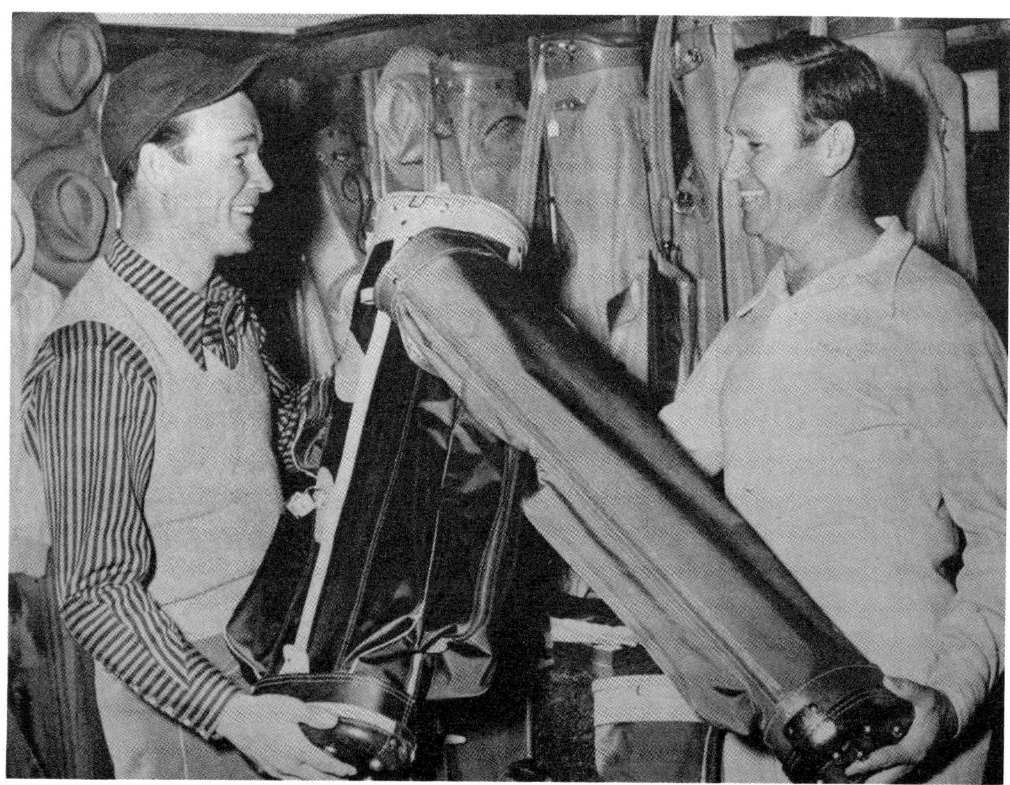

roy and

FINE POINTS of new driver are explained to Roy and Gene by pro Harry Cooper. Cooper reports two stars well-matched, usually shooting around high 80's and 90's.

ON THE PUTTING GREEN, Roy lines up a few so he'll be in top form. Star of *Twilight in the Sierras* felt plenty cheerful that morning. On his hunting trip, he'd bagged two 300-pound bears, four deer, and he hoped his sporting luck would hold while he was on the course.

GENE LETS GO with the first drive, a good long one; caddy has to squint to see where that ball's flying. Average drive for both Gene and his opponent is about 200 to 220 feet. Pro believes they're both good natural golfers, would attain real expertness if their work permitted them to play each week end, like most addicts.

gene play golf!

Continued

ROY MATCHES IT—looks like a hot game. He and Gene, usually loyal to Western-style garb on all occasions, play golf in "civvies." But Roy couldn't resist just one characteristic cowboy touch: light-colored piping along seams and pockets of his pants.

NOW TO SEE whether those practice shots pay off. Measuring putt carefully, Roy's sure it's a cinch, but Gene ribs him anyhow. Progress of the pair around Lakeside course was accompanied by much gag-swapping.

TUSSLING with a really tough lie, Gene gets helpful suggestion from Roy: "What you need is a curved cue!" Par for Lakeside is 70; membership list includes dozens of big names in addition to Rogers and Autry. Bing and Bob often battle it out there; other regulars are Errol Flynn (when he isn't globe-trotting), John Wayne, Bogart, Rooney, and Bergen.

IN SPITE of tense moments, game was really relaxing for two busy stars. Gene was furnishing new home, finishing *Beyond the Purple Hills,* getting set for rugged 71-day tour.

PAIR AGREED it was a pleasant novelty to stroll leisurely across wide open spaces for once, with no ornery rustlers to chase.

roy and gene play golf!

Continunued

IT'S GENE'S TURN to take it easy, while Roy blasts out of sand-trap. Roy says he's going to raise a new breed of dogs: golf-ball retrievers. Actually, he's just acquired rare breed of pooch called the Weimaraner, a German hunting dog.

SESSIONS in the rough leave those pretty white pills grubby. Halfway along, Roy and Gene stop to clean golf balls, so clinging earth won't spoil balance and speed.

BEFORE STARTING, Gene tried some shots on the putting green, too, as Roy sized up his style. Republic's Rogers and Columbia's Autry found skills closely matched on the course as well as on film.

PRACTICE SHOTS prove profitable again in Gene's case. As he's about to sink a putt, photog sets up camera just behind the cup, shows ball rolling true. Seems this marksman's as handy with a putter as he is with the trusty six-shooter.

roy and gene play golf!

Continued

APPETITES SHARPENED by brisk game, pair polish off hearty lunch, take a look at new comic strip on Roy's adventures, syndicated by King Features. Each star lends his name to many products outside the film field—kids's cowboy suits, toy guns, etc.

OVER COFFEE, Gene and Roy exchange news about Ina and Dale and the Rogers youngsters, compare notes on the movie-cowboy business. Perennially popular Westerns have become such big business that practically every star wants to get into the saddle, and top cowhands like Rogers and Autry seldom get a chance to get out of it for a get-together like this. Below, they climb back into Western boots for their return to range-riding.

(The preceding publicity release was originally published in *Movie Life*, April, 1950.)

How time flies when you're having fun! Here we see Gene and Roy at the 1978 Cowboy Hall of Fame induction ceremony in Oklahoma City, Oklahoma.

Q - What television series (other than his own) did Gene's production company produce?

A - "The Range Rider" (78 half-hour episodes) with Jock Mahoney and Dick Jones starring; the first 39 episodes of "Death Valley Days" with Stanley Andrews as the Old Ranger; "Annie Oakley" (81 half-hour episodes) starring Gail Davis; "Buffalo Bill, Jr." (42 half-hour films) starring Dick Jones; and "The Adventures of Champion" (26 half-hour episodes starring Champion and Jim Bannon.

Dick Jones and Jock Mahoney are pictured here on location for their Autry-produced television series, "The Range Rider." The series was noteworthy for the stunt work of its two stars.

Jocko and Dick made many rodeo personal appearances across the country to publicize their series, "The Range Rider." After that series concluded, Dick Jones went on to star in another of Gene's Flying A Productions, "Buffalo Bill, Jr." There were forty-two half-hour episodes made in the series.

Call their home Welcome Mat Manor, 'cause when Gene and Ina Autry entertain, it's hospitality all the way.

guesting with Gene

Both Mr. and Mrs. A. were on hand when young Dick Jones pulled up in his car for a few days with the Autrys. He plays part of Jack Mahoney's sidekick in the Range Rider TV film series which Gene produces under Flying A Productions.

Off to bed so he can rise early, Dick starts unpacking chore. All beds at chez Autry are oversized; Mr. and Mrs. A's is 7 by 7 ft. The one in the guest room has specially built footboard from old oxbow Mrs. A. acquired years ago.

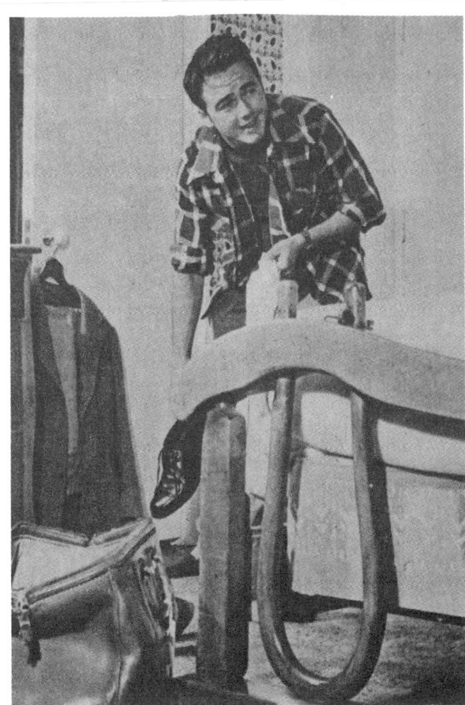

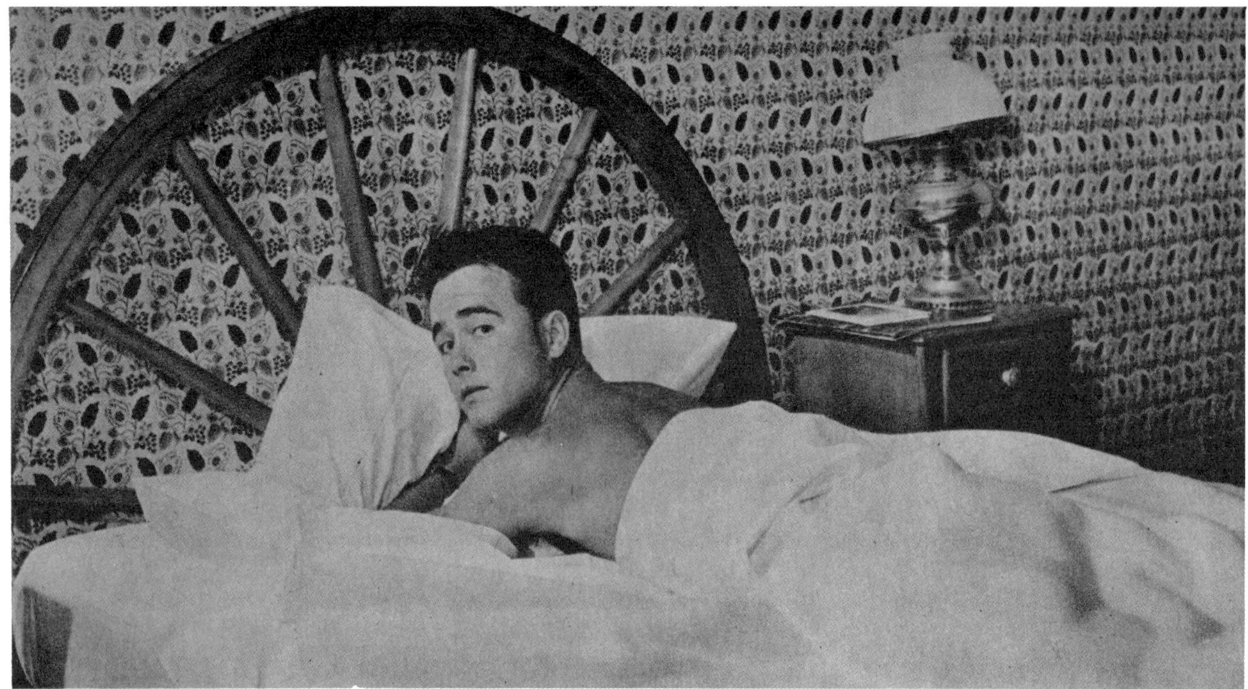

Morning found Dick fresh from night's rest. Used to early rising, Dick often has 5 a.m. camera calls to take advantage of early sunlight.

Gene's breakfast generally consists of ham and eggs with orange or grapefruit juice. Ina likes to serve morning meal in small nook at one end of their kitchen. Dick, a Texan, is twenty-three.

The Autry's town house in Laurel Canyon was completed in 1950, is built of white adobe brick with red tile roof and green blinds. Here Gene tells Dick of plans for building pool.

guesting with Gene *Continued*

Carpentering is more Dick's speed, or even riding and roping, but he's game when the boss suggests a bit of pruning. It's a rare day that Gene gets to catch up on his puttering chores, with movie, TV and p.a. schedules piling up.

He wouldn't do this at his own place—Dick hires a handyman to cut the lawn around his Burbank home, but this is different. Despite his youth, Dick's appeared in more than 200 movies, has been in films since days as child actor.

Mike, the boxer, was Xmas gift from Mrs. Autry to Gene last year. Dick has appeared in Gene's westerns, most recent, Col.'s Wagon Team.

guesting with Gene

continued

Dick helps Gene get a fire started in the den. Panelled in ash, the room features a rope design carved into the woodwork, plus a bright red carpet on the floor. Gene and Ina like to spend evenings here.

Columbia Records presented Gene with this platinum record of the hit tune, "Rudolph the Rednosed Reindeer," after its 2½ millionth pressing. Dick holds trophy Gene received from the American Legion.

"Come again!" Friendly Autry grins match Dick's and it seems everybody had a good time. Though he usually wears westerns, Dick prefers California type sports clothes.

Gene's favorite at home diversion is running home movies. His favorite movie is a short subject depicting the life and times of Will Rogers, who discovered Gene in Oklahoma.

The preceding publicity release originally appeared in Movies, December, 1952.)

Q - On what date did Gene get approval to operate the California Angels baseball team? What made the date the butt of later jokes?
A - December 7, 1960. During some of the difficult times which followed for the Angels, a wag referred to it as a "day of infamy" not unlike the day nineteen years before when Peal Harbor was bombed.

* * *

Q - The Angels played their first league game against what team?
A - The Baltimore Orioles. The date was April 11, 1961.

* * *

Q - Did the Angels win their first league game?
A - Yes. The score was 7-2.

Q - Where did Gene's Angels first play their games in California?
A - Wrigley Field, the old minor league stadium which held just over 20,000 people.

* * *

Q - Gene first offered the job of Angels' manager to what old pro in baseball?
A - Casey Stengel, who was then seventy years old. Because of other commitments Casey was not able to accept the position.

* * *

Q - Who was Gene's first manager for the Angels?
A - Bill Rigney. Rigney had formerly been with the Giants.

* * *

Q - In what year did the California Angels move

Gene is pictured here in the mid 1960s checking over the progress on the construction of the Anaheim Stadium, the new home being built for his California Angels baseball team.

Take me out to the ballgame! Left to right: Gene's business associate Bob Reynolds, President Richard Nixon, and Gene. Ina Autry is seated behind President Nixon. The photo was taken on July 26, 1970.

into their new stadium in Anaheim?

A - 1966.

* * *

Q - The Anaheim Stadium quickly acquired a nickname from the fans. What is it?

A - "The Big A," because of its million-dollar A-frame scoreboard.

* * *

Q - Was there a "Melody Ranch" television series?

A - Yes. It was telecast on Gene's Los Angeles station KTLA for seven years during the 1960s. Gene was not a regular on the show, but he made occasional guest appearances. The show was later syndicated to a few stations across the country.

Q - In what year was Gene elected to the Country Music Hall of Fame?

A - 1969. The commemorative plaque was engraved as follows:

America's great singing cowboy paved the way for others with his Western songs on radio and in the movies, where he set box office records. He was among the first country and Western performers to win world-wide acclaim. Born a cowboy, he overcame every adversity to move to the top of his field, always lending dignity to the industry. Best known as an artist and actor, he also was an accomplished writer.

* * *

Q - Which of the Beatles idolized Gene as his boyhood hero?

A - Ringo Starr.

Gene and his bride, Jacqueline Ellam, are standing outside the First United Methodist Church in Burbank after their wedding on July 19, 1981.

Q - In what major 1977 movie did some of Gene's old recordings serve as background for several key scenes?
A - SEMI-TOUGH. The Burt Reynolds character in the film loves Gene's old recordings and plays them as often as possible.

* * *

Q - What was Gene's reaction to the use of his old recordings in SEMI-TOUCH, especially "Back in the Saddle Again," which was played by Burt Reynolds when co-stars Kris Kristofferson and Jill Clayburgh slipped off into the bedroom?
A - Gene commented at the time, "I did give them the right to use the song. I got a lot of mail about it, and I figured I'd get a lot of criticism, but most people I heard from thought it was kind of fun."

* * *

Q - Who played the young Gene Autry in the television tribute, "Gene Autry, An American Hero" (1979)?
A - Henry Crowell, Jr.

* * *

Q - Who played Will Rogers in the television tribute, "Gene Autry, An American Hero"?
A - Will Rogers, Jr.

* * *

Q - What was Gene's response when asked in 1980 who his closest friend had been over the years?
A - Gene said his closest friend had been his wife Ina Mae, who had died a few months earlier on May 19, 1980. They had been happily married for 48 years.

Q - Did Gene and his wife Ina ever have any children.
A - No. Their children were the children of the world who idolized the cowboy star.

* * *

Q - In what year was Gene named to the Cowboy Hall of Fame of Great Westerners at the annual Western Heritage Awards in Oklahoma City, Oklahoma?
A - 1980. Gene was lauded as "one of the most famous men, not only in America but in the world."

* * *

Q - After so many successes in his life, what particular goal does Gene still seek with great zeal?
A - A World Series win for his California Angels baseball team. As of this writing (summer of 1987), Gene is still seeking that goal.

* * *

Q - What is the identification on Gene's car license plate?
A - California
9 ANGELS

* * *

Q - How did Gene meet Jackie Ellam, who was to become his second wife?
A - She was the vice president at the Security-Pacific Bank in Palm Springs. Gene had known her in that capacity for about 15 years.

* * *

Q - When does Gene plan to retire?
A - He doesn't!

CHAPTER 3

LITTLE-KNOWN FACTS ABOUT A WELL-KNOWN COWBOY

* Gene tried to learn to play the saxophone when he was a youngster. He finally gave up the sax and turned successfully to the guitar.

* When he was a young man, Gene received an offer from a professional baseball team to become a player. Gene turned the offer down because it would have meant a fifty dollar a month pay cut from his telegrapher's job.

* In the late 1930s Gene turned down an offer of $3,000 to endorse a brand of cigarette.

* When it went on the air in 1940, Gene's "Melody Ranch" radio series replaced Wrigley's "Gateway to Hollywood" program.

* Early in Gene's film career he owned a golden palomino named Pal which he planned to use in later color movies. Of course, Roy Rogers and Trigger came along before that could occur.

* In his Republic films Gene, one of the country's great businessmen, encountered a multitude of villains who were crooked businessmen.

* Early in his film career Gene received a grateful note from a Hugo R. Awtrey, who had spent years in vain trying to get people to pronounce his last name correctly. Now with Gene's fame, everybody pronounced Awtrey's name correctly.

* In 1940 (and probably for several years before and after) the Gene Autry cap pistol was the main industry in Kenton, Ohio, a town of (then) 7,000.

* When Gene enlisted in the Air Force, his squadron commander was Barry Goldwater.

* Gene has stated through the years that the only shoes he owns are golf shoes.

* Gene has always preferred his sponsor's product (Wrigley's Doublemint Gum) to smoking.

* Gene's favorite food is steak.

* Gene's favorite drink is Scotch and water.

* Gene's first Champion was purchased from an Ardmore, Oklahoma, man named Hardy Murphy.

* Gene was the first Western star to perform at Madison Square Garden in New York City.

* In 1950 Gene was named one of "America's Ten Best-Dressed Men."

* Gene's Western film attire in his post-war films at Columbia was far more subdued than the fancy Western garb he wore during his years at Republic Pictures.

* Gene's frequent expression when ending a conversation or while changing a subject is "Well, all right, sir."

* Gene is a collector of poems.

* Gene has 1,000 square feet of closet space in his North Hollywood home.

* Gene still holds the all-time box office record for a rodeo in Madison Square Garden.

* One of Gene's favorite nobbies over the years has been home movies.

* Gene once received a record 80,000 fan letters in one month.

* The official publication of the Gene Autry Fan Club was called "Autry's Aces."

* Gene's hometown of Tioga, Texas, once planned to change its name to Autry Wells, but Berwyn,Oklahoma, beat them to the name change with their conversion to Gene Autry, Oklahoma.

* According to a 1948 *Life* magazine article, Gene's records, "if they were all shipped to one place, would make up a freight train solid with Western songs and be more than a mile long."

* According to a 1953 fan magazine estimate, if all the recordings Gene has sold were stacked one atop of the other, the pile would be 57 miles high.

* Gene has the ability to take instant, brief catnaps, awakening a few minutes later refreshed and ready for the next task.

* By 1948 the Dell Publishing Company was turning out over one million *Gene Autry Comics* each year.

* Gene and his horse trainer Johnny Agee "schooled" the Champion horses with loudspeaker applause machines and brass band recordings so that the horses would be accustomed to such sounds while on personal appearances.

* Gene does not attend funerals.

* Gene was one of the last to see John Wayne before his death. Gene commented on the visit: "Wayne said he hoped I'd live 100 years. I'm the last one to shake his hand and say good-bye."

* Gene's television production schedule called for him to shoot two episodes of his half-hour TV series at the same time.

* When the famous "Hollywood" sign in the hills over the film capital fell into disrepair by 1978, various entertainers agreed to buy a letter for $27,777.77. Gene bought the first "L."

* In Gene's office there is a life-sized carved wooden Indian sitting in a chair to the right of his desk. There is long, black, braided hair falling over the Indian's chest and a menacing expression on his face. When the author visited Gene's office, the Indian was wearing an Angels baseball cap.

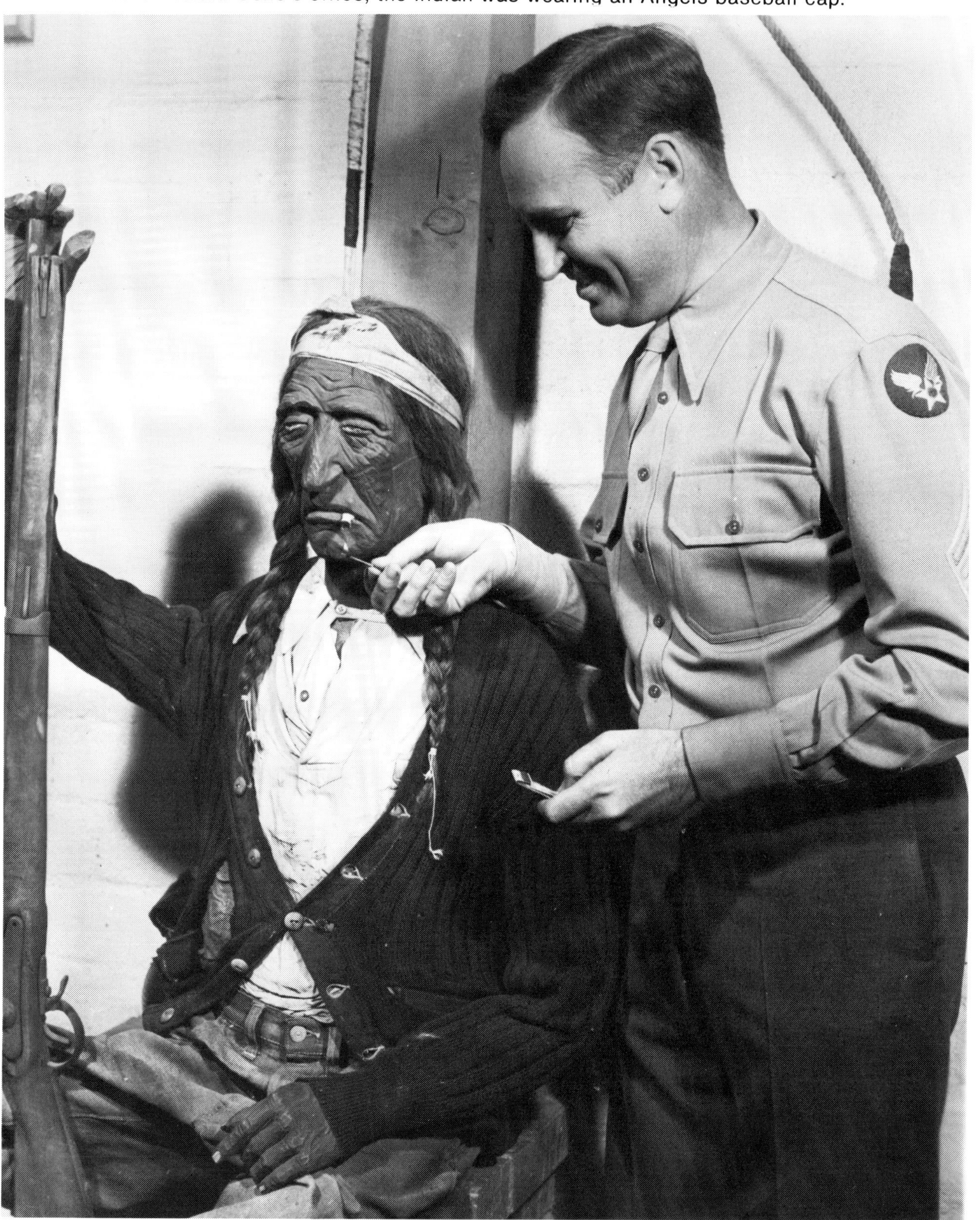

Gene offers his wooden Indian friend a light. This rare photo was taken while Gene was in the service during World War II.

* Gene has been a dinner guest of every American President since Herbert Hoover, with the exception of Jimmy Carter.

* Former President Richard Nixon has been Gene's guest at many of the California Angels baseball games. The former President is a great Angels fan.

* Gene is a compulsive gatherer of information and reads three or four papers a day.

* The California State Museum of Science and Industry at Exposition Park in Los Angeles honored Gene during the summer of 1980 with a 13-week exhibit and film retrospective.

CHAPTER 4
THE WIT AND WISDOM OF GENE AUTRY

I thought of myself as a showman, not a great entertainer. I never tried to be more or less than Gene Autry.

"Out our way a fellow has to judge a man pretty well—if he expects to stay healthy. Life in the West shows what stuff your sidekick is made of in a hurry. That's why cowboys pick their pals by what they *are*—not by race, religion or where they came from. Those fellows sure have no truck with prejudice of any kind—they can't afford to."

SPONSORED BY SCHOLASTIC MAGAZINES FOR DISTRIBUTION IN AMERICAN SCHOOLS

I am secure about who I am and what my place has been. I was the first of the full-time singing cowboys. I am not sure I was the best but when you are first it really doesn't matter. Even if everybody else is better, no one can ever be first again.

* * *

I'm not a great actor; I'm not a great rider; I'm not a great singer; but what the hell is my opinion when fifty million people think I do pretty good.

* * *

I was never an actor. An actor would be someone like Paul Muni or Spencer Tracy. I was a personality. And there's a hell of a lot of difference.

* * *

The old days were not necessarily better. I only know they were slower and less cynical. You could talk about setting an example for young people without blushing.

* * *

I've loved baseball all my life. I think what I would have liked most of all was to have been a big league ballplayer. My friends back in Oklahoma were ballplayers, and in the early years I played sandlot and semipro. In fact, some scouts came to look at me in Tulsa, but I knew I'd never be that good.

* * *

It occurs to me that music, with the possible exception of riding a bull, is the most uncertain way to make a living I **know.** *In either case you can get bucked off, thrown, stepped on, trampled—if you get on at all. At best, it is a short and bumpy ride.*

* * *

We always had three choices of travel in a Western. We could mosey, hightail it, or skedaddle.

* * *

Regarding the content of his films:

We had to have a decent story, good music, comic relief, enough action with chases and gunfights, and a little romance. But we had to treat that love angle **real** *careful. Almost no clinches or embraces. I could put my arm around the girl only if it was necessary to stop her fallin' off a cliff.*

* * *

Regarding his acting in his first films:

I moved like my parts needed oiling, and I didn't like the way I looked or sounded.

* * *

Westerns were to movies what the sports page is to the daily newspaper: the best part of it. The toy department.

* * *

Regarding Will Rogers' comment that he never met a man he didn't like:

Well, he actually didn't say that. What Will Rogers did say was, "I never **knew** *a man that I didn't like." There's a difference, because I think that every person in the world has at one time or another met someone and said, "I can't stand that man" or "I can't stand that woman." But if you really know them, then I think you do learn to like them. What I would like to truthfully say when I bale out of this life is that I never* **knew** *a man or a woman that I didn't like.*

* * *

Management is the important thing in business. If you've got good management, you'll get fat profits. And that's what I always remember.

I had the best of two eras—mine and the one I re-created on the movie screen.

* * *

Stay in business with people who know what they're doing. Stay out of the kind of business you don't know. Every day I get propositions that "will make you rich overnight." They're from promoters that you shouldn't get involved with.

* * *

I have read stories estimating the value of companies I control at around seventy million dollars. Of course, that figure refers to property and assets. No one has that kind of cash. The funny thing is, at no time in my life have I ever thought of myself as being rich. I sort of think of myself as independently poor.

* * *

When asked if he is as rich as people think:

Hell no. I don't know anybody who can write a check for a million dollars, except Howard Hughes. And he's dead!

* * *

My movies offered crimes of cunning, instead of violence. Dishonest salesmen and financial pirates were my villains. I ran a kind of one-man Better Business Bureau, out in the wide-open spaces.

When early in his career it was suggested that he change from a Western star to a romantic actor:

A cowboy, if he doesn't let his public down, is good until he is fifty years old. A matinee idol doesn't last five years.

* * *

A comment from 1940 regarding his films rarely playing the big cities:

Some of 'em play in towns so small even Mrs. Roosevelt hasn't been there.

About the arrival of "adult" Westerns:

Until I quit films, most movie fans thought dance hall girls actually danced.

Regarding his many screen fights:

I fought more rounds than Dempsey.

After a major purchase for his Angels:

If I can't make it with them, I'll have to hock the horse.

* * *

When the baseball players threatened to strike:

If they strike we'll just close down the ballpark. We'll tell those boys to go back to driving their tractors, to go back to the farm.

About Howard Cosell as a baseball broadcaster:

Howard calls a good game. It's just not the one you're watching.

* * *

I've had several offers to come back and make a picture, but I've seen too many try it. People remember you in your prime. I have no desire to make another movie. To tell you the truth, though, I think there's room for a singing cowboy today.

When in 1980 the California Museum of Science and Industry marked Gene's 50th anniversary in show business with an elaborate exhibit of memorabilia and a film retrospective, Gene commented at the opening festivities:

I really don't deserve all of this; but I had arthritis and I didn't deserve that either.

If your youngster has a faith to live by he'll never wander off the trail. As any cowhand will tell you, it's easier to keep 'em on a well marked trail than to hunt for a maverick once he's wandered away. Even when you find 'em, they don't always want to come back. It's like that with youngsters. Give them a trail to follow—something to guide them when problems come along—and you'll never have a maverick on your hands. Even when the grazing looks greener away from the path, if your kids are sure the path leads to something—even though they can't see the destination—they'll stick to it. It's all in believing—in having faith. I guess that's the biggest gift any parent can give a child—and it's more valuable than anything money can buy.

On growing older:

I think it's kind of a crime to go back and daydream. You can't make yourself young again.

*It **is** pleasant to look back, though not nearly so much as to be able to look ahead.*

CHAPTER 5
GENE AUTRY—ON THE RECORD

Gene Autry has had a tremendously prolific recording career. He started recording phonograph records on October 9, 1929, by best accounts, and continued until the early 1960s. Not only has Gene recorded hundreds of songs, but he has also written or had a hand in writing many of the songs he recorded.

As one examines the Gene Autry discography, it becomes very apparent that the Marvin brothers from Oklahoma, Frankie and Johnny, had a considerable impact on Gene's recording career. Both of these men were composers and musicians of outstanding talent. Their contributions to Gene Autry's career are not commonly known to the public, but those who have been near him over the years are very aware of the close bond the three men have shared.

Johnny Marvin had had some success in New York as a recording artist for Victor prior to Gene's first sojourn to the Big Apple. Johnny's mother, who lived in Butler, Oklahoma, told Gene to "look Johnny up" when he got to New York. Gene did just this and also met up with brother Frankie, who was a struggling musician like Gene. They all became immediate friends and continued the relationship throughout the successful years which soon followed. Frankie and Johnny Marvin played backup guitars on Gene's very first recording session. They also contributed dozens of compositions to the Autry list of recordings that were to come flooding forth.

When the movie years commenced for Gene, Frankie appeared in just about every Autry film, usually in minor roles back in the crowd. Ardent Autry fans, however, soon "discovered" Frankie and looked for him in each film. Frankie was not only in the background of those films, but he also provided backup music, compositions, some comic relief, and was always a trusted pal that Gene found nice to have close at hand. Johnny Marvin became associated with Gene in business matters and cut back on his performing career. During World War II Johnny went out on tours to entertain the troops. While performing in the South Pacific, he became very ill with a tropical sickness and died.

Another person who was a strong influence on Gene in those early years was Jimmy Long. Starting out together as telegraph dispatchers in Oklahoma, they discovered a common love for composing songs. Together they wrote "That Silver-haired Daddy of Mine," Gene's first and one of his biggest hits. Jimmy also sang with Gene on the recording of "Silver-haired Daddy" and other early recordings. As the Gene Autry discography reveals, they joined forces for the composition of many successful songs. (As a side note, Gene, of course, married Jimmy's niece Ina Mae Spivey in 1932.)

Without question, Gene has influenced several generations of country-Western singers, but who greatly influenced him as he struggled to establish his career? The answer is singer-composer Jimmie Rodgers. From 1927 to 1933 Rodgers, a tubercular railroad man, singer, composer, and recording artist became a country music legend. During these six brief years he is acknowledged to have laid the foundation for commercial country music while selling some twenty million records. Many of Gene's early songs were composed by Jimmie Rodgers, and upon Rodgers' death in 1933, Gene recorded "The Life of Jimmy Rodgers" and "The Death of Jimmie Rodgers" in tribute to this country artist who had meant so much to him.

Gene's most frequent collaborator on song compositions was Fred Rose. Gene has often commented that he recorded more than three hundred songs and helped write a third or them, mostly with Fred Rose.

Rose was from Nashville and is credited with discovering Hank Williams. Fred Rose and Gene worked well together and frequently would knock out songs overnight or even in a couple of hours when they were needed quickly for particular scenes in Gene's movies.

The Gene Autry discography which follows was compiled from such sources as *55 Years of Recorded Country-Western Music* by Jerry Osborne, Gene's own discography from his autobiography, and a very detailed Autry discography provided by Autry collector Gary Parmenter of Memphis. Jon Guyot Smith was especially helpful in providing obscure bits of information that nobody else seemed to have. These sources and others that were examined did not always agree. In any cases of discrepancies an attempt was made to determine and use the best evidence available.

* * *

GENE AUTRY DISCOGRAPHY

The song title of the recording is followed by the name(s) of the composer(s) and (where possible) the date on which the recording was made.

"A Boy from Texas, A Girl from Tennessee" (McCarthy, Jr.-Segal-Brooks)
No recording date ascertained.

"A Broken Promise Means a Broken Heart" (Autry-Rex Allen-Dave Bohm)
March 5, 1947.

"A Cowboy's Prayer" (Public Domain) 1964.

"A Cowboy's Serenade" (Nick Kenny-C. Kenny-Fina) December 2, 1949.

"A Face I See at Evening" August 20, 1940.

"A Gangster's Warning" (Autry) February 17, 1931.

"A Gold Mine in Your Heart" (Autry-Rose-J. Marvin) September 12, 1939.

"A Heartsick Soldier on Heartbreak Ridge" (Fiddler-Kane) December 27, 1951.

"A Hillbilly Wedding in June" (Freddie Owen-Frankie More) October 4, 1953.

"A New Star Is Shining in Heaven" (Tinturin) December 8, 1949.

"A Voice in the Choir" (Autry-Carr) October 29, 1953.

"A Year Ago Tonight" (Autry-Rose) June 18, 1941.

"Address Unknown" (Autry-Darling-Horton) June 13, 1945.

"After Tomorrow" (Autry-Rose) June 18, 1941.

"After 21 Years" (Autry) March 26, 1934, (sung with Jimmy Long).

"Ages and Ages Ago" (Autry-Rose-Whitley) June 11, 1946.

"Alone With My Sorrows" (Autry-Long) June 28, 1932.

"Amapola" (Gamse-Lacalle) September 26, 1941.

"Am I Just a Past Time" (Bond-Autry) December 27, 1951.

"Angel Boy" (Long-Paul-Dennis) January 14, 1935 (sung with Jimmy Long and Smiley Burnette).

"Angel Song" (Curt-Massey-Millard-Autry) March 5, 1947.

"Angels in the Sky" (Glasser) December 12, 1953.

"Anniversary Blue Yodel #7" (J. Rodgers) November 16, 1930.

"An Old Fashioned Tree" (Becker-Williams) August 28, 1947.

"Answer To Nobody's Darling" (Davis) May 12, 1936.

"Answer To Red River Valley" (Burnette-Autry) January 15, 1935.

"Answer to Twenty-one Years" (Bob Miller) March 2, 1933.

"Any Old Time" (J. Rodgers) February 28, 1931.

"As Long As I've Got My Horse" (J. Marvin-Rose-Autry) June 22, 1938.

"At Mail Call Today" (Autry-Rose) December 6, 1944.

"At the Old Barn Dance" (Tinturin-Lawrence) November 24, 1937.

"At the Rodeo"—Parts 1-4 (Henry Walsh) July 18, 1950.

"Back Home in the Blue Ridge Mountains" (Autry) June 28, 1932.

"Back in the Saddle Again" (Autry-Ray Whitley) April 18, 1939, February 13, 1946, and June 19, 1952.

"Back to Old Smokey Mountain" (Autry) June 24, 1932.

"Barney the Bashful Bull Frog" (Gene Evans) July 19, 1954.

"Be Honest With Me" (Autry-Rose) August 20, 1940, and February 27, 1956.

"Bear Cat Mama from Horner's Corners" (Jimmie Davis) April 1, 1931.

"Bear Cat Papa Blues" (F. Marvin) April 16, 1931.

"Beautiful Texas" (W. Lee O'Daniel) March 31, 1934 (sung with Jimmy Long).

"Bible on the Table" (Cunningham-Whitcup-Bennett) December 31, 1948.

"Big Corral" (Public Domain) December 27, 1951.

"Bimbo" (Rodney Morris) December 12, 1953.

"Birmingham Daddy" (Autry) November 11, 1931.

"Black Bottom Blues" (Autry) June 30, 1932.

"Blue Canadian Rockies" (Walker) April 24, 1950.

"Blue Days" (Autry) November 18, 1930.

"Blue-eyed Elaine" (Ernest Tubb) August 27, 1941.

"Blue Hawaii" (Robin-Rainger) October 11, 1937.

"Blue Montana Skies" (Autry-Rose-J. Marvin) April 13, 1939.

"Blue Shadows on the Trail" (Lange-Daniel) April 25, 1948.

"Blue Yodel #5" (Jimmie Rodgers) October 24, 1929.

"Blue Yodel #8" (Jimmie Rodgers) January 29, 1931 (sung with C. Keiser and B. Long).

"Blueberry Hill" (A. Lewis-L. Stock V. Rose) August 20, 1940.

"Broomstick Buckaroo" (Autry-J. Marvin-Frank Harford) August 21, 1940, and April 24, 1950.

"Bucky the Bucking Bronco" (Gerald Marks-Milton Pascal) July 28, 1950.

"Buffalo Bill" (Jay Glass-Nelson-Fred Wise) July 13, 1951.

"Bunny Round-up Time" (Stephen Gale-Leo Israel) January 31, 1951.

"Buon Natale" (Bob Saffer-Frank Linale) 1959.

"Buttons and Bows" (Livingstone-Evans) December 26, 1947.

"California Blues #4" (J. Rodgers) December 6, 1929.

"Call for Me and I'll Be There" (Autry-Rose) March 26, 1942.

"Call of the Canyon" (Hill) August 20, 1940.

"Candy Roundup" (Autry-Haldeman) June 25, 1953.

"Champion"—Parts 1-4 (Henry Walsh-Peter Steele) December 3, 1949.

"Clementine" (Public Domain) December 27, 1951.

"Closing the Book" (Smiley Burnette) January 4, 1954.

"Convict's Dream" (Autry-Hadley Hooper) March 22, 1937.

"Cowboy Blues" (Autry-Walker) July 2, 1946.

"Cowboy Yodel" (Autry) June 5, 1930.

"Cowboy's Heaven" (F. Marvin-Autry) January 27, 1933.

"Cowboy's Trademark" (arranged by Autry) August 27, 1940.

"Crime I Didn't Do" (Autry-Long) June 29, 1932 (sung with Jimmy Long).

This Gene Autry song book was published in 1938 and featured small still photographs from Gene's films in the upper corner of each page.

"Crime Will Never Pay" (Robinson-Pepper) March 26, 1951.

"Dad in the Hills" (Autry) November 20, 1930.

"Daddy and Home" (J. Rodgers) December 6, 1929.

"Dallas County Jail Blues" (F. Marvin) April 14, 1931.

"Darling, How Can You Forget So Soon?" (Autry-King-Frank) September 12, 1939.

"Darling, What More Can I do?" (Autry-Jenny Lou Carson) November 29, 1944, and June 6, 1957.

"Dear Little Dream Girl of Mine" (Autry-Rose) August 1, 1941.

"Dear Old Dad of Mine" (Autry-J. Marvin) August 11, 1941.

"Dear Old Western Skies" (Smiley Burnette) March 27, 1934.

"Death of Jimmie Rodgers" (Miller) June 22, 1933.

"Death of Mother Jones" (Public Domain) February 25, 1931.

"Deep in the Heart of Texas" (Hershey-Swander) February 24, 1942.

"Deisel Smoke, Dangerous Curves" (Martin) March 25, 1952.

"Dixie Cannonball" (Autry-Red Foley-Horton) September 9, 1946.

"Do Right Daddy Blues" (F. Marvin) February 18, 1931.

"Don't Believe a Word They Say" (Cunningham-Manners) March 25, 1952.

"Don't Bite the Hand That's Feeding You" (Hoier-Morgan) August 27, 1941.

"Don't Do Me That Way" (F. Marvin) March 31, 1931.

"Don't Hang Around Me Anymore" (Autry-Denver Darling-Vaughn Horton) June 13, 1945.

"Don't Live a Lie" (Autry-Johnny Bond) June 13, 1945.

"Don't Send Your Love" (Haldeman-R. Wright) April 12, 1950.

"Don't Take Me Back to the Chain Gang" (Autry) March 2, 1933.

"Don't Take Your Spite Out on Me" (Autry-Rose) June 15, 1945, (unissued until 1983 in THE GENE AUTRY COLLECTION album) and November 1, 1945.

"Don't Waste Your Tears on Me" (Autry) December 5, 1935.

"Down a Mountain Trail" (Thompson-Autry) June 2, 1937, (sung with Jimmy Long and unissued until 1983 in THE GENE AUTRY COLLECTION album).

"Dude Ranch Cowhands" (Autry-Rose-J. Marvin) June 23, 1938.

"Dust" (J. Marvin-Autry) October 11, 1937.

"Dust Pan Blues" (F. Marvin) December 3, 1929.

"Dying Cowgirl" (F. Marvin-Autry) June 22, 1933.

"Easter Mornin'" (June Winters-Mary Alice Ruffin) January 4, 1954.

"El Rancho Grande" (Uranga-Costello) March 12, 1940.

"Eleven Months in Leavenworth" (Autry) March 26, 1934.

"Ellie Mae" (Autry-Favilla) March 21, 1949.

"End of My Roundup Days" (Pee Wee King-J. Frank-Estes) May 9, 1937, (unissued until 1983 in THE GENE AUTRY COLLECTION album) and October 15, 1937.

"End of the Trail" (Smiley Burnette) December 5, 1935.

"Everyone's a Child at Christmas" (Marks) October 17, 1956.

"Eyes to the Sky" (J. Marvin-Autry) October 11, 1937.

"Frankie and Johnny" (Public Domain) December 3, 1929.

"Freddy and the Little Fir Tree" (Travis-Fairchild) June 24, 1953.

"Frosty the Snowman" (Nelson-Rollins) June 12, 1950.

"Funny Little Bunny" (Autry-Bond) March 2, 1950.

"Galivantin' Galveston Gal" (Nelson-Leeds-Wise) July 2, 1946.

"Girl I Left Behind" (J. Marvin) June 5, 1930.

"God Bless America" (Irving Berlin) April 20, 1951.

"God Must Have Loved America" (Autry-Rose) August 1, 1941.

"God's in the Saddle" (J. Hope-Moraine) July 19, 1954.

"God's Little Candles" (Kennedy) July 19, 1952.

"Gold Can Buy Anything But Love" (B. Sherman-D. Sherman) March 26, 1951.

"Gonna' Build a Big Fence Around Texas" (Friend-Phillips-Olsen) November 19, 1944.

"Good Luck, Old Pal" (Autry) November 1, 1933.

"Good Old Fashioned Hoedown" (Autry-Le Penney) August 27, 1940.

"Goodbye, Little Darling, Goodbye" (Autry-J. Marvin) March 12, 1940.

"Goodbye Pinto" (J. Marvin-Freddie Rose-Autry) June 22, 1938.

"Goodnight, Irene" (Huddy Ledbetter-John Lomax) January 12, 1952.

"Gosh, I Miss You All the Time" (Long) March 2, 1933 (sung with Jimmy Long).

"Guffy the Goofy Gobbler" (G. Marks-Pascal) January 12, 1952.

"Guns and Guitars" (Oliver Drake-Autry) August 25, 1936.

"Half Your Heart" (Blair-Duhig) June 6, 1957.

"Happy Little Island" (Gale-Hector Marchese) June 26, 1953.

"Have I Told You Lately That I Love You?" (Scott Wiseman) November 1, 1945.

"Have Your Found Someone Else?" (Long) June 30, 1932 (sung with Jimmy Long).

"He'll Be Comin' Down the Chimney" (J. Fred Coots-Al Neilburg) July 11, 1951.

"Here Comes Santa Claus" (Autry-Haldeman-Melka) August 28, 1947.

"Here's to the Ladies" (Autry-Walker) September 9, 1946.

"He's a Chubby Little Fellow" (Autry-Haldeman) June 27, 1949.

"High Powered Mama" (J. Rodgers) November 14, 1930.

"High Steppin' Mama Blues" (F. Marvin) March 31, 1931.

"Hobo Bill's Last Ride" (Waldo Lafayette O'Neal) August 4, 1930.

"Hobo Yodel" (Autry) December 3, 1929.

"Hold On, Little Doggies, Hold On" (Burnette) January 16, 1935.

"Home on the Range" (Public Domain) June 5, 1946.

"Horse with the Easter Bonnet" (Al Hoffman-Dick Manning) January 4, 1954.

"How Long Is Forever?" (Marks) March 26, 1951.

"I Can't Shake the Sands of Texas from My Shoes" (Autry-Pitts-Johnson) August 30, 1946.

"I'd Love a Home in the Mountains" (Burnette-Autry) September 22, 1935 (sung with Jimmy Long).

"I Don't Belong in Your World" (Autry-Rose), September 22, 1938, (unissued until 1983 in THE GENE AUTRY COLLECTION album) and April 13, 1939.

"I Don't Want to Set the World on Fire" (Sieler-Marcus-Benjamin-E. Durham) September 26, 1941.

"I Guess I've Been Asleep for All These Years" (Autry-Rose) December 6, 1944.

"I Hang My Head and Cry" (Autry-Rose-Whitley) December 13, 1941, and 1956.

"I Hate to Say Goodbye to the Prairie" (Autry-Thompson) May 29, 1937.

"I Just Want You" (Autry-Rose-J. Marvin) April 13, 1939.

Texas Frank's Original

25¢

COWBOY MUSIC WORLD

AMERICA'S NUMBER ONE WESTERN AND HILLBILLY RADIO NEWS MAGAZINE

Cowboy Music World was a small publication dedicated to promoting what its title suggested. It was jammed with photos, song lyrics, music news, and country-Western performer radio listings. It was all edited and published by Texas Frank. This was the September-October 1947 issue.

"I Left My Gal in the Mountains" (Carson Robinson) October 24, 1939.

"I Lost My Little Darlin'" (Oakley-Haldeman-Kraus-Coburn) December 31, 1948.

"I Love You Because" (Leon Payne) April 24, 1950.

"I Want a Pardon for Daddy" (Charles Roat) October 18, 1937.

"I Want To Be Sure" (Autry-Merle Travis) June 13, 1945.

"I Was Just Walking out the Door" (Walker) January 12, 1952.

"I Wish All My Children Were Babies Again" (Jack Baxley) September 26, 1941.

"I Wish I Had Never Met Sunshine" (Autry-Dale Evans-Haldeman) June 11, 1946.

"I Wish I Had Stayed Over Yonder" (Autry-Whit) March 21, 1949.

"I Wish My Mom Would Marry Santa Claus" (Autry-Carr) October 29, 1953.

"I Wonder If You Feel the Way I Do?" (Bob Wills) April 18, 1939.

"If I Could Bring Back My Buddy" (Long) March 1, 1933.

"If It Doesn't Snow on Christmas" (Pascal-Marks) August 4, 1949.

"If It Wasn't for the Rain" (Autry-Rose) April 14, 1939.

"If Today Were the End of the World" (Autry) June 23, 1938, and 1955.

"If You'll Let Me Be Your Little Sweetheart" (Autry-Slim Bryant) June 22, 1933.

"If You Only Believed in Me" (Autry-Rose) August 27, 1941.

"I'll Always Be a Rambler" (F. Marvin) February 25, 1931.

"I'll Be Back" (Autry-Dean-Rex Preis-Bill Bryan) November 29, 1944.

"I'll Be Thinking of You, Little Girl" (Autry) March 5, 1930.

"I'll Be True While You're Gone" (Autry-Rose) July 1941.

"I'll Go Riding Down That Texas Trail" (Smiley Burnette) August 25, 1936.

"I'll Never Let You Go, Little Darlin'" (Jimmy Wakely) July 1941.

"I'll Never Smile Again" (Lowe) August 27, 1940.

"I'll Wait for You" (Autry-Rose) August 1941.

"I'm a Cowpoke Pokin' Along" (Autry-Rose) June 10, 1942.

"I'm a Fool to Care" (Ted Daffan) December 5, 1947.

"I'm Always Dreaming of You" (Long-Autry) October 30, 1931 (sung with Jimmy Long).

"I'm a Railroad Man" (Autry) November 16, 1931.

"I'm Atlanta Bound" (Autry) October 29, 1931.

"I'm a Truthful Fellow" (F. Marvin) April 1, 1931.

"I'm Beginning to Care" (Autry-Rose-J. Marvin) September 12, 1939.

"I'm Blue and Lonesome" (Fleming-Townsend) April 1, 1931.

"I'm Comin' Home, Darlin'" (Autry-Eddie Dean-Hoefle) August 11, 1941.

"I'm Gonna' Roundup My Blues" (Autry-J. Marvin) April 18, 1939.

"I'm in the Jailhouse Now #2" (Rodgers) November 6, 1930.

"I'm Innocent" (King-Redd Stewart) May 18, 1954.

"I'm Learning to Live Without You" (Autry-Bond-Billy Folger) November 1, 1945.

"I'm Thinking Tonight of My Blue Eyes" (A.P. Carter) February 24, 1942.

"In a Garden" (Miles) April 20, 1950 (duet with Dinah Shore).

"In the Cradle of My Dreams" (Long) June 30, 1932.

"In the Hills of Caroline" (Autry-Burton) June 30, 1932.

"In the Shadow of the Pine" (Raskin-Brown-Eliscu) June 5, 1930.

"In the Valley of the Moon" (Burke-Tobias) June 22, 1933.

"It Just Don't Seem Like Home When You're Gone" (Tex Atchison) May 18, 1954.

"It Makes No Difference Now" (Davis-Floyd Tillman) June 18, 1941.

"It's My Lazy Day" (Burnette) January 4, 1954.

"It's Roundup Time in Reno" (Owens-Lawrence-Autry) October 15, 1937.

"I've Lived a Lifetime for You" (Whitley-B. Newman) December 5, 1947.

"Jailhouse Blues" (Autry) April 10, 1931.

"Jimmie the Kid" (J. Rodgers) March 31, 1931.

"Jingle Bells" (arranged by Carl Cotner) 1957.

"Jingle Jangle Jingle" (Loesser-Lilley) June 10, 1942.

"Johnny Appleseed"—Parts 1-2 (Henry Harvey Walsh-Gale) July 20, 1952.

"Johnny Reb and Billy Yank" (Charles Tobias) May 3, 1957.

"Joy to the World" (arranged by Carl Cotner) 1957.

"Keep Rollin', Lazy Longhorns" (Autry-J. Marvin) August 27, 1941.

"Kentucky Babe" (Buck-Geibel) December 6, 1947.

"Kentucky Lullaby" (Autry) June 23, 1932.

"Kit Carson" (Glass-Nelson-Wise) July 13, 1951.

"Last Letter, The" (Rex Griffin) August 27, 1940.

"Last Mile, The" (Autry-Haldeman-Rose) September 9, 1946.

"Last Roundup, The" (Billy Hill) October 9, 1933, February 13, 1946.

"Last Straw, The" (Tillman) April 24, 1950.

"Leaf of Love" (Tex Williams-Bob Newman) March 5, 1947.

"Let Me Cry on Your Shoulder" (Hershey-Swander) September 13, 1950.

"Life Is So Misleading" (Autry-Simms) December 8, 1949.

"Life of Jimmie Rodgers" (Miller) June 22, 1933.

"Little Old Band of Gold" (Autry-Charles Newman-F. Glickman) April 14, 1939.

"Little Farm Home" (Burnette-Long-Autry) March 27, 1934 (sung with Jimmy Long).

"Little Johnny Pilgrim" (Kane-Fidler) January 12, 1950.

"Little Partner" (Autry-Rose-J. Marvin) September 11, 1939.

"Little Peter Pumpkin Eater" (Langeston-Hampton-Moore-Underwood) July 19, 1954.

"Little Ranch on the Old Circle B" (Autry-Blanchard) January 27, 1933.

"Little Sir Echo" (Smith-Fearis) April 14, 1939.

"Living in the Mountains" (F. Marvin) 1930.

"Loaded Pistols and Loaded Dice" (Johnny Lange-Hy Heath) December 26, 1947.

"Lone Star Moon" (Friend-Franklin) December 26, 1947.

"Lonely River" (Autry-Rose-Whitley) August 1, 1941.

"Look Out the Window" (Lew Porter-Tee Pee Mitchell) June 10, 1952.

"Louisiana Moon" (Autry) January 27, 1933.

"Love Is So Misleading" (Autry-A. Simms) December 8, 1949.

"Lullaby Yodel" (J. Rodgers) December 5, 1929.

"Maria Elena" (Russell-Barcelata) September 26, 1941.

"Mary Dear" (Public Domain, arranged by Autry and Cactus Mack) March 12, 1940.

"Mean Mama Blues" (J. Rodgers) January 29, 1931.

"Memories of That Silver-haird Daddy of Mine" (Autry) March 26, 1934.

"Merry Christmas Waltz" (Inez Loewer-Bot Batson) September 30, 1955.

"Merry Go Roundup" (Autry-Rose-J. Marvin) September 11, 1939.

"Merry Texas Christmas, You All" (Harris, Jr.-Miller) July 20, 1952.

"Methodist Pie" (Public Domain) April 10, 1931.

"Mexicali Rose" (H. Stone-J.B. Tenney) December 24, 1935, and February 13, 1946.

"Mississippi Valley Blues" (Autry-Long) October 30, 1931 (sung with Jimmy Long) and April 12, 1950.

"Missouri Is Calling" (Autry) October 29, 1931 (sung with Jimmy Long).

"Missouri Waltz (Shannon-Eppel-Logan) December 6, 1947.

"Mister and Mississippi" (Irving Gordon) March 21, 1951.

"Money Ain't No Use Anyway" (Autry) February 28, 1931.

"Moonlight and Skies" (Rodgers) June 29, 1932.

"Moonlight Down in Lover's Lane" (Pitman-Kortlander) October 9, 1933.

"Mule Train" (Lange-Heath-Glickman) December 2, 1949.

"My Alabama Home" (Jimmy Long) October 9, 1929.

"My Carolina Mountain Rose" (Long) June 30, 1932.

"My Carolina Sunshine Girl" (J. Rodgers) August 4, 1930.

"My Cross-eyed Gal That Lived Upon the Hill" (Long-Autry) October 30, 1931.

"My Dreaming of You" (Johnny Marvin) October 9, 1929.

"My Empty Heart" (Autry-Porter-Mitchell) March 21, 1949.

"My Heart Cries for You" (Percy Faith-Carl Sigman) December 1, 1951.

"My Oklahoma Home" (F. Marvin) September 15, 1930.

"My Old Pal of Yesterday" (Long-Autry) October 30, 1931.

"My Old Saddle Pal" (Autry-Odie Thompson) December 5, 1935.

"My Rose of the Prairie" (Long-Autry) May 29 1937 (unissued until 1983 in THE GENE AUTRY COLLECTION album).

"My Rough and Rowdy Ways" (J. Rodgers) March 5, 1930.

"My Shy Little Bluebonnet Girl" (Long) May 31, 1934.

"My Star of the Sky" (Autry) May 29, 1937, (unissued until 1983 in THE GENE AUTRY COLLECTION album) and October 18, 1937.

"Night Before Christmas in Texas That Is" (Leon A. Harris, Jr.-B. Miller) July 20, 1952.

"Night Before Christmas Song" (Marks) June 20, 1952.

"Nine Little Reindeer" (Autry-Marks-Travis) 1959.

"No Back Door to Heaven" (Dave Burgess) 1957.

"No One to Call Me Darling" (Autry) December 3, 1929.

"Nobody's Darling But Mine" (Davis) September 22, 1935, and February 27, 1956.

"Oklahoma Hills" (Guthrie) April 8, 1946 (unissued until 1983 in THE GENE AUTRY COLLECTION album).

"Old Buckaroo, Goodbye" (J. Marvin-Autry) October 15, 1937.

"Old Chisholm Trail" (Public Domain) December 27, 1951.

"Old Covered Wagon" (Burnette-Autry) January 15, 1935.

"Old Folks Back Home" (Long) March 1, 1933 (sung with Jimmy Long).

"Old Grey Mare" (F. Marvin) August 25, 1936 (sung with Frankie Marvin).

"Old Man Duff" (Publc Domain) April 1, 1931.

"Old Missouri Moon" (Long-Dennis) January 17, 1935 (sung with Jimmy Long).

"Old November Moon" (J. Marvin-Autry) April 13, 1939.

"Old Rugged Cross" (Reverend George Bennard) April 20, 1950 (duet with Dinah Shore).

"Old Soldiers Never Die" (arranged by Autry) April 20, 1951.

"Old Trail" (Autry-Rose-J. Marvin) June 23, 1938.

"Old Woman and the Cow" (F. Marvin) April 1, 1931.

"Ole Faithful" (Michael Carr-Jimmy Kennedy) January 17, 1935, and June 5, 1946.

"On Top of Old Smoky" (Public Domain) December 27, 1951.

"One Rose" (Lani-McIntire-Del Lyon) May 29, 1937.

"One Solitary Life" (Public Domain) 1964.

"Onteora (Great Land in the Sky)" (Anderson-Andrea) June 12, 1950.

"Over and Over Again" (Autry-Walker) April 8, 1946.

"Panhandle Pete" (J. Marvin-Rose-Autry) June 23, 1938 (unissued until 1983 in THE GENE AUTRY COLLECTION album).

"Paradise in the Moonlight" (Autry-Rose) April 13, 1939.

"Peter Cottontail" (Melson-Jack Rollins) March 2, 1950.

"Pictures of My Mother" (Autry) November 18, 1930.

"Pistol Packin' Papa" (J. Rodgers-O'Neal) January 29, 1931.

"Place Where I Worship" (Carr-Foster-Goodhart) December 1, 1951.

"Play Fair" (Whitley-Leeds-Hayes) December 7, 1947.

"Poison Ivy" (George Wyle-Eddie Pola) December 8, 1949.

"Poppy the Puppy" (Johnston) July 11, 1951.

"Pretty Mary" (Autry-Haldeman-Mitchell-MacDonald) August 28, 1947.

"Private Buckaroo" (Wrubel-Bob Newman) March 26, 1942.

"Purple Sage in the Twilight" (Autry-Jules Styne-Meyer) August 11, 1941.

"Railroad Boomer" (Robinson) December 5, 1929.

"Rainbow on the Rio Colorado" (Autry-Rose) February 24, 1942.

"Rainbow Valley" (Burnette-Autry) September 22, 1935.

"Red River Valley" (Public Domain) August 30, 1946.

"Returning to My Cabin Home" (Autry-Burton) June 29, 1932.

"Rheumatism Blues" (Autry) October 30, 1931.

"Rhythm of the Hoofbeats" (Autry-Rose-J. Marvin) April 14, 1939.

"Rhythm of the Range" (J. Marvin-Autry) October 11, 1937.

"Ride, Tenderfoot, Ride" (Johnny Mercer- Richard Whiting) June 22, 1938.

"Ridin' All Day" (Burnette) May 12, 1936.

"Ridin' Down the Canyon" (Burnette-Autry) January 15, 1935, and June 4, 1946.

"Ridin' the Range" (Fleming Allan-Autry-Nelson Shawn) December 5, 1935.

"Riders in the Sky" (Stan Jones) August 16, 1949.

"Roll Along, Kentucky Moon" (Bill Halley) June 20, 1933.

"Rolling Along" (Kotel-Cooper) December 6, 1947.

"Roly Poly" (Autry-Rose) December 12, 1953.

"Rose-colored Memories" (Autry-Haldeman-Wright) September 18, 1950.

"Roses" (Tim Spencer-Glen Spencer) April 12, 1950.

"Roses I Picked for Our Wedding" (Peter Tinturin-Autry) December 8, 1949.

"Round and Round the Christmas Tree" (Fred Stryker) September 30, 1955.

"Rounded Up in Glory" (Public Domain) June 4, 1946.

"Round-up in Cheyenne" (Smiley Burnette) March 26, 1934.

GENE AUTRY'S HIT KIT was published in 1946.

"Rudolph the Red Nosed Reindeer" (Johnny Marks) June 27, 1949.

"Rusty the Rocking Horse" (John Jacob Loeb) January 12, 1950.

"Sail Along, Silvery Moon" (Tobias-Wenrich) November 24, 1937.

"Same Old Fashioned Girl" (Autry) December 6, 1944 (unissued until 1982 album entitled GENE AUTRY COLUMBIA HISTORIC EDITION).

"Santa Claus Is Comin' to Town" (Haven-Gillespie-Coots) 1957.

"Santa, Santa, Santa" (Autry-Haldeman) August 4, 1949.

"Santa's Comin' in a Whirlybird" (Ashley Dees) 1959.

"Serenade of the Bells" (Twomey-Goodhart-Urbano) December 26, 1947.

"Seven More Days" (Autry-Long) May 29, 1934.

"She Wouldn't Do It" (F. Marvin) March 31, 1931.

"She's a Humdinger" (Jimmy Davis) April 1, 1931.

"She's a Low Down Mama" (F. Marvin) April 1, 1931.

"She's Always On My Mind" (Fleming-Townsend) April 1, 1931.

"She's Just That Kind" (Fleming-Townsend) April 1, 1931.

"Sierra Sue" (Joseph Carey) August 22, 1940.

"Silent Night" (Public Domain) 1957.

"Silver Bells" (Livingston-Evans) 1957.

"Silver Spurs" (Autry-Cindy Walker) November 1, 1945.

"Sing Me a Song of the Saddle" (Autry-Frank Hartford) May 29, 1937.

"Singing Hills" (Mack David-Dick Sanford-Samy Mysels) March 12, 1940.

"Sioux City Sue" (Dick Thomas-R. Freedman) April 8, 1946.

"Sleigh Bells" (Autry-Carr) 1957.

"Slue Foot Sue" (F. Marvin) December 5, 1929.

"Smoky the Bear" (Nelson-Rollins) June 19, 1952.

"Someday You'll Want Me to Want You" (Jimmy Hodges) October 15, 1937 and July 2, 1946.

"Someday in Wyoming" (Burnette-Autry) January 14, 1935 (sung with Jimmy Long).

"Sonny the Bunny" (Tommy Johnston) January 31, 1951.

SOUTH OF THE BORDER
(DOWN MEXICO WAY)
by
JIMMY KENNEDY
and
MICHAEL CARR
March 28, 1940.
As Featured by
Gene Autry
in the REPUBLIC production
"SOUTH OF THE BORDER"
SHAPIRO, BERNSTEIN & Co. Inc
MUSIC PUBLISHERS
NEW YORK
By Arrangement with
THE PETER MAURICE MUSIC CO. LTD.
LONDON, ENGLAND.

"South of the Border" (Carr-Kennedy) September 11, 1939, and June 4, 1946.

"Spend a Night in Argentina" (Autry-Rose)

"Stampede" Parts 1-4 (Henry Walsh-Peter Steele) June 29, 1949.

"Statue in the Bay" (Monte-Hale-Wagner-Carlyle) September 18, 1950.

"Stay Away from My Chicken House" (F. Marvin) December 5, 1929.

"Stop Your Gambling" (Robison-Pepper) March 21, 1951.

"Story Book of Love" (Eaton) August 4, 1949.

"Story of Little Champ, The" Parts 1-4 (Walsh-Steele) July 26, 1950.

"Story of the Nativity, The" Parts 1-4 (Public Domain) July 17, 1950.

"Sunflower" (Mack David) March 21, 1949.

"Sweethearts or Strangers" (Davis) December 13, 1941.

"Sycamore Lane" (Autry-Rose) August 21, 1940.

"Take Me Back Into Your Heart" (Autry-Rose) December 13, 1941.

"Take Me Back to My Boots and Saddle" (Powell-Whitcup-Samuels) October 18, 1937, and February 13, 1946.

"T. B. Blues" (J. Rodgers) March 31, 1931.

"Teardrops from My Eyes" (Rudolph Toombs) December 1, 1951.

"Tears on My Pillow" (Autry-Rose) August 22, 1940.

"Texans Never Cry" (Haldeman-Autry-Hank Fort) August 16, 1949.

"Texas Blues" (J. Rodgers) August 4, 1930.

"Texas Plains" (Stuart Hamblen) September 23, 1935 (sung with Jimmy Long).

"That Little Kid Sister of Mine" (Autry-Rose) August 22, 1940.

"That Mother and Dad of Mine" (Autry) June 20, 1933.

"That Old Feather Bed on the Farm" (Autry-Louis O'Connell) June 23, 1933.

"That Ramshackle Shack" (Autry-Hugh Cross) June 24, 1932.

"That Silver-haired Daddy of Mine" (Autry-Long) October 29, 1931, (sung with Jimmy Long) and December 2, 1949 (sung with Bert Dodson).

"That's How I Got My Start" (Autry) February 17, 1931.

"That Why I Left the Mountains" (F. Marvin) March 3, 1930.

SIOUX CITY SUE
music by
DICK THOMAS
lyrics by
RAY FREEDMAN
GENE AUTRY
and
CHAMPION
Wonder Horse of the West
in
"SIOUX CITY SUE"
with
LYNNE ROBERTS • STERLING HOLLOWAY
CASS COUNTY BOYS
Directed by Frank McDonald • Original Screen Play by Olive Cooper
Associate Producer—Armand Schaefer
A REPUBLIC PICTURE
EDWIN H. MORRIS & CO., INC.
MUSIC PUBLISHERS
by arrangement with
NATIONAL MUSIC PUBLISHING CORP.

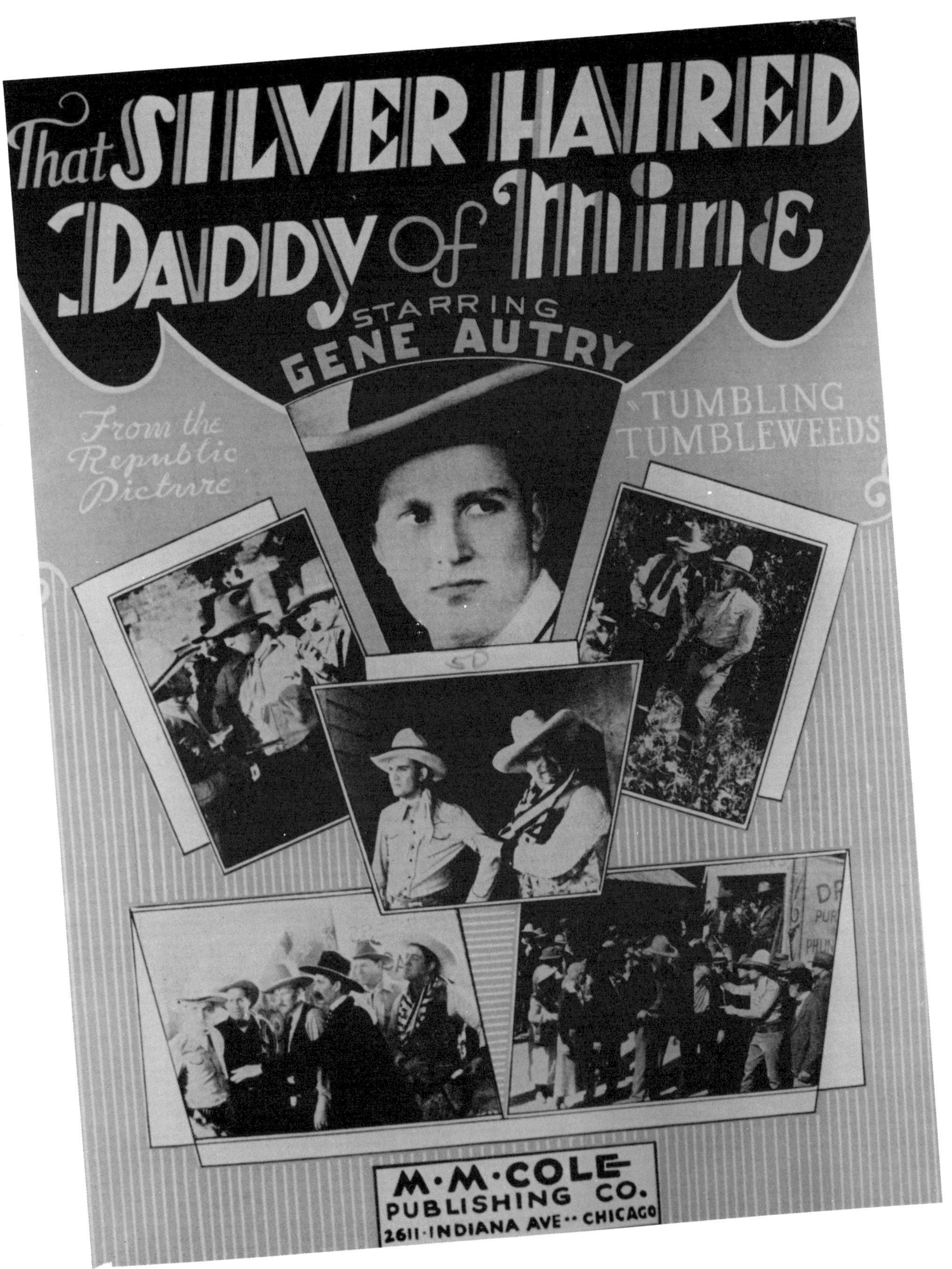
That SILVER HAIRED
DADDY of Mine
STARRING
GENE AUTRY
From the Republic Picture
"TUMBLING TUMBLEWEEDS"
M·M·COLE
PUBLISHING CO.
2611·INDIANA AVE·· CHICAGO

"That's Why I'm Blue" (J. Rodgers-Elsie MacWilliams) August 4, 1930.

"That's Why I'm Nobody's Darling" (Davis) March 22, 1937.

"There Ain't No Use in Crying Now" (Autry-Marvin) August 21, 1940.

"There'll Never Be Another Pal LIke You" (Autry-Marvin-Tobias) August 21, 1940.

"There's a Gold Mine in the Sky" (Charles and Nicky Kenny) November 24, 1937 and February 13, 1946.

"There's a Good Gal in the Mountains" (Autry) April I, 1931.

"There's a Little Old Lady Waltlng" (Burnette-Autry-Long) April 28, 1934 (sung with Jimmy Long).

"There's an Empty Cot in the Bunkhouse Tonight" (F. Marvin-Autry) June 23, 1933, and June 5, 1946.

"There's Only One Love in a Lifetime" (Autry-Marvin-Tobias) March 12, 1940.

"They Cut Down the Old Pine Tree" (Raskin-Brown-Eliscu) June 5, 1930.

"They Warned Me About You" (Autry-Bond) December 5, 1947.

"Thirty-two Little Feet, Eight Little Tails" (John Redmond-James Cavanaugh-Frank Weldon) July 11, 1951.

"Three Little Dwarfs" (Hamblen) July 11, 1951.

"Too Late" (Jimmy Wakely) September 1941.

"Train Whistle Blues" (J. Rodgers) August 4, 1930.

"Travelin' Blues" (J. Rodgers-Shelly Lee Alley) March 31, 1931.

"True Blue Bill" (F. Marvin) February 17, 1931.

"Tumbling Tumbleweeds" (Bob Nolan) November 11, 1935, and June 5, 1946.

"Tweedle-O-Twill" (Autry-Rose) February 24, 1942.

"20/20 Vision and Walking Around Blind" (Allison-Estes) May 19, 1954.

"Twilight on the Trail" (Mitchell-Alter) August 30, 1946.

"Two Cheaters in Love" (J. Toombs) October 4, 1955.

"Uncle Noah's Ark" (Burnette) November 11, 1935 (sung with Smiley Burnette).

"Under Fiesta Skies" (Autry-Rose) 1941.

"Under the Old Apple Tree" (Autry) November 16, 1931.

"Up on the House Top" (Jane Whitman) June 26, 1953.

"Valley in the Hills" (Public Domain) April 1, 1931.

"Vine Covered Cabin in the Valley" (Burnette) September 22, 1935.

TUMBLING TUMBLEWEEDS
by
BOB NOLAN
Dick McConnell
Sung by
GENE AUTRY
in
"TUMBLING TUMBLEWEEDS"
A REPUBLIC PICTURE
MELOTONE RECORD No. M13315
by GENE AUTRY TRIO
SAM FOX PUB. CO.
CLEVELAND NEW YORK
LONDON-PARIS-BERLIN-MELBOURNE
SOROKIN

"Wagon Train" (Burnette) January 17, 1935 (sung with Smiley Burnette).

"Waiting for a Train" (arranged by J. Rodgers) December 5, 1929.

"Watching the Clouds Roll By" (Long) March 2, 1933 (sung with Jimmy Long).

"Wave to Me, My Lady" (Loesser-Stein) April 8, 1946.

"Way Out West in Texas" (Autry) June 22, 1933.

"We Never Dream the Same Dream Twice" (Autry-Rose) August 27, 1940.

"Were You Sincere?" (Autry-Mark Halliday) October 15, 1937.

"We've Come a Long Way Together" (Sam Stept-Koehler) April 18, 1939.

"What's Gonna' Happen to Me?" (Autry-Rose) August 22, 1940.

"When He Grows Tried of You" (Aldrich) May 18, 1954.

"When I First Laid Eyes on You" (Autry-Marshall) April 14, 1939.

"When I'm Gone You'll Soon Forget" (Keith) March 12, 1940.

"When It's Lamplighting Time in the Valley" (Joe Lyons-Sam Hart) March 2, 1933.

"When It's Roundup Time in Heaven" (Davis) June 4, 1946.

"When It's Roundup Time in Reno" (Owens-Lawrence-Autry) October 15, 1937.

"When It's Springtime in the Rockies" (Woolsey-Taggart-Sauer) October 18, 1937.

"When Jimmie Rodgers Said Goodbye" (Dwight Butcher-Lou Herscher) November 1, 1933.

"When Santa Claus Gets Your Letter" (Marks) June 12, 1950.

"When the Golden Leaves Are Falling" (C.A. Havens) June 2, 1937.

"When the Humming Birds Are Humming" (Autry) June 22, 1933.

"When the Moon Shines on the Mississippi Valley" (Burnette) May 28, 1934.

"When the Silver Colorado Turns to Gold" (Paul Herrick-Mitchell) August 16, 1949.

"When the Snowbirds Cross the Rockies" (Autry-Joy Howard) March 5, 1947.

"When the Swallows Come Back to Capistrano" (L. Rene) August 27, 1940.

"When the Tumbleweeds Come Tumbling Down Again" (Autry) October 18, 1937.

"Where Did the Snowman Go?" (Venis-S. Mann-Poser) June 24, 1953.

"Whirlwind" (Stan Jones) August 16, 1949.

"Whisper Your Mother's Name" (Braisted-Rogers) June 5, 1930.

"Why Don't You Come Back to Me?" (Autry) December 3, 1929, and October 30, 1931 (sung with Jimmy Long).

"Wildcat Mama" (F. Marvin) October 30, 1931.

"Wildcat Mama Blues" (F. Marvin) November 16, 1931.

"With a Song in My Heart" (Richard Rogers-Larry Hart) July 6, 1937.

"Yellow Rose of Texas" (Public Domain) January 27, 1933.

"Yesterday's Roses" (Autry-Rose) March 26, 1942.

"Yodeling Hobo" (Autry) November 14, 1930.

"You Are My Sunshine" (Davis-Charles Mitchell) June 18, 1941, and February 27, 1956 (sung with Rosemary Clooney and the Tunesmiths).

"You Are the Light of My Life" (Autry-Rose) August 1, 1941.

"You Can See Old Santa Claus" (J. Johnson-L. Frizzell-B. Adams) No recording date ascertained.

"You Gotta' Take the Bitter with the Sweet" (Fotine-Miles) September 30, 1955.

"You Laughed And I Cried" (Whitley-Milton Leeds-Billy Hayes) April 8, 1946.

"You Only Want Me When You're Lonely" (Autry-Steve Nelson) June 11, 1946.

"You Waited Too Long" (Autry-Whitley-Rose) August 22, 1940.

"You'll Be Sorry" (Autry-Rose) December 13, 1941.

"Your Voice Is Ringing" (Percy Wenrich) January 27, 1933.

"You're An Angel" (Byrum) May 19, 1954.

"You're Not My Darling Anymore" (Rosalie Allen-Rose-Sam Martin) June 11, 1946.

"You're the Only Good Thing That Happened to Me" (J. Toombs) May 18, 1954.

"You're the Only Star in My Blue Heaven (Autry) December 5, 1935, and April 13, 1939.

* * *

GENE AUTRY FAVORITES album (circa 1961)

"Tweedle-O-Twill" (Autry-Rose)
"Be Honest With Me" (Autry-Rose)
"Hang Your Head in Shame" (Rose-Nelson)
"Darling, What More Can I Do?" (Autry-Carson)
"Trouble in Mind" (Richard Jones)
"Ages and Ages Ago" (Rose-Whitley)
"Blues Stay Away From Me" (Delmore-Raney-Glover)

"I'll Wait for You" (Rose-Autry)
"You're the Only Star in My Blue Heaven" (Autry)
"Goodbye, Little Darling, Goodbye" (Autry-Marvin)

* * *

Most of the foregoing recordings were originally released as singles, one 78rpm record with a song on each side. With the arrival of the 45rpm and the LP recordings in the early 1950s, many Autry singles were compiled into albums. The result has been that original single recordings now appear in several albums which have been released at various times over the last thirty-five years in many countries around the world and on numerous labels. In addition, Gene has authorized the LP record release of several albums comprised of songs originally performed "live" on the weekly "Melody Ranch" radio programs

between 1940 and 1956. These extracted songs are not record releases in the usual sense, and yet they add to the Autry library of recorded material. Also, there are several album releases of *entire* "Melody Ranch" radio programs with songs, of course, included.

Thus, it is at this juncture that the discography becomes a trail hard to follow. The tracks—some very dim—lead in all directions. Rather than try to follow all trails and get lost in trail dust (and perhaps lose my reader, too), I have decided to provide a listing of the albums which are most widely accessible and which offer the Autry devotee a potpourri of what are probably the best and most representative of the Gene Autry albums released over the years.

Albums of the very earliest Gene Autry recordings:

THE VERY RAREST OF YOUNG GENE AUTRY - Peace-Maker Discs
YOUNG GENE AUTRY - New Country Loon Recordings
LIVE SOUND OF THE LEGENDARY GENE AUTRY - New Country Loon
YOUNG GENE AUTRY, VOL. 3 - New Country Loon Recordings.

Albums of Autry favorites compiled from early discs and a few "Melody Ranch" radio transcriptions:

GENE AUTRY, BACK IN THE SADDLE AGAIN	- Harmony/Columbia
GENE AUTRY, BACK IN THE SADDLE AGAIN	- CBS Records/Encore, 1979
GENE AUTRY, YOU ARE MY SUNSHINE	- Harmony/Columbia
20 GOLDEN PIECES OF GENE AUTRY	- Bulldog Records (England)
GENE AUTRY FAVORITES-LIVE FROM MADISON SQUARE GARDEN (two-record set)	- Republic Records
GENE AUTRY SINGS SOUTH OF THE BORDER-GENE AUTRY, ALL AMERICAN COWBOY (two-record set)	- Republic Records
GENE AUTRY SINGS SONGS OF FAITH	- Republic Records, 1977
GENE AUTRY FAVORITES—COLLECTOR'S EDITION	- Republic Records, 1976
GENE AUTRY CLASSICS, VOLUME I	- Republic Records, 1977

Albums of Autry favorites (some rare) that could be categorized as commemorative in nature:

GENE AUTRY'S COUNTRY MUSIC HALL OF FAME ALBUM	- Columbia Records, 1969
GENE AUTRY 50TH ANNIVERSARY (two-record set)	- Republic Records, 1978
GENE AUTRY—COLUMBIA HISTORIC EDITION	- Columbia Records, 1982
THE GENE AUTRY COLLECTION (four-record set)	- Murray Hill/CBS, 1983

Albums of Autry Christmas favorites:

THE ORIGINAL: GENE AUTRY SINGS RUDOLPH THE RED NOSED REINDEER AND OTHER CHRISTMAS FAVORITES	- Grand Prix Records
CHRISTMASTIME WITH GENE AUTRY	- Mistletoe Records

Albums of "Melody Ranch" radio program in their entirety:

GENE AUTRY'S MELODY RANCH (three complete shows)	- Golden Age Records, 1977
GENE AUTRY'S MELODY RANCH (four-record album featuring eight complete shows)	- Murray Hill Records

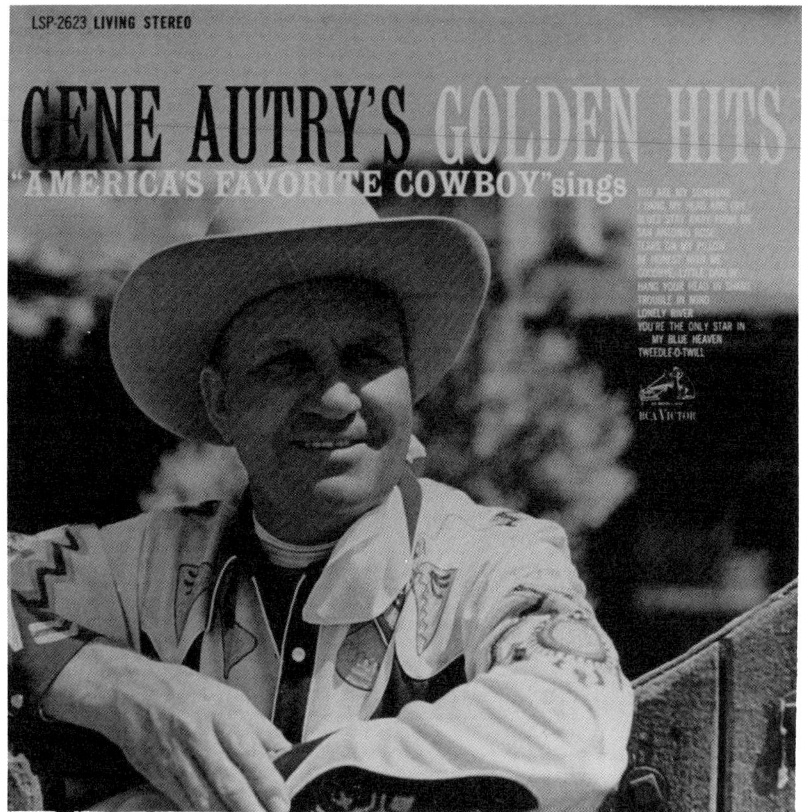

The recordings in the two albums shown above have been released in other albums, too. The recordings in GENE AUTRY'S GOLDEN HITS, for example, can also be found in 20 GOLDEN PIECES OF GENE AUTRY.

CHAPTER 6
LIVING IN REEL TIME
THE FILMS OF GENE AUTRY

Gene Autry made his film debut as a dude ranch cowboy singer in a 1934 Ken Maynard film entitled IN OLD SANTA FE. He quickly followed that performance by playing a bit role in a Maynard serial called MYSTERY MOUNTAIN (1934). By this time IN OLD SANTA FE had been released and the public reaction to the youthful cowboy singer proved very positive. This, of course, did not go unnoticed by the officials at Mascot Studio, which had made the film.

About this same time Ken Maynard was due to star in another serial for the studio. This one was to be called PHANTOM EMPIRE. Suddenly Maynard went on one of his frequent rampages with Mascot, a company which had grown weary of its temperamental Western star. Nat Levine, the head of Mascot, decided to fire Maynard and to take a chance on the young, inexperienced cowboy singer who had screen-tested so well in IN OLD SANTE FE. The rest, as they say, is history.

From 1935 until 1953 Gene Autry starred in a total of ninety motion pictures. He quickly rose to the top of the B Western field and remained in first or second place among cowboy stars in terms of box office draw throughout his long film career.

I have attempted a slightly different approach to the Gene Autry filmography for this book. After my own years of viewing and analyzing these films; reading what trade paper, magazine, and book critics have had to say about them; and discussing Gene's films with other Western film aficionados, I have come to the conclusion that one can't really compare, for instance, an Autry film with a Hopalong Cassidy. They are both Westerns, but they are basically two completely different types of Western films. Even the films of another singing cowboy — Roy Rogers, for example—are in sharp contrast. Roy and Gene's personal appeal was very different, and their use of music, comedy, romance, production values, and overall Western tone were decidedly different. Therefore, the ratings you will find in the Gene Autry filmography are determined from within the Gene Autry collection rather than as compared with films outside the collection.

For the following filmography I called upon the assistance of six Gene Autry authorities and film collectors—people who have followed Gene's career closely over the years and who have viewed his films many times. I asked them to rate the Autry films on a four-star basis, with four stars representing best and one star indicating a lesser film. I also asked them, if they wished, to comment on the films. I asked them as Autry buffs to examine Gene's total film output and to provide ratings and comments—guidelines, if you will—from an admittedly partisan perspective.

The filmography which you are about to read is not, therefore, an objective analysis; it is the considered opinions of six men who know the Gene Autry films intimately and, admittedly, like Gene Autry films. You will discover that the star ratings are slightly higher than you might find in a Leonard Maltin Guide, but, within the framework I've outlined, you just may end up with a deeper appreciation and sounder comments regarding the films than you might garner from an impartial critic who had given each film only a cursory viewing and had only a limited knowledge of the Autry films as a body of work to be studied and analyzed.

I am deeply indebted to six gentlemen who so kindly agreed to assist me with the Gene Autry filmography. I am confident that their efforts will provide new insights into these films. The six Gene Autry authorities who consented to rate and comment on the films are the following:

Truman L. Evitt (TE) - Fort Worth, Texas
Jimmy Glover (JG) - Northport, Alabama
Gary Parmenter (GP) - Memphis, Tennessee
Charlie Rhine, Sr. (CR) - Davisburg, Michigan
Jesse Rush (JR) - Guntersville, Alabama
John Guyot Smith (JGS) - White Plains, New York

THE GENE AUTRY FILMOGRAPHY

PHANTOM EMPIRE (Mascot, 1935) Serial

Rating: ***

Producer, Nat Levine; directors, Otto Brower and B. Reeves Eason; screenplay, John Rathmell and Armand Schaefer; story, Wallace McDonald, Gerald Geraghty, and Hy Freedman.

Cast: Gene Autry, Smiley Burnette, Frankie Darro, Betsy King Ross, Dorothy Christy, Wheeler Oakman, Charles K. French, Warner Richmond, Frank Glendon, Bill Moore, Wally Wales, Edward Piel, Stanley Blystone, Champion.

Comment: In the highly fanciful story Gene, a Western radio singer, gets involved with people from an underground city called Murania in one cliff-hanging chapter after another. Gene and his sidekick, Smiley Burnette, get plenty of opportunities over the many weeks of the serial's run to sing some Western ditties—most of which were written by the two of them.

"Enjoyed the story" -CR

"A charming fantasy, as ingenuous and guileless as of the world of childhood itself, (the serial) provided a marvelous escape from depression-era problems." -JGS

Songs: "Uncle Noah's Ark," "That Silver-haired Daddy of Mine," "I'm Getting a Moon's Eye View of the World," "I'm Oscar; I'm Pete," "Uncle Henry's Vacation," "Just Come On Back," "No Need to Worry," and "My Cross-eyed Gal."

* * *

TUMBLING TUMBLEWEEDS (Republic, 1935) 57 M.

Rating: ***

Producer, Nat Levine; director, Joseph Kane; screenplay, Ford Beebe; story, Alan Ludwig.

Cast: Gene Autry, Smiley Burnette, Lucile Browne, Norma Taylor, George Hayes, Edward Hearn, Jack Rockwell, Frankie Marvin, George Chesebro, Eugene Jackson, Charles King, Charles Whitaker, George Burton, Tom London, Cornelius Keefe, Tracy Layne, Champion.

Comment: Gene, returning from a five-year exile from his estranged father, discovers that the prosperous cattleman has been murdered and his (Gene's) childhood companion is accused of the crime. With the assistance of his medicine show companions, Smiley Burnette and George Hayes, Gene rounds up the real villains.

"The prototype for all Gene Autry features to come—fast paced and thoroughly entertaining." —JGS

Songs: "Tumbling Tumbleweeds," "That Silver-haired Daddy of Mine," "Ridin' Down the Canyon," "Corn Fed and Rusty," "I'll Yodel My Troubles Away," "Wagon Train," "Cowboy Medicine Show," and "Oh, Susanna."

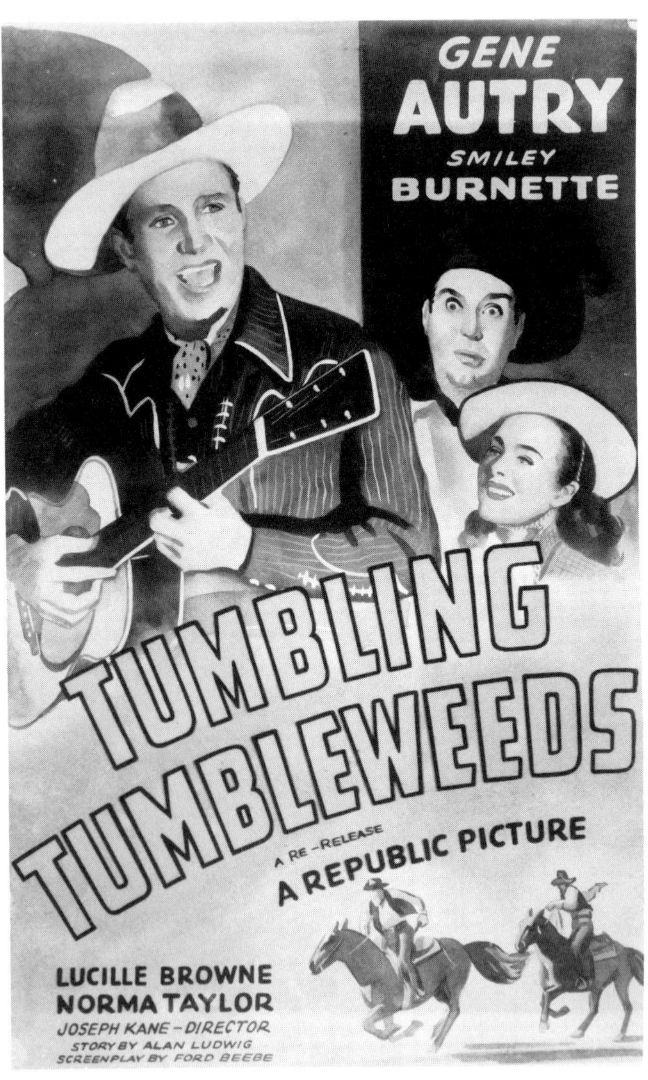

MELODY TRAIL (Republic, 1935) 57 M.

Rating: **½

Producer, Nat Levine; director, Joseph Kane; screenplay, Sherman Lowe.

Cast: Gene Autry, Smiley Burnette, Ann Rutherford, Wade Boteler, Alan Bridge, Gertrude Messinger, Willy Castello, Marie Quillan, Tracey Layne, Fern Emmett, Jane Barnes, Iona Reed, Champion.

Comment: Gene loses his rodeo winnings to a gypsy thief and seeks a job at a ranch owned by the father of a pretty girl he had spied in the stands at the rodeo. Gene and Smiley eventually catch the gypsy as well as some rustlers who have been tormenting the rancher.

"Smiley was assigned the name "Frog Millhouse"—a screen appelation he would use for the next ten years. The film is essentially a comedy with a thrilling action-packed climax." -JGS

Songs: "On the Melody Trail," "A Lone Cowboy on the Lone Prairie," "Western Lullaby," "Hold On, Little Dogies, Hold On," "My Neighbor Hates Music," "Way Down on the Bottom," and "Where Will the Wedding Supper Be?"

* * *

SAGEBRUSH TROUBADOUR (Republic, 1935) 57 M.

Rating: **½

Producer, Nat Levine; director, Joseph Kane; screenplay, Oliver Drake.

Cast: Gene Autry, Smiley Burnette, Barbara Pepper, Frank Glendon, Denny Meadows, Hooper Atchely, Fred Kelsey, Julian Rivero, Champion.

Comment: Murder, mystery, and music are the plot ingredients that go into this sagebrush stew. Gene and Frog are Rangers, assigned to the task of tracking down the murderer of a half-blind old rancher who was killed with a guitar string.

"A wonderfully dusty, well-photographed location; a characteristically droll Oliver Drake screenplay; and Gene and Smiley in excellent musical form make this Western murder mystery great fun." -JGS

Songs: "The End of the Trail," "I'd Love a Home Out in the Mountains," "I'd Love to Wed (on the Prairie)," "Way Out West in Texas," "Looking for the Lost Chord," "My Prayer for Tonight," "The Hurdy Gurdy Man," "Someday in Wyoming."

* * *

SINGING VAGABOND (Republic, 1935) 55 M.

Rating: **½

Producer, Nat Levine; director, Carl Pierson; screenplay, Oliver Drake, Betty Burbridge.

Cast: Gene Autry, Smiley Burnette, Ann Rutherford, Barbara Pepper, Warner Richmond, Frank LaRue, Grace Goodall, Niles Welch, Tom Brower, Robinson Neeman, Ray Benard, Hanry Roquemore, Allan Sears, Chief Big Tree, Champion.

Comment: The plot concerns Captain Tex Autry and his Singing Plainsmen. They are trusted scouts with flawless military records, but when the crafty Utah Joe frames Tex (Gene) in a horse theft, the Captain is court-martialed and sentenced to hang. At the last minute Tex escapes from prison and vindicates himself by stopping Utah Joe from leading renegade Indians on a wagon train attack. The story is set in 1860.

". . . a period piece with memorable characters and a compelling plot. . . ." -JGS

Songs: "Down Honeymoon Trail," "Rounded Up in Glory," "Singing Vagabonds," "Wagon Train," and "Friends of the Prairie, Farewell."

* * *

RED RIVER VALLEY (Republic, 1936) 60 M.

Rating: ***

Producer and director B. Reeves Eason; screenplay, Stuart McGowan, Dorrell McGowan.

Cast: Gene Autry, Smiley Burnette, Frances Grant, Boothe Howard, Jack Kennedy, Sam Flint, George Chesebro, Charles King, Eugene Jackson, Edward Hearn, Frank LaRue, Ken Cooper, Frank Marvin, Champion.

Comment: The plot concerns the efforts of unknown evildoers to foil the efforts to complete an irrigation project that will bring water to the drought-parched valley. Gene takes the job of ditch-rider in order to personally look into the trouble. The TV title is *MAN OF THE FRONTIER.*

"Superbly constructed. . .there is literally a thrill every five minutes...with serial-like pacing, atmospheric and imaginative photography." -JGS

Songs: "Red River Valley, "Fetch Me Down My Trusty .45." "Yodeling Cowboy," "Where a Waterwheel Keeps Turning On," and "Construction Song."

* * *

COMIN' ROUND THE MOUNTAIN (Republic, 1936) 60 M.

Rating: ***

Producer, Nat Levine, director, Mack Wright; screenplay, Oliver Drake, Dorrell and Stuart McGowan.

Cast: Gene Autry, Smiley Burnette, Ann Rutherford, Roy Mason, Raymond Brown, Ken Cooper, Tracy Lane, Robert McKenzie, John Ince, Frank Lackteen, Champion.

Comment: Pony express rider Gene Autry befriends the lovely Dolores Moreno (Ann Rutherford), whose ranch is about to be sold for non-payment of taxes. After he tames a beautiful wild stallion on Miss Moreno's range, Gene proposes a race between Dolores' wild mustangs and the thoroughbreds belonging to Matt Ford (LeRoy Mason)—the winner to receive the valuable contract to sell horses to the Pony Express.

". . . beautiful photography and young Gene at his best! —JGS

Songs: "When the Campfire Is Low on the Prairie," "Chiquita," "Don Juan of Sevillio," and "Comin' Round the Mountain."

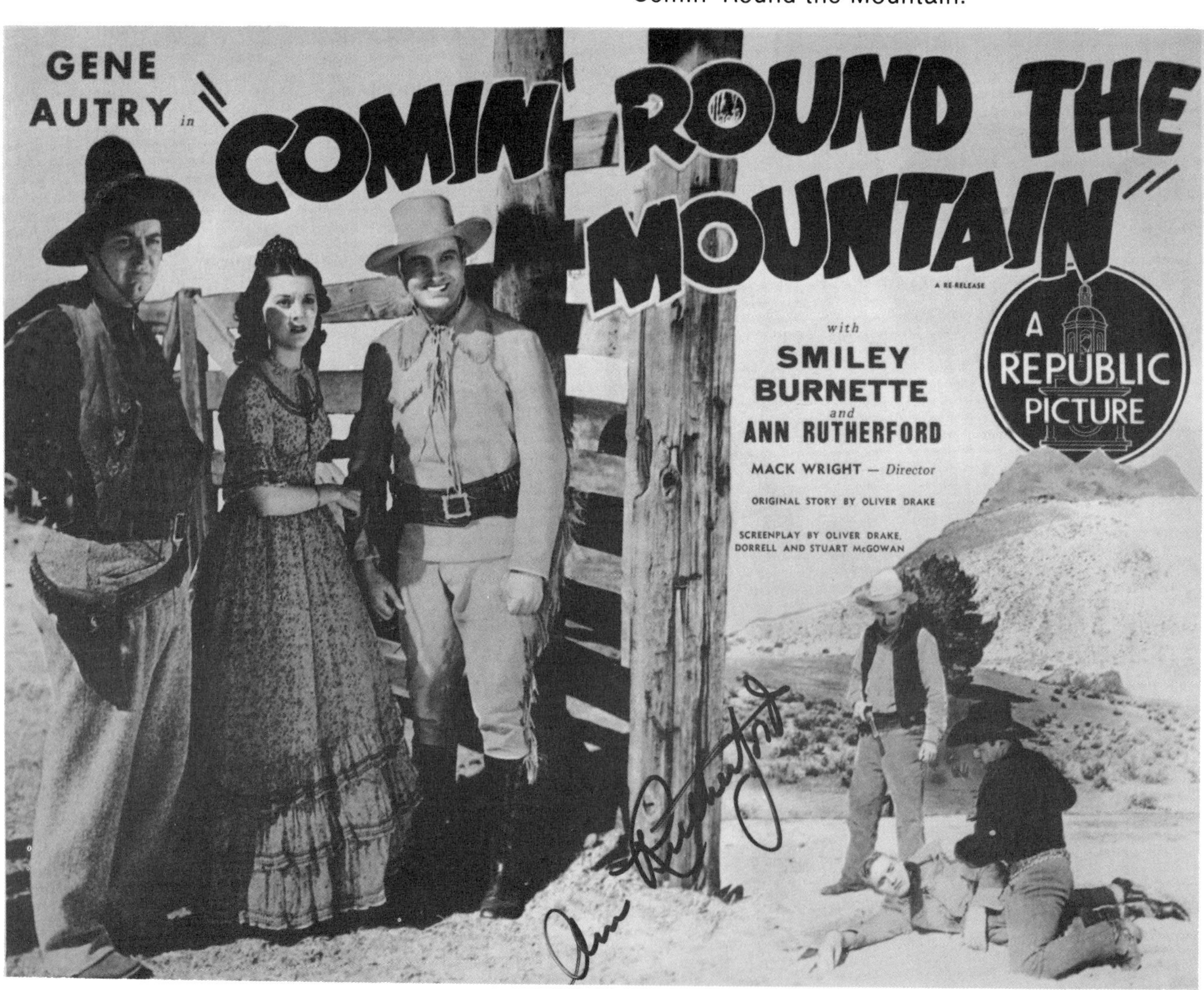

THE SINGING COWBOY (Republic, 1936) 60 M.

Rating: ***

Producer, Nat Levine; director, Mack Wright, screenplay, Dorrell and Stuart McGowan.

Cast: Gene Autry, Smiley Burnette, Lois Wilde, Lon Chaney, Jr., Ann Gillis, Earl Hodgins, Harvey Clark, John Van Pelt, Earl Eby, Ken Cooper, Harrison Green, Wes Warner, Jack Rockwell, Tracy Layne, Oscar Gahan, Frankie Marvin, Jack Kirk, Audrey Davis, George Pearce, Charles McAvoy, Alfred P. James, Snowflake, Pat Coron, Champion.

Comment: Unless Gene and his pals can raise some money for an operation, a little girl will be a cripple for life. Gene goes off to the city and rounds up a sponsor for a radio series. As a stunt to attract a big audience, the prairie broadcasts are televised. (Don't ask who watches!)

"Very heart-warming story." -CR

"Mack Wright's direction keeps it moving from thrill to thrill, but comedy and music abound." -JGS

Songs: "Down in Slumberland," "Rainbow Trail," "My Old Saddle Pal," "There's an Empty Cot in the Bunkhouse Tonight," "I'll Be Thinking of You, Little Gal," "True Blue Bill," "New Jassackophone," and "Covered Wagon Coffee Theme."

* * *

GUNS AND GUITARS (Republic, 1936) 55 M.

Rating: ***

Producer, Nat Levine; director, Joseph Kane; screenplay, Dorrell and Stuart McGowan.

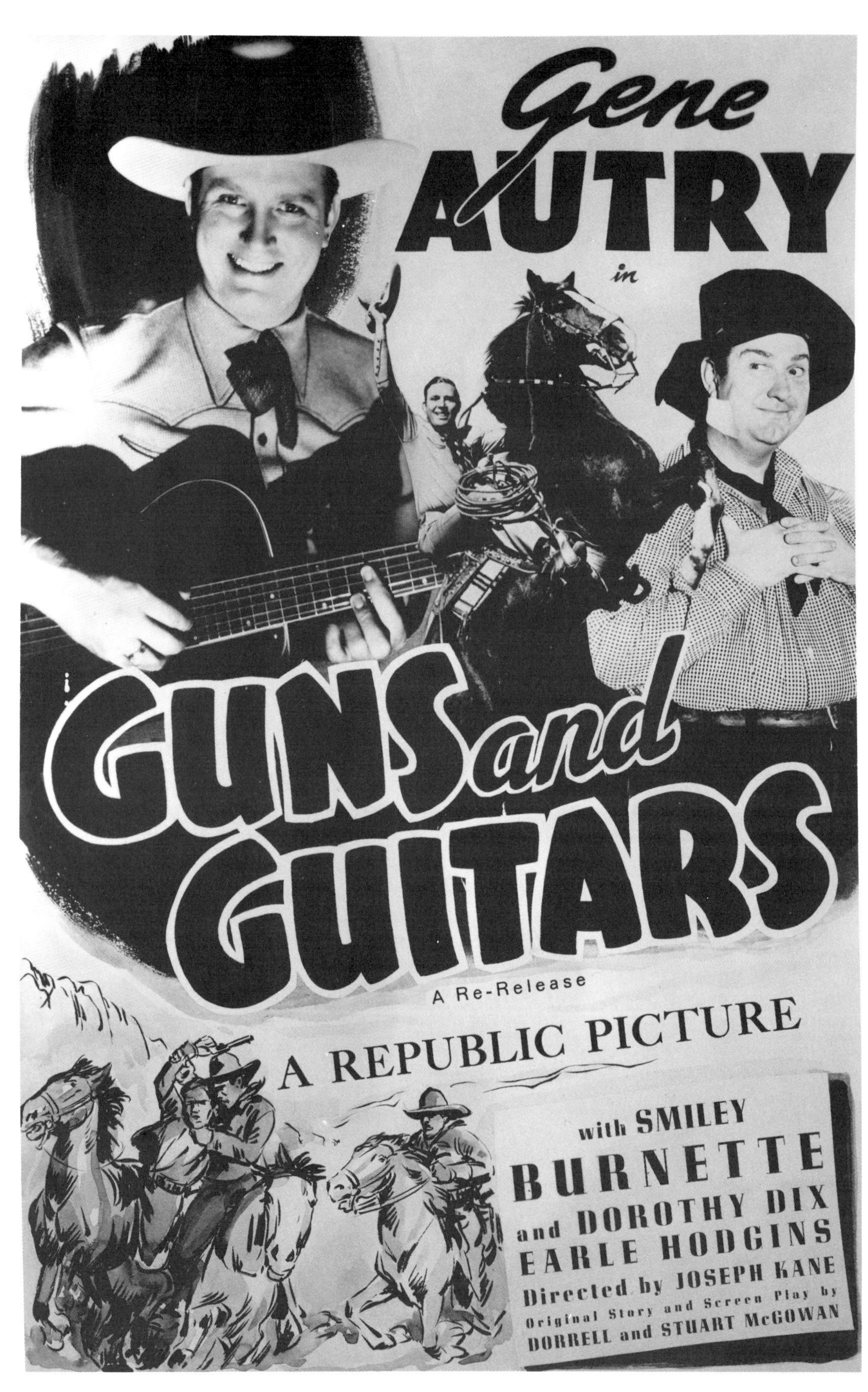
Gene
AUTRY
in
GUNS and
GUITARS
A Re-Release
A REPUBLIC PICTURE
with SMILEY
BURNETTE
and DOROTHY DIX
EARLE HODGINS
Directed by JOSEPH KANE
Original Story and Screen Play by
DORRELL and STUART McGOWAN

Cast: Gene Autry, Smiley Burnette, Dorthy Dix, Tom London, Charles King, J.P. McGowan, Earl Hodgins, Frankie Marvin, Eugene Jackson, Jack Rockwell, Ken Cooper, Tracy Lane, Wes Warner, Jim Corey, Frank Stravenger, Harrison Greene, Pascale Perry, Bob Burns, Champion.

Comment: The plot has Autry accused of the local sheriff's murder, but through the many plot twists Gene gets himself elected new sheriff and catches the real murderer.

"I consider this as one of the best of Gene's early films. It just has something intangible above the others." -TE

"The McGowan brothers wrote a part for their illustrious father (J.P.)." —JGS

Songs: "Guns and Guitars," "Riding' All Day," "Dreamy Valley," "I've Got Fine Relations," and "The Cowboy Medicine Show."

*   *   *

OH, SUSANNA (Republic, 1936) 60 M.

Rating: ***

Producer, Nat Levine; director, Joseph Kane; screenplay, Oliver Drake.

Cast: Gene Autry, Smiley Burnette, Francis Grant, Earl Hodgins, Donald Kirke, Boothe Howard, Clara Kimball Young, Carl Stockdale, Frankie Marvin, Ed Piel, Sr., Light Crust Doughboys Band, Champion.

Comment: On his way to Mineral Springs by train, Gene gets mugged, robbed of his clothes and belongings, and tossed from the moving train. He is befriended by two wandering minstrels (Burnette and Hodgins), who patch him up and accompany him to Mineral Springs. Gene finds the one who "done him wrong" and gets his clothes, guns, and honor back. Songs include the title song and "I'll Go Ridin' Down That Old Texas Trail," written by Autry and Burnette.

"Good action!" -CR

"Oliver Drake outdid himself this time around, providing Gene and Smiley with one of their most delightful scripts." -JGS

Songs: "I'll Go Ridin' Down That Texas Trail," "Oh, Susanna," "As Our Pals Ride By," "That Old Texas Trail Is Calling Me," "Dear Old Western Skies," "Whiskey Bill," "Where a Waterwheel Keeps Turning On," "Tiger Rag," "He Never Came Through with the Ring," "Ride On, Vaquero," "Heebie Jeebie Blues," and "Down Honeymoon Trail."

*   *   *

RIDE, RANGER, RIDE (Republic, 1936) 63 M.

Rating: **½

Producer, Nat Levine; director, Joseph Kane; screenplay, Dorrell and Stuart McGowan.

Cast: Gene Autry, Smiley Burnette, Kay Hughes, Monte Blue, George Lewis, Max Terhune, Robert E. Homans, Lloyd Whitlock, Chief Thundercloud, Tennessee Ramblers, Champion.

Comment: Autry is a Texas Ranger working undercover as a scout for the Army. He's trying to stop the Comanches from looting a wagon train loaded down with ammunition.

"Extraordinary showman Max Terhune made his screen debut in this one with an unusually good role, and turning in such a pleasing performance that he was asked to remain in Hollywood." -JGS

Songs: Ride, Ranger, Ride," "On the Sunset Trail," "The Yellow Rose of Texas," "I'm Doomed to Follow the Bugle," "When You and I Were Young, Maggie," "The Song of the Pioneers," "The Old Gray Mare," "Going Down the Trail," "La Cucaracha," and "Merry Mix-up."

*   *   *

THE BIG SHOW (Republic, 1936) 70 M.

Rating: ***½

Producer, Nat Levine; director, Mark V. Wright, screenplay, Dorrell and Stuart McGowan.

Cast: Gene Autry, Smiley Burnette, Kay Hughes, Sally Payne, William Newell, Max Terhune, Charles Judels, Rex King, Harry Worth, Mary Russell, Christine Maple, The Sons of the Pioneers, The Light Crust Doughboys Band, The Jones Boys, The Beverly Hills Billies, Champion.

Comment: The story has Gene playing a dual

role—a temperamental Western film star and his double. When the star skips out on a personal appearance at the Texas Centennial in Dallas (the scenic background for the story) Gene, the double, is persuaded to take over. The resulting comedy (mistaken identity engagements to two girls) and action (a fracas with Texas gangsters) make this film a high point of Gene's career to this time.

"Billed as a Gene Autry 'special' and sold as such to exhibitors, this was Republic's first attempt to place their most popular attraction in a more elaborate setting. . .many great songs and comic situations. . ." -JGS

Songs: "I'm Mad About You," "Ole Faithful," "Nobody's Darling But Mine," "The Lady Known As Lulu," "The Martins and the Coys," "Wild and Wooly West," "Roll, Wagons, Roll," Traveling' Along," and "Ride, Ranger, Ride."

* * *

THE OLD CORRAL (Republic, 1936) 52 M.

Rating: ***

Producer, Armand Schaefer; director, Joseph Kane; screenplay, Joseph Poland, Sherman Lowe.

Cast: Gene Autry, Smiley Burnette, Hope Manning, Sons of the Pioneers, Cornelius Keefe, Lon Chaney, Jr., John Bradford, Milburn Morante, Abe Lefton, Merrill McCormick, Charles Sullivan, Buddy Roosevelt, Lynton Brent, Frankie Marvin, Oscar and Elmer, Champion.

Comment: Autry, a sheriff and local singing cowboy star, is pursuing a group of singing bandits (The Sons of the Pioneers), Chicago gangsters loaded down with Tommy guns, and a singing heroine on the lam after witnessing a murder back in gangster-infested Chicago.

"I love it! A total escape from so-called reality. . .a classic! The universe created here—that of the singing cowboy— is a pretty special place." —JGS

Songs: "The Old Corral," "Old Pinto," "One Man Band," "Money Ain't No Use Anyway," "In the Heart of the West," "Silent Trails," "He's Gone up the Trail," "Down Along the Sleepy Rio Grande," and "La Cucaracha."

ROUNDUP TIME IN TEXAS (Republic, 1937) 63 M.

Rating: ***

Producer, Nat Levine; director, Joseph Kane; screenplay, Oliver Drake.

Cast: Gene Autry, Smiley Burnette, Maxine Davis, Cabin Kids, LeRoy Mason, Earle Hodgins, Dick Wessel, Buddy Williams, Elmer Fain, Cornie Anderson, Frankie Marvin, Ken Cooper, Champion.

Comment: Gene's brother, a diamond prospector in South Africa, has hit a strike and needs some horses to work the mine. He contacts Gene in Texas. Gene hops the next ship to Africa with Smiley and a herd of horses. Villains led by LeRoy Mason have their eyes on the diamonds, too.

"One of my favorites." -TE

"The funniest of all the films. . .Smiley delivers a truly brilliant performance, with some of the best material he was ever given." -JGS

Songs: "When the Bloom Is on the Sage," "The Old Chisholm Trail," "Prairie Rose," "Uncle Noah's Ark," "English Drinking Song," "The Caveman Song," "On Revival Day," "Dinah," "Witch Doctor Serenade," "Indian Song," and "Moon of Desire."

* * *

GIT ALONG, LITTLE DOGIES (Republic, 1937), 60 M.

Rating: ***

Producer, Armand Schaefer; director, Joseph Kane; screenplay, Dorrell and Stuart McGowan.

Cast: Gene Autry, Smiley Burnette, Maple City Four, Judith Allen, Weldon Heyburn, William Farnum, Willie Fung, Carleton Young, Will and Gladys Ahearn, The Cabin Kids, Champion.

Comment: The story concerns the conflict between cattle ranchers and a crooked oil drilling operation. Through the efforts of Gene and Frog real oil is discovered and the would-be swindlers are brought to justice.

"First of the Gene-versus-leading-lady plot lines. . . ." -JGS

Songs: "Git Along, Little Dogies," "In the Valley Where the Sun Goes Down," "A Cowboy's A.B.C.'s," "Honey, Bringin' Honey to You," "Chinatown, My Chinatown," "After You're Gone," "Happy Days Are Here Again," Medley: "Wait for the Wagon," "Long, Long, Ago," "Red River Valley," "Comin' Round the Mountain," "He's a Jolly Good Fellow," "Oh, Susanna," and "Goodnight, Ladies."

* * *

ROOTIN' TOOTIN' RHYTHM (Republic, 1937) 60 M.

Rating: **½

Producer, Armand Schaefer; director, Mark V. Wright; sceenplay, Jack Natteford.

Cast: Gene Autry, Smiley Burnette, Armida, Monte Blue, Al Clauser and The Outlaws, Hal Taliaferro, Ann Pendleton, Max Hoffman, Jr., Charles King, Frankie Marvin, Nina Campana, Champion.

Comment: The plot has Gene and Smiley trying to round up some cattle rustlers and in the process being suspected themselves of the cattlenapping.

"Great songs and an offbeat plot. . .Frankie Marvin has his biggest role here. . .Al Clauser and his Oklahoma Outlaws from WHO in Des Moines, Iowa, are featured. Visiting the band, WHO's sportcaster Ronald Reagan spent his first day on a movie set during the filming of this feature. Gene paid his friend several return visits many years later in the White House." -JGS

Songs: "Mexicali Rose," "I Hate To Say Goodbye to the Prairie," "Little Black Bronc," "On the Old Home Place," "The Dying Cowgirl."

* * *

YODELIN' KID FROM PINE RIDGE (Republic, 1937) 62 M.

Rating: ***

Producer, Armand Schaefer; director, Joseph Kane; screenplay, Jack Natteford, Dorrell and Stuart McGowan.

Cast: Gene Autry, Smiley Burnette, Betty Bronson, LeRoy Mason, Charles Middleton, Russell Simpson, Tennessee Ramblers, Jack Dougherty, Guy Wilkerson, Frankie Marvin, Henry Hall, Snowflake, Champion.

Comment: Set in the Georgia turpentine forests, this film is a partial reworking of the TUMBLING TUMBLEWEEDS theme, wherein Gene is banished by his father only to return to his home town with a wild West show five years later and find that the old man has been murdered by villains who are using a land-feud to cover up their own lawless deeds.

"Very good story." -CR

"Gene's mounts and riding are exceptionally good here." -JGS

Songs: "Sing Me a Song of the Saddle," "Down in Santa Fe," "At the Millhouse Wild West Show," "Travelin' Slow," and "Swing Low, Sweet Chariot."

* * *

PUBLIC COWBOY NO. 1 (Republic, 1937) 60 M.

Rating: ***

Producer, Sol C. Siegel; director, Joseph Kane; screenplay, Oliver Drake.

Cast: Gene Autry, Smiley Burnette, Ann Rutherford, William Farnum, James C. Morton, Frank LaRue, Marston Williams, Arthur Loft, Frankie Marvin, House Peters, Jr., Milburn Morante, King Mojave, Hal Price, Jack Ingram, Champion.

Comment: The plot takes place in the West of "today" with cattle rustlers using refrigerated trucks, planes, and two-way radios to purloin the cattle, slaughter them, and send them off to market—all in one quick operation.

"Gene at his best!" -CR

"This one had a strong appeal to me." -TE

"Bill Farnum is wonderful as the old sheriff, and Ann Rutherford is always a joy to watch." -JGS

Songs: "Wanderers of the Wasteland," "I Picked Up The Trail When I Found You," "The West Ain't What It Used to Be," "Old Buckaroo, Goodbye," and "The Defective Detective from Brooklyn."

* * *

BOOTS AND SADDLES (Republic, 1937) 60 M.

Rating: ***

Producer, Sol C. Siegel; director, Joseph Kane; screenplay, Jack Nattefod and Oliver Drake.

Cast: Gene Autry, Smiley Burnette, Judith Allen, Ra Hould, Guy Usher, Gordon Elliott, John Ward, Frankie Marvin, Chris Marvin, Stanley Blystone, Bud Osborne, Champion.

Comment: Ranch foreman Gene quickly wins over an uppity teen-age English boy who has just inherited his father's ranch. Together they then contend with villains who want to take the ranch away from them.

"Great songs!" -CR

". . .This picture (the first of Gene's to play Broadway) could be enjoyed by Western and non-Western audiences alike. When Dallas Burnette (Smiley's wife) and I ran this one at Iverson's Ranch in 1972, she turned to me and said, 'Smiley and I had thirty wonderful years of marriage, but I had forgotten how funny he really was until I saw this movie again!' " -JGS

Songs: "Take Me Back To My Boots and Saddles," "The One Rose," "Ridin' the Range," "Dusty Roads," "Cielito Lindo," and "Salud, Vaquero."

* * *

MANHATTAN MERRY-GO-ROUND (Republic, 1937)

Gene, along with many other recording artists, makes a guest appearance in this Phil Regan feature.

Song: "When It's Round-Up Time in Reno."

* * *

SPRINGTIME IN THE ROCKIES (Republic, 1937) 60 M.

Rating: ***½

Producer, Sol C. Siegel; director, Joseph Kane; screenplay, Gilbert Wright and Betty Burbridge.

Cast: Gene Autry, Smiley Burnette, Polly Rowles, Ula Love, Ruth Bacon, Jane Hunt, George Chesebro, Alan Bridge, Tom London, Edward Hearn, Frankie Marvin, William Hole, Edmund Cobb, Fred Burns, Jimmy's Saddle Pals, Champion.

Comment: Gene is the foreman of a cattle ranch owned by the absent Polly Rowles. A student of animal husbandry back East, she suddenly arrives at the ranch with a flock of sheep. All of Gene's tact is taxed as he tries to keep peace at home and with the other ranchers in the territory.

"Interesting story." -CR

"Human-interest plot. . .Smiley continued to quote the line, 'Sheep! sheep at Thorpe's Ranch!' throughout the years whenever he was confronted with a minor crisis in his daily life. . . ." -JGS

Songs: "When It's Springtime in the Rockies," "You're the Only Star In My Blue Heaven," "The Moon and I," "Give Me a Pony and an Open Prairie," "Down in the Land of Zulu," "Way Down Low," and "Hayride Wedding in June."

* * *

THE OLD BARN DANCE (Republic, 1938) 60 M.

Rating: ***

Producer, Sol C. Siegel; director, Joseph Kane; screenplay, Bernard McConville and Charles Francis Royal.

Cast: Gene Autry, Smiley Burnette, Helen Valkis, Sammy McKim, Walter Shrum and His Colorado Hillbillies, Stafford Sisters, Dick Weston (Roy Rogers), Maple City Four, Ivan Miller, Earl Dwire, Hooper Atchley, Raphael Bennett, Carleton Young, Frankie Marvin, Earle Hodgins, Gloria Rich, Champion.

Comment: Gene and his pals earn their living by selling work horses to ranchers. A tractor firm comes along and kills the horse-selling business for them. Soon they discover that the ranchers are having trouble with malfunctioning tractors. Gene doesn't need a Better Business Bureau to see that the tractor company is composed of a pack of crooks. With a little help from the ranchers, Gene saves the day.

"Fast-paced classic. . .Gene's last in the "early" Autry period, prior to his walkout. . ." -JGS

Songs: "At the Old Barn Dance," "Rocky Mountain Rose," "Let's Go Roaming around the Range," "The Old Gray Mare," "You're the Only Star in My Blue Heaven," "Only Eight Little Miles Left to Go," "The Old Mill," "The New Jassackophone," "Chewing Gum," and "She'll Be Comin' Round the Mountain."

GOLD MINE IN THE SKY (Republic, 1938) 60 M.

Rating: ***½

Producer, Charles E. Ford; director, Joseph Kane; screenplay, Jack Natteford and Betty Burbridge.

Cast: Gene Autry, Smiley Burnette, Carol Hughes, Craig Reynolds, Cupid Ainsworth, LeRoy Mason, Frankie Marvin, Robert Homans, Eddie Cherkose, Ben Corbett, Milburn Morante, Jim Corey, George Guhi, Stafford Sisters, J.L. Frank's "Golden West Cowboys," Champion.

Comment: The plot is again "simple cowboy in conflict with haughty, pseudosophisticated city girl who thinks he's just a dumb cowpoke." After the usual verbal and physical skirmishes with him, she grows to respect and even—heaven forfend—love him. He teaches her the "ways of the West," mostly by crooning prairie hymns in the moonlight.

"Very good plot." -CR

"Great music. J.L. Frank, the kindly promoter who first introduced Gene and Smiley in 1933, got his son-in-law, Pee Wee King, and the Golden West Cowboys a part in this film." -JGS

Songs: "There's a Gold Mine in the Sky," "The Dude Ranch Cowboys," "As Long As I've Got My Horse," "I'd Love To Call You My Sweetheart," "That's How Donkeys Were Made," "I'm a Tumbleweed Tenor," and "Comin' Round the Mountain."

* * *

MAN FROM MUSIC MOUNTAIN Republic, 1938) 58 M.

Rating: ***

Producer, Charles E. Ford; director, Joseph Kane; screenplay, Betty Burbridge and Luci Ward; original story, Bernard McConville.

Cast: Gene Autry, Smiley Burnette, Carol Hughes, Sally Payne, Ivan Miller, Edward Cassidy, Lew Kelly, Howard Chase, Albert Terry, Frankie Marvin, Earl Dwire, Lloyd Ingraham, Lillian Drew, Al Taylor, Joe Yrigoyen, Polly Jenkins and Her Plowboys, Champion.

Comment: The plot to this episode concerns unscrupulous land developers that Autry and company must thwart. Polly Jenkins and Her Plowboys add musical merriment to the feature.

"Very fast-paced and great fun." -JGS

Songs: "The Man from Music Mountain," "Goodbye Pinto," "I'm Beginning to Care," "Love, Burning Love," "She Works Third Tub at the Laundry," "There's a Little Deserted Town on the Prairie," and "All Nice People."

* * *

PRAIRIE MOON (Republic, 1938) 58 M.

Rating: ***½

Producer, Harry Grey; director, Ralph Staub; screenplay, Betty Burbridge and Stanley Roberts.

Cast: Gene Autry, Smiley Burnette, Shirley Deane, Tommy Ryan, Walter Tetley, David Gorcey, Stanley Andrews, William Pawley, Warner Richmond, Raphael Bennett, Tom London, Bud Osborne, Jack Rockwell, Peter Potter, Champion.

Comment: Three tough city kids (Chicago, as usual) are left a ranch when their father dies. Autry is the foreman of the ranch and assumes custody of the delinquents. The plot utilizes a background of cattle rustling for Autry to teach the young toughs the difference between right and wrong.

"Ralph Staub, director of Columbia's long-running short subject series, SCREEN SNAPSHOTS, excellently blended comedy, music and dramatic content in this superior film. . .Tommy Ryan, Leo Gorcey's brother David, and Walter Tetley (radio actor best remembered as The Great Gildersleeve's nephew, LeRoy) are excellent as the gangster's tough sons." -JGS

Songs: "The West, a Nest, and You," "Rhythm of the Hoofbeats," "He's In the Jailhouse Now," "Good Old-fashioned Hoedown," "The Story of Trigger Joe," and "The Girl In the Middle of My Heart."

* * *

RHYTHM OF THE SADDLE (Republic, 1938) 58 M.

Rating: ***

Producer, Harry Grey; director, George Sherman; screenplay, Paul Franklin.

Cast: Gene Autry, Smiley Burnette, Pert Kelton, Peggy Moran, LeRoy Mason, Arthur Loft, Ethan Laidlaw, Walter de Palma, Archie Hall, Eddie Hart, Eddie Acuff, Champion.

Comment: The story concerns a young female ranch owner/Frontier Week Rodeo manager (Peggy Moran) who is in danger of losing her rodeo contract. Her foreman, Gene Autry, helps her overcome the obstacles of chief heavy, LeRoy Mason, that include a bum murder rap, burning barns, fixed rodeo events, and a to-the-death stagecoach race for the finale.

"Good songs." -GP

"Pert Kelton and Smiley make a very funny team." -JGS

Songs: "Let Me Call You Sweetheart," "When Mother Nature Sings Her Lullaby," "The Old Trail," "The Merry-Go-Roundup," and "Oh, Ladies!"

* * *

WESTERN JAMBOREE (Republic, 1938) 57 M.

Rating: ***

Producer, Harry Grey; director, Ralph Staub; screenplay, Gerald Geraghty from original story by Pat Harper.

Cast: Gene Autry, Smiley Burnette, Jean Rouverol, Ester Muir, Joe Frisco, Frank Darien, Margaret Armstrong, Harry Holmon, Edward Raquelio, Bently Hewlett, Kermit Maynard, George Walcott, Ray Teal, Eddie Dean, Champion.

Comment: Helium gas bandits are the novel owlhoots this time. When the theives can't lay claim to the helium well any other way, they secretly lay a pipeline to tap the well. Gene takes time between the songs he sings to figure out what's up and to get the sheriff and his posse to help him capture the crooks.

"Offbeat characters and situations...a lesser entry in some respects, but pleasing because of its uniqueness. Smiley really is floating above the treetops with the helium balloon; it is not a process shot, and Smiley later commented that he was more than slightly jittery being up there!" -JGS

Songs: "Old November Moon," "Roll On, Little Dogies, Roll On," "When the Bloom Is on the Sage," "El Rancho Grande," "Cielito Lindo," "I Love the Morning," and "The Balloon Song."

* * *

HOME ON THE PRAIRIE (Republic, 1939) 58 M.

Rating: ***

Producer, Harry Grey; director, Jack Townley; screenplay, Charles Arthur Powell and Paul Franklin.

Cast: Gene Autry, Smiley Burnette, June Storey, George Cleveland, Jack Mulhall, Walter Miller, Gordon Hart, Hal Price, Earl Hodgins, Ethan Laidlaw, John Beach, Jack Ingram, Bob Woodward, The Rodeoliers, Sherven Brothers, Champion.

Comment: June Storey, playing the owner of a cattle ranch, makes her first of many appearances in this Autry film. Gene's a border inspector whose job is to see to it that no germ-carrying materials or animals cross into the territory. As you might expect, there is an outbreak of hoof-and-mouth disease that forces Gene to quarantine the area. Some unscrupulous cattlemen attempt to ship their diseased cattle to market anyway, causing Gene one heck of a lot of trouble.

Songs: "Moonlight On the Ranch House," "There's Nothin' Like Work," "I'm Gonna Round Up My Blues," and "Big Bull Frog."

* * *

MEXICALI ROSE (Republic, 1939) 58 M.

Rating: ****

Producer, Harry Grey; director, George Sherman; screenplay, Gerald Geraghty from an original story by Luci Ward and Connie Lee.

Cast: Gene Autry, Smiley Burnette, Noah Beery, Luana Walters, William Farnum, William Royle, LeRoy Mason, Wally Albright, Kathryn Frye, Roy Barcroft, Dick Botiller, Vic Demourelle, John Beach, Henry Otho, Champion.

Comment: This feature is one of four or five Autry films that possess the quintessence of the Autry

GENE AUTRY
MEXICALI ROSE
with
SMILEY BURNETTE
NOAH BEERY LUANA WALTERS WILLIAM FARNUM
Directed by GEORGE SHERMAN
A Republic PICTURE

film style. All the ingredients are here: a popular title song and other Western ballads sung by Gene; Smiley Burnette's slapstick comedy and novelty songs; some ne'er-do-wells to keep the thrill quota sufficient for action buffs; a charming leading lady; and lots of kids involved in the sentimental story about a mission padre trying to help poor Mexican children while having to protect the mission land from oil swindlers.

"One of my favorites." -GP

"Liked the story very much." -CR

"A fresh, appealing film." -TE

Songs: "Mexicali Rose," "You're the Only Star In My Blue Heaven," "El Rancho Grande," "My Orchestra's Driving Me Crazy," and "Robin Hood."

BLUE MONTANA SKIES (Republic, 1939) 56 M.

Rating: ***½

Producer, Harry Grey; director, B. Reeves Eason; screenplay, Gerald Geraghty from an original story by Norman S. Hall and Paul Franklin.

Cast: Gene Autry, Smiley Burnette, June Storey, Harry Woods, Tully Marshall, Al Bridge, Glenn Strange, Dorothy Granger, Edmund Cobb, Robert Winkler, Jack Ingram, Augie Gomez, John Beach, Walt Shrum and The Colorado Hillbillies, Champion.

Comment: Fur smuggling is the plot ploy in this Autry adventure. When Gene and Frog try to discover the murderer of their partner, they come upon a fur smuggling ring operating from a dude ranch near the Canadian border.

"Very good outdoor action." -CR

"On the set Smiley bedeviled the cast and crew by saying 'smur fugglers' instead of 'fur smugglers.' Some retakes were needed." -JGS

Songs: "Blue Montana Skies," "I Just Want You," "Rockin' In the Saddle All Day," "The Old Geezer," and "Rootin' Tootin' Figures of the West."

* * *

MOUNTAIN RHYTHM (Republic, 1939) 57 M.

Rating: ***

Producer, Louis Grey; director, B. Reeves Eason; screenplay, Gerald Geraghty from a story by Connie Lee.

Cast: Gene Autry, Smiley Burnette, June Storey, Maude Eburne, Ferris Taylor, Walter Fenner, Jack Pennick, Hooper Atchley, Bernard Suss, Ed Cassidy, Jack Ingram, Tom London, Frankie Marvin, Champion.

Comment: Frog's Aunt Mathilda and other ranchers are about to lose their valuable grazing land when the cunning owner or a nearby resort hotel schemes to buy the land at a low price for his own future development. Gene helps the ranchers to round up and sell their cattle in order to buy the grazing land which they had been using without charge during many long years.

"The film blends exciting action with top-notch music and tomfoolery." -JGS

Songs: "It Makes No Difference Now," "Highways Are Happy Ways," "It Was Only a Hobo's Dream," "A Gold Mine In Your Heart," "Knights Of the Open Road," Medley: "Put On Your Old Gray Bonnet," "Long, Long Ago," "Oh, Dem Golden Slippers," "Old MacDonald's Farm."

* * *

COLORADO SUNSET (Republic, 1939) 58 M.

Rating: ***½

Producer, William Berke; director George Sherman; screenplay, Betty Burbridge and Stanley Roberts from an original story by Luci Ward and Jack Natteford.

Cast: Gene Autry, Smiley Burnette, June Storey, Barbara Pepper, Larry "Buster" Crabbe, Robert Barrat, Patsy Montana, The CBS-KMBC Texas Rangers, Purnell Pratt, William Farnum, Kermit Maynard, Jack Ingram, Elmo Lincoln, Frankie Marvin, Champion.

Comment: A milk war provides the impetus for this Autry film. It seems milk ranchers are being coerced into joining a "protective" association, otherwise their milk runs the risk of never making it to market.

"Liked all the stars." -CR

"One of his best." -TE

Songs: "Colorado Sunset," "Seven Years With the Wrong Woman," "Poor Little Dogie," "Beautiful Isle of Somewhere," "I Want To Be a Cowboy's Sweetheart," "On the Merry Old Way Back Home," and "Vote for Autry."

* * *

IN OLD MONTEREY (Republic, 1939) 74 M.

Rating: ***½

Producer, Armand Schaefer; director, Joseph Kane; screenplay, Gerald Geraghty, Dorrell and Stuart McGowan.

Cast: Gene Autry, Smiley Burnette, June Storey, George Hayes, Hoosier Hot Shots, Sarie and Sallie, The Rand Boys, Stuart Hamblen, Billy Lee, Jonathan Hale, Robert Warwick, William Hall, Eddie Conrad, Champion.

Comment: The topical plot deals with 1939 army preparedness for the war abroad. Gene's an army attache assigned to acquire out-of-the-way land for use in bombing practice exercises. Some unscrupulous persons try to make an illegal profit from the trying times until Gene straightens things out.

"An impressive, excellent film. . .one of his best." -TE

"The death of the child seems excessively melodramatic in a film which devotes so much footage to the hijinks of the Hoosier Hot-Shots and Sarie and Sallie." -JGS

Songs: "It Happened in Monterey," "Little Pardner," "My Buddy," "Born to the Saddle,"

"The Vacant Chair," "Tumbling Tumbleweeds," "Columbia, Gem of the Ocean," "It Looks Like Rain," and "Virginia Blues."

* * *

ROVIN' TUMBLEWEEDS (Republic, 1939) 62 M.

Rating: ***

Producer, William Berke; director, George Sherman; screenplay, Betty Burbridge, Dorrell and Stuart McGowan.

Cast: Gene Autry, Smiley Burnette, Mary Carlisle, Douglas Dumbrille, William Farnum, Lee "Lasses" White, Ralph Peters, Gordon Hart, Vic Potel, Jack Ingram, Sammy McKim, Reginald Bartow, Eddie Kane, Gay Usher, Pals of the Golden West, Champion.

Comment: A crooked Washington politician is stalling a flood control bill long enough to set himself up for a huge land sale profit when the bill goes through. The poor, common people who are affected by the scheme finally rise up and elect radio singer Gene Autry to Congress.

"This vastly underrated film is one of the finest of Gene's career." -JGS

Songs: "Back in the Saddle Again," "Paradise in the Moonlight," "Ole Peaceful River," "Away Out Yonder," "Rocky Mountain Express," "A Girl Like You and a Night Like This," "The Sunny Side of the Cell," and "We've Got a Date with Nolan."

* * *

SOUTH OF THE BORDER (Republic, 1939) 71 M.

Rating: ****

Producer, William Berke; director, George Sherman; screenplay, Betty Burbridge and Gerald Geraghty from an original story by Dorrell and Stuart McGowan.

Cast: Gene Autry, Smiley Burnette, June Storey, Lupita Tovar, Mary Lee, Duncan Renaldo, Frank Reicher, Alan Edwards, Claire DuBrey, Dick Botiller, William Farnum, Selmer Jackson, Sheila Darcy, Rex Lease, The Checkerboard Band, Champion.

Comment: The stylistic presentation of the title song is first heard as part of the prediction of a fortune teller. In the main plot line Gene and Smiley are U.S. agents sent to quell a potential Mexican revolution.

"Great!" -GP

"Gene Autry's best-loved film. . . ." -JGS

"A top film--possibly my favorite of all he made." -TE

Songs: "South of the Border," "Goodbye, Little Darling, Goodbye," "Girl of my Dreams," "Come to the Fiesta," "Yippi-Yaddi-Yah!" "Fat Caballero," "Moon of Manana," "We'll Be With You," "The Merry-Go-Roundup."

* * *

RANCHO GRANDE (Republic, 1940) 68 M.

Rating: ***½

Producer, William Berke; director, Frank McDonald; screenplay, Bradford Ropes, Betty Burbridge, Peter Milne from an original story by Peter Milne and Connie Lee.

Cast: Gene Autry, Smiley Burnette, June Storey, Mary Lee, Dick Hogan, Ellen D. Lowe, Ferris Taylor, Joseph De Stefani, Roscoe Ates. Rex Lease, Ann Baldwin, Roy Barcroft, Edna Lawrence, Pals of the Golden West, Boys' Choir of St. Joseph's School, Brewer Kids, Champion.

Comment: June Storey is a "madcap Eastern heiress" who takes over Rancho Grande, which was willed to her by her grandfather. She and foreman Gene don't always agree on how the ranch should be run. When some baddies try to upset the new irrigation system, Gene goes into action.

"A highly enjoyable film of the type which could be widely appreciated by audiences not usually attracted to Westerns." -JGS

Songs: "El Rancho Grande," "I Don't Belong in Your World," "There'll Never Be Another Pal Like You," "You Can Take the Boy Out of the Country," "The Dude Ranch Cowhands," "Whistle," and "Swing of the Range."

* * *

SHOOTING HIGH (Twentieth Century-Fox, 1940) 65 M.

SOUTH OF THE BORDER
A SCREEN SENSATION!
STARRING
Gene AUTRY
WITH
SMILEY BURNETTE
JUNE STOREY
LUPITA TOVAR
MARY LEE
DUNCAN RENALDO
DIRECTED BY
GEORGE SHERMAN
A Republic
PICTURE

Rating: ***

Producer, John Stone; director, Alfred E. Green; screenplay, Lou Breslow and Owen Francis.

Cast: Gene Autry, Jane Withers, Marjorie Weaver, Robert Lowery, Katherine Aldridge, Hobart Cavanaugh, Frank M. Thomas, Jack Carson, Hamilton MacFadden, Charles Middleton, Ed Brady, Tom London, Eddie Acuff, Pat O'Malley, George Chandler, Champion.

Comment: This is Gene's first film away from Republic and the first starring feature in which he does not play himself. There is a movie company coming to Gene's Western town to film the life of his grandfather, who was quite a hero in his time. Gene is induced to play the role. When some gangsters pull a bank robbery while the film is rolling, Gene, himself, becomes a hero by capturing the bandits.

"I didn't like the name change (from 'Gene Autry')." -TE

"...a pleasant entry...no more no less...." -JGS

Songs: "Little Old Band of Gold," "There's Only One Love in a Lifetime," "Wanderers of the Wasteland," and "In Our Little Shanty of Dreams."

This publicity photo is from GAUCHO SERENADE (1940). Gene has just finished singing "A Song at Sunset" as the scene occurs in the film. The horse is the Champion, Jr., which was used primarily on personal appearances.

GAUCHO SERENADE (Republic, 1940) 66 M.

Rating: ***½

Producer, William Berke; director, Frank McDonald; screenplay, Betty Burbridge and Bradford Ropes.

Cast: Gene Autry, Smiley Burnette, June Storey, Duncan Renaldo, Mary Lee, Clifford Severn, Jr., Lester Matthews, Smith Ballew, Joseph Crehan, William Ruhl, Wade Boteler, Ted Adams, Wendell Niles, The Velascos, Jose Eslava's Orchestra, Champion.

Comment: Gene works with cattle ranchers to overcome the corrupt leaders of a packing company.

"An underrated film... (It) has the funniest dialogue and whole sequences of all the Autry films." -TE

"... Gene at the peak of his career, giving the public... his kind, reassuring personality...." -JGS

Songs: "Gaucho Serenade," "Keep Rolling' Lazy Longhorns," "A Song At Sunset," "The Singing Hills," "We're Heading for the Wide Open Spaces," "The Wooing of Kitty McFootie," and "Give Out with a Song."

* * *

CAROLINA MOON (Republic, 1940) 65 M.

Rating: ***½

Producer, William Berke; director, Frank McDonald; screenplay, Winston Miller from an original story by Connie Lee.

Cast: Gene Autry, Smiley Burnette, June Storey, Mary Lee, Eddy Waller, Hardie Albright, Frank Dae, Terry Nibert, Robert Fiske, Etta McDaniel, Paul White, Fred Ritter, Ralph Sanford, Jimmie Lewis and His Texas Cowboys, Champion.

Comment: Gene finds himself in the South trying to save some old plantations from a local land wheeler-dealer.

"Good action." -CR

"Smiley is hilarious!!" -JGS

Songs: "Carolina Moon," "Say Si, Si," and "Dreams That Won't Come True."

* * *

RIDE, TENDERFOOT, RIDE (Republic, 1940) 66 M.

Rating: ***½

Producer, William Berke; director, Frank McDonald; screenplay, Winston Miller from an original story by Betty Burbridge.

Cast: Gene Autry, Smiley Burnette, June Storey, Mary Lee, Warren Hull, Forbes Murray, Joe McGuinn, Joe Frisco, Isobel Randolph, Herbert Clifford, Mildred Shay, Cindy Walker, The Pacemakers, Champion.

Comment: This is another Autry film that deserves careful study by those who wish to better understand the fantastic success of the Autry pictures with audiences of the late thirties and early forties. The plot has Gene the heir to a meatpacking company. Snooty June Storey owns the rival company, whose underhanded executives are trying to run Autry out of business. Gene successfully exposes the dirty dealers and finds time to sing a number of songs.

"Great songs and story." -CR

"This is as out-and-out a comedy as Gene ever made, with very little traditional 'Western' content." -JGS

Songs: "Ride, Tenderfoot, Ride," "The Woodpecker Song," "When the Work's All Done This Fall," "Leaning On the Old Top Rail," "On the Range," "Eleven More Months and Ten More Days," "That Was Me by the Sea," and "Oh! Oh! Oh!"

* * *

MELODY RANCH (Republic, 1940) 80 M.

Rating: ***½

Producer, Sol C. Siegel; director, Joseph Santley; screenplay, Jack Moffitt and F. Hugh Herbert.

Cast: Gene Autry, Jimmy Durante, Ann Miller, Barton MacLane, Barbara Jo Allen (Vera Vague), George "Gabby" Hayes, Jerome Cowan, Mary Lee, Joseph Sawyer, Horace MacMahon, Clarence Wilson, William Benedict, Champion.

Comment: This Autry special is titled after his popular radio series and features some big show business names of the era. Jimmy Durante is particularly effective playing the radio announcer for the singing cowboy. The plot has radio singing star Gene Autry invited to return home to Torpedo, Arizona, to be honorary sheriff for the Frontier Days Celebration. Some town hoods rough up acting Sheriff Autry and try to send him packing back to the big city. His dander now up, Gene stays on to clean up the town just as it's done in Western films.

"Gene sang and looked his very best." -GP

"An elaborate, impressive film that was very enjoyable." -TE

"The songs are beautiful and Gene does an excellent job throughout, but the script does not present our hero in situations Autry enthusiasts like best. . .the film simply lacks the solid entertainment values of earlier releases." -JGS

Songs: "We Never Dream the Same Dream Twice," "Call of the Canyon," "Melody Ranch," "Vote for Autry," "Rodeo Rose," "Back in the Saddle Again," "My Gal Sal," and "Torpedo Joe."

* * *

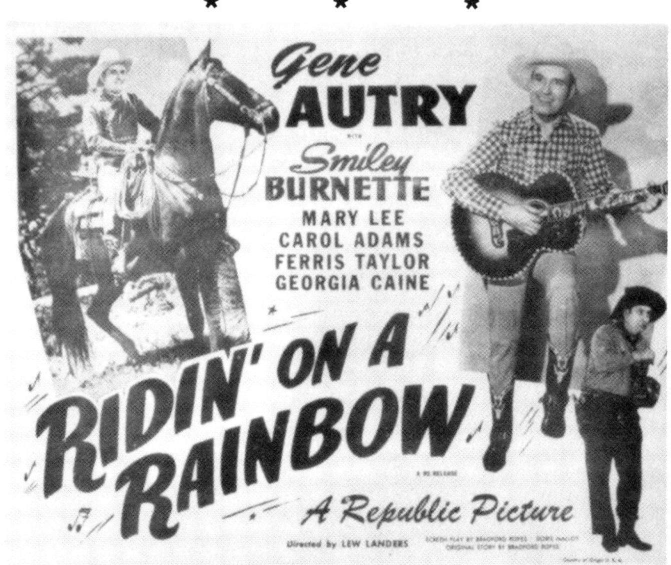

RIDING' ON A RAINBOW (Republic, 1941) 79 M.

Rating: ***½

Producer, Harry Grey; director, Lew Landers; screenplay, Bradford Ropes, Doris Malloy from a story by Ropes.

Cast: Gene Autry, Smiley Burnette, Mary Lee, Carol Adams, Ferris Taylor, Georgia Caine, Byron Fougler, Ralf Harolde, Jimmy Conlin, Guy Usher, Anthony Warde, Forrest Taylor, Burr Caruth, Champion.

Comment: The investigation of a local bank robbery leads Gene to a showboat where teen-aged Mary Lee and her father are the entertainers. It soon becomes apparent that Mary Lee's father has cooperated with the robbers. Gene gets the whole matter resolved to everybody's satisfaction.

"This one set the tone for all the 1941 entries, blending top-notch songs (such as the Oscar-nominated 'Be Honest with Me') with strong dramatic plot elements." -JGS

Interestingly, even though Gene starred in the movie and his picture appears on the sheet music, he never recorded the song.

Songs: "Riding' on a Rainbow," "Hunky Dunky Dory," "Steamboat Bill," "Be Honest with Me," "Carry Me Back to the Lone Prairie," "I'm the Only Lonely One," "Sing a Song of Laughter," and "What's Your Favorite Holiday."

* * *

BACK IN THE SADDLE (Republic, 1941) 73 M.

Rating: ***½

Producer, Harry Grey; director, Lew Landers; screenplay, Richard Murphy and Jesse Lasky, Jr.

Cast: Gene Autry, Smiley Burnette, Mary Lee, Edward Norris, Jacqueline Wells, Addison Richards, Arthur Loft, Edmund Elton, Joe McGuinn, Edmund Cobb, Robert Barron, Champion.

Comment: A copper mine is opened near the ranch young Tom Bennett (Edward Norris) has just inherited, and the pollution from the mine is fast poisoning the cattle on the range. Gene tries to solve the problem by reasoning with both sides, but Tom's impetuous behavior leads everyone into more trouble. The story ends with a shoot-out in which the boom town is destroyed and the copper mine is finally shut down.

"Very good from start to finish." -CR

Songs: "Back in the Saddle Again," "You Are My Sunshine," "In the Jailhouse Now," "I'm an Old Cowhand," "When the Cactus Is in Bloom," "Ninety-nine Bullfrogs," and "Swingin' Sam, the Cowboy Man."

* * *

THE SINGING HILL (Republic, 1941) 65 M.

Rating: ***

Producer, Harry Grey; director, Lew Landers; screenplay, Olive Cooper from a story by Jesse Lasky, Jr. and Richard Murphy.

Cast: Gene Autry, Smiley Burnette, Virginia Dale, Mary Lee, Spencer Charters, Gerald Oliver Smith, George Meeker, Wade Boteler, Harry Stubbs, Cactus Mack Peters, Jack Kirk, Champion.

Comment: Josephine Adams (Virginia Dale), a wild and irresponsible young heiress who owns the Circle R Ranch, plans to sell it, thus preventing neighboring ranchers from using the rich grazing lands any longer. Gene tries to prevent this by asking a friendly old judge to declare her mentally unbalanced—at least long enough so that she may be convinced not to sell.

" 'Realism' turns to downright somberness here. Comic and tragic elements not blended too smoothly." -JGS

Songs: "The Singing Hills," "Blueberry Hill," "Good Old-Fashioned Hoedown," "The Last Round-up," "Ridin' Down That Ole Texas Trail," "Let a Smile Be Your Umbrella," "Sail the Seven Seas," "Tumbledown Shack in Havana," and "Patsy's Birthday."

* * *

SUNSET IN WYOMING (Republic, 1941) 65 M.

Rating: ***

Producer, Harry Grey; director, William Morgan; screenplay, Ivan Goff and Ann Morrison Chapin.

Cast: Gene Autry, Smiley Burnette, George Cleveland, Maris Wrixon, Robert Kent, Sarah Edwards, Monte Blue, Dick Elliott, John Dilson, Stanley Blystone, Champion.

Comment: In this episode Gene is attempting to teach a logging company a few things about land conservation. His efforts take him to a swanky country club, fancy swimming pools, and even a ball where everyone shows up in formal gowns or tails, including Frog.

". . .blends frivolity with an unusually austere story." -JGS

Songs: "I Was Born in Old Wyoming," "Casey Jones," "There's a Home in Wyoming," "Sing Me a Song of the Saddle," and "Twenty-one Years."

* * *

UNDER FIESTA STARS (Republic, 1941) 68 M.

Rating: ***

Producer, Harry Grey; director, Frank McDonald; screenplay, Karl Brown and Eliot Gibbons.

Cast: Gene Autry, Smiley Burnette, Carol Hughes, Frank Darien, Joseph Strauch, Jr., Pauline Drake,

Ivan Miller, Sam Flint, John Merton, Jack Kirk, Elias Gamboa, Inez Palange, Champion.

Comment: Gene and Barbara Erwin (Carol Hughes) each inherit half of the late Dad Erwin's ranch and mining property. Neither can sell without the other's consent. Gene is interested in following the wishes of Dad Erwin to the letter, but Barbara wants to sell out for ready cash. She hires some men to "convince" Gene to sell, too.

". . .enough Autry elements to keep us happy." -JGS

Songs: "Under Fiesta Stars," "Purple Sage in the Twilight," "I've Got No Use for the Women," "Keep It in the Family," and "When You're Smiling."

* * *

DOWN MEXICO WAY (Republic, 1941) 77 M.

Rating: ****

Producer, Harry Grey; director, Joseph Santley; screenplay, Olive Cooper and Albert Duffy from an original story by Dorrell and Stuart McGowan.

Cast: Gene Autry, Smiley Burnette, Fay McKenzie, Harold Huber, Sidney Blackmer, Joe Sawyer, Andrew Tombes, Murray Alper, Arthur Loft, Duncan Renaldo, Paul Fix, Julian Rivero, Ruth Robinson, Thornton Edwards, The Herrara Sisters, Champion.

Comment: The plot takes Gene and Frog south of the border in pursuit of con men who have fleeced the citizens of Sage City out of their hard-earned savings.

"Very, very good in the uncut version!" -GP

"Gene was great!" -CR

". . . the beautiful songs and leisurely Autry-like pace make this a big winner!" -JGS

Songs: "Down Mexico Way," "South of the Border," "Maria Elena," "The Cowboy and the Lady," "Beer Barrel Polka," "Guadalajara," "Las Altenitas," and "La Cachita."

* * *

SIERRA SUE (Republic, 1941) 64 M.

Rating: ***

Producer, Harry Grey; director, William Morgan; screenplay, Earl Felton and Julian Zimet.

Cast: Gene Autry, Smiley Burnette, Fay McKenzie, Frank Thomas, Robert Homans, Earle Hodgins, Dorothy Christy, Kermit Maynard, Jack Kirk, Eddie Dean, Budd Buster, Rex Lease, Champion.

Comment: There is a weed growing on the grazing land that has been poisoning the cattle. Government inspector Autry calls for chemical spraying of the area by airplanes, but the troublesome head of the cattlemen's association wants to burn the infected area. He finally relents, but during the air spraying, a hired gun who has not gotten the word shoots the plane out of the sky. Some days nothing goes right!

"Gorgeous photography, beautiful singing, and some very funny sequences (including Smiley's being shot out of a cannon) make this a most entertaining entry." -JGS

Songs: "Sierra Sue," "Be Honest with Me," "I'll Be True While You're Gone," "Ridin' the Range," and "Heebie Jeebie Blues."

* * *

COWBOY SERENADE (Republic, 1942) 66 M.

Rating: ***½

Producer, Harry Grey; director, William Morgan; screenplay, Olive Cooper.

Cast: Gene Autry, Smiley Burnette, Fay McKenzie, Cecil Cunningham, Addison Richards, Rand Brooks, Tristram Coffin, Lloyd "Slim" Andrews, Melinda Leighton, Johnnie Berkes, Champion.

Comment: Gene is attempting to break up a gambling ring and finds matters complicated when the leader turns out to be the father of the girl, Miss McKenzie.

". . . serious undertones are expertly worked in by director William Morgan. A fine cast. . . ." -JGS

Songs: "Sweethearts or Strangers," "Cowboy Serenade," "Nobody Knows," and "Tahiti Honey."

* * *

HEART OF THE RIO GRANDE (Republic, 1942) 68 M.

Rating: ***½

Producer, Harry Grey; director, William Morgan; screenplay, Lillie Hayward and Winston Miller from a story by Newlin B. Wildes.

Cast: Gene Autry, Smiley Burnette, Fay McKenzie, Edith Fellows, Pierre Watkin, Joe Strauch, Jr., William Haade, Sarah Padden, Jean Porter, The Jimmy Wakely Trio, Champion.

Comment: In this entry we have the situation of a wealthy and spoiled big-city girl taken to a dude ranch out West where the great outdoors and a singing cowboy save her soul.

". . . the classic Autry pacing which endeared him to audiences in theatres and which infuriates dull-witted 1980s Western film buffs. . . ." -JGS

Songs: "Deep in the Heart of Texas," "Cimarron (Roll On)," "Rocky Canyon," "I'll Wait for You," "Rancho Pillow," "Dusk on the Painted Desert," "Oh, Woe Is Me!" "A Rumble Seat for Two," and "A Rainbow in the Night."

* * *

HOME IN WYOMIN' (Republic, 1942) 67 M.

Rating: ***½

Producer, Harry Grey; director, William Morgan; screenplay, Robert Tasker and M. Coates Webster.

Cast: Gene Autry, Smiley Burnette, Fay McKenzie, Olin Howlin, Chick Chandler, Joseph Strauch, Jr., Forrest Taylor, James Seay, George Douglas, Charles Lane, Hal Price, Champion.

Comment: Gene plays a singing radio performer who goes home to Wyoming to help out a friend who's having financial problems with a rodeo he owns.

". . . this 'mystery-Western' is among Gene's best. . . ." -JGS

Songs: "Tweedle-O-Twill," "I'm Thinkin' Tonight of My Blue Eyes," "Any Bonds Today," "Twilight in Old Wyoming," "Clementine," "Be Honest With Me," and "Modern Design."

* * *

STARDUST ON THE SAGE (Republic, 1942) 65 M

Rating: ***

Producer, Harry Grey; director, William Morgan; screenplay, Betty Burbridge from a story by Dorrell and Stuart McGowan.

Cast: Gene Autry, Smiley Burnette, Bill Henry, Edith Fellows, Louise Currie, Emmett Vogan, George Ernest, Vince Barnett, Betty Farrington, Roy Barcroft, Tom London, Champion.

Comment: A Girl who operates a radio station deceives the townsfolk into believing Gene Autry advises them to buy stock in a mine in which the girl's brother has invested the cattlemen's money illegally. Gene and Frog attempt to discover whether or not the mine operations are legitimate.

". . . some extra-good comic and physical action sequences." -JGS

Songs: "I'll Never Let You Go, Little Darlin'," "You'll Be Sorry," "When the Roses Bloom Again," "Wouldn't You Like to Know?" "Goodnight Sweetheart," "Perfidia," Medley: "You Are My Sunshine," "Home on the Range," "Roll on, Little Dogies, Roll On," and "Deep in the Heart of Texas."

* * *

CALL OF THE CANYON (Republic, 1942) 71 M.

Rating: ***

Producer, Harry Grey; director, Joseph Santley; screenplay, Olive Cooper from an original story by Maurice Rapf and Olive Cooper.

Cast: Gene Autry, Smiley Burnette, Sons of the Pioneers Ruth Terry, Thurston Hall, Joe Strauch, Jr., Cliff Nazarro, Dorothea Kent, Edmund MacDonald, Marc Lawrence, John Harmon, John Holland, Champion.

Comment: The plot deals with cattlemen, a crooked purchasing agent for the packing company, and the head of the packing company. Gene, the cattlemen's representative, is called on to straighten out the trouble.

"Illogical script. . . but many nice touches compensate for these lapses. . . ." -JGS

Songs: "The Call of the Canyon," "Take Me Back To My Boots and Saddle," "Montana Plains," "Chilly Down in Chile," and "Somebody Else Is Taking My Place."

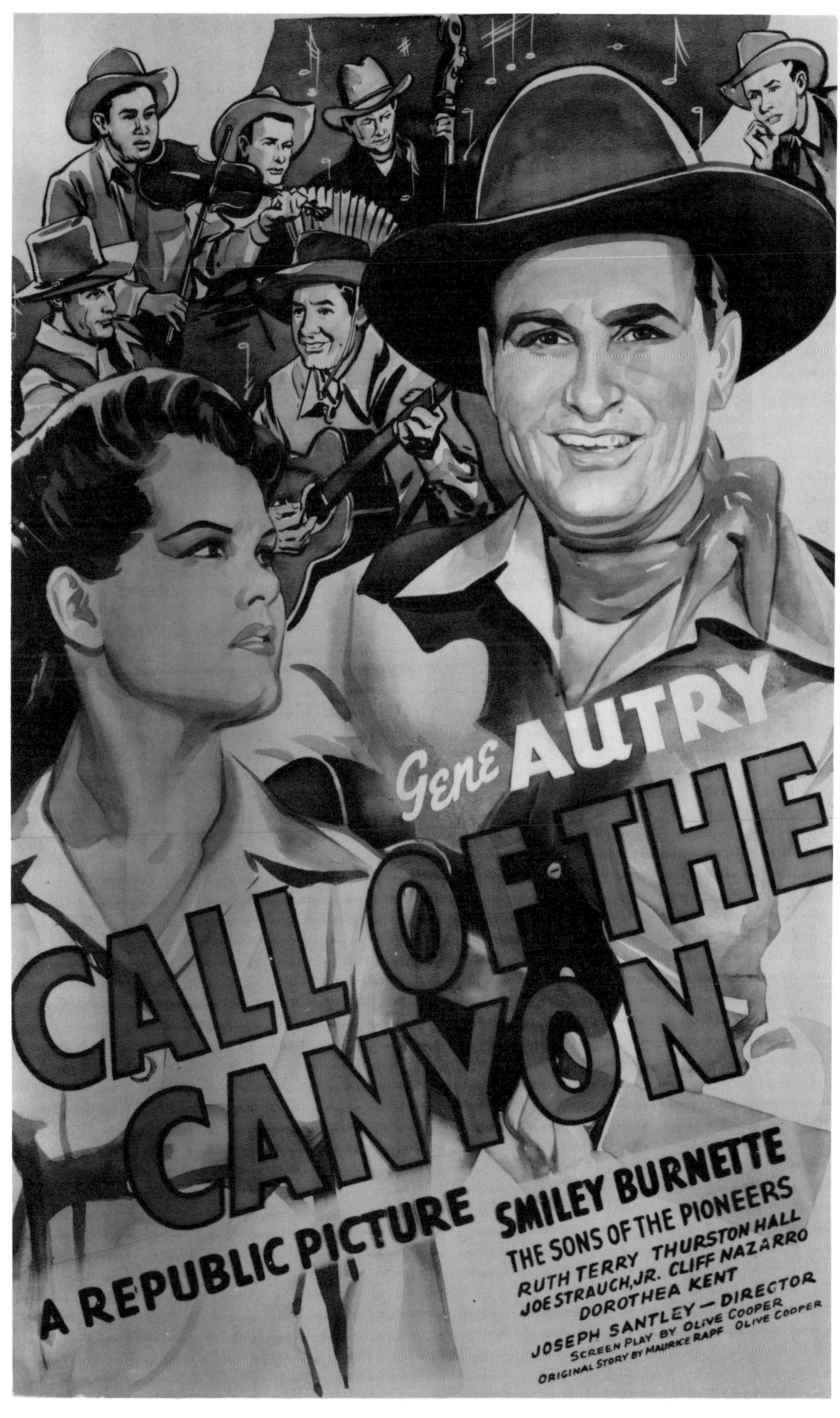
Gene AUTRY
CALL OF THE CANYON
A REPUBLIC PICTURE
SMILEY BURNETTE
THE SONS OF THE PIONEERS
RUTH TERRY THURSTON HALL
JOE STRAUCH, JR. CLIFF NAZARRO
DOROTHEA KENT
JOSEPH SANTLEY — DIRECTOR
SCREEN PLAY BY OLIVE COOPER
ORIGINAL STORY BY MAURICE RAPF OLIVE COOPER

BELLS OF CAPISTRANO (Republic, 1942) 73 M.

Rating: *** ½

Producer, Harry Grey; director, William Morgan; screenplay, Lawrence Kimple.

Cast: Gene Autry, Smiley Burnette, Virginia Grey, Lucien Littlefield, Morgan Conway, Claire DuBrey, Charles Lane, Joe Strauch, Jr., Maria Shelton, Tristram Coffin, Champion.

Comment: Two traveling rodeos are in competition with each other in this film. Gene goes to help out Virginia Grey, the owner of one of the shows. Prospects start to brighten for Miss Grey until her competitor introduces a little sabotage into the story. This was Gene's last feature before entering the service during World War II.

"One of the all-time greatest Gene Autry films—well-written, well-directed, beautifully acted. . . " -JGS

Songs: "At Sundown," "Don't Bite the Hand That's Feeding You," "Forgive Me," "Fort Worth Jail," and "In Old Capistrano."

* * *

SIOUX CITY SUE (Republic 1946) 69 M.

Rating: *** ½

Producer, Armand Schaefer; director Frank McDonald; screenplay, Olive Cooper.

Cast: Gene Autry, Lynne Roberts, Sterling Holloway, Richard Lane, Ralph Sanford, Ken Lundy, Helen Wallace, Pierre Watkin, Kenne Duncan, Cass County Boys, Champion.

Comment: This is the first postwar Autry Western musical. The story concerns a film company that is looking for a good Western singing voice for a cartoon donkey series. Lynne Roberts is a film scout who discovers cattleman Gene and lures him to Hollywood with the promise of a starring film career when in reality he turns out to be the tonsils for the animated donkey.

"Good songs and a pleasant story make a fitting welcome back." -JGS

Songs: "Sioux City Sue," "Oklahoma Hills," "Someday You'll Want Me To Want You," "Yours," "Ridin' Double," and "The Old Chisholm Trail."

* * *

TRAIL TO SAN ANTONE (Republic, 1947) 67 M.

Rating: ***

Producer, Armand Schaefer; director, John English; screenplay, Jack Natteford and Luci Ford.

Cast: Gene Autry, Peggy Stewart, Sterling Holloway, William Henry, John Duncan, Tristram Coffin, Dorothy Vaughan, Edward Keane, Ralph Peters, Cass County Boys, Champion.

Comment: The film is a horse-racing, human-interest story with Autry trying to help in the rehabilitation of a crippled jockey before the big race.

"Another good story and some pleasant songs and memorable characters." -JGS

Songs: "Down the Trail to San Antone," "That's My House," "By the River of the Roses," and "Shame On You."

* * *

TWILIGHT ON THE RIO GRANDE (Republic, 1947) 71 M.

Rating: *** ½

Producer, Armand Schaefer; director, Frank McDonald; screenplay, Dorrell and Stuart McGowan.

Cast: Gene Autry, Sterling Holloway, Adele Mara, Bob Steele, Charles Evans, Martin Garralaga, Howard J. Negley, George J. Lewis, Nacho Galinda, Tex Terry, Cass County Boys, Champion.

Comment: When Gene's partner is murdered one rainy evening in Mexico, Gene and The Cass County Boys follow the killer's trail, which leads through a mysterious path of smuggling and espionage.

"Liked the mystery." -CR

"Intriguingly different." -JGS

Songs: "Twilight on the Rio Grande," "The Old Lamplighter," "I Tipped My Hat and Slowly Walked Away," and "Great Grand-Dad."

* * *

SADDLE PALS (Republic, 1947) 71 M.

Rating: ***

Producer, Sidney Picker; director, Lesley Selander; screenplay, Bob Williams and Jerry Sackheim from an original story by Dorrell and Stuart McGowan.

Cast: Gene Autry, Lynne Roberts, Sterling Holloway, Irving Bacon, Damian O'Flynn, Charles Arnt, Jean Van, Tom London, Charles Williams, Francis McDonald, George Chandler, Edward Gargan, Cass County Boys, Champion.

Comment: The plot is about villains attempting to bankrupt a rich land-owner so that they can buy him out for a fraction of the true land value.

"Just great!" -CR

Songs: "I Wish I Had Never Met Sunshine," "You Stole My Heart," "Amapola," "The Covered

Wagon Rolled Right Along," and "They Went That-A-Way!"

*   *   *

ROBIN HOOD OF TEXAS (Republic, 1947) 71 M.

Rating: ***

Producer, Sidney Picker; director, Lesley Selander; screenplay, Jon K. Butler and Earle Snell.

Cast: Gene Autry, Lynne Roberts, Sterling Holloway, Adele Mara, James Cardwell, John Kellogg, Ray Walker, Michael Branden, Paul Bryar, James Flavin, Dorothy Vaughan, Stanley Andrews, Alan Bridge, Cass County Boys, Champion.

Comment: The plot concerns a bank stick-up and the resulting search for the missing loot. The windup has Gene giving chase to the robbers, who try escaping via buckboard. Gene finally intercepts them by jumping from that familiar rock into the buckboard and subduing them as the wagon careens along the trail.

"A real winner!" -GP

Songs: "Goin' Back to Texas," "Just To Know You," and "The Merry-Go-Roundup."

THE LAST ROUND-UP (Columbia, 1947) 76 M.

Rating: ****

Producer, Armand Schaefer; director, John English; screenplay, Jack Townley and Earl Shell.

Cast: Gene Autry, Jean Heather, Ralph Morgan, Carol Thurston, Mark Daniels, Bobby Blake, Russ Vincent, George "Shug" Fisher, Trevor Bardette, Lee Bennett, John Holloran, Sandy Sanders, Roy Gordon, Silverheels Smith (Jay Silverheels), Frances Rey, Bob Cason, Champion.

Comment: This is Gene's first Columbia release and first feature produced under his Gene Autry Productions banner. The film is one of the best features of his career and is his particular favorite. The story, placed in the modern West, deals with Gene's attempt to relocate a tribe of Indians onto new lands so that an aqueduct can be built on their barren, former homeland.

"Very good story!" -CR

Songs: "The Last Round-Up," "An Apple for the Teacher," "A Hundred and Sixty Acres in the Valley," "You Can't See the Sun When You're Crying," and "She'll Be Comin' 'Round the Mountain."

* * *

THE STRAWBERRY ROAN (Columbia, 1948) 76 M. Cinecolor

Rating: ****

Producer, Armand Schaefer; director, John English; screenplay, Dwight Cummins and Dorothy Yost from a story by Julian Zimet.

Cast: Gene Autry, Gloria Henry, Jack Holt, Dick Jones, Pat Buttram, Rufe Davis, John McGuire, Eddy Waller, Redd Harper, Jack Ingram, Eddie

THE SCREEN'S MIGHTIEST DRAMA
OF A STALLION OUTLAW...
in magnificent
outdoor CINECOLOR!
IT'S THE FIRST AUTRY COLOR PICTURE
COLUMBIA
PICTURES
presents
GENE AUTRY
and his famous horse,
CHAMPION
The STRAWBERRY
ROAN
HEAR
AUTRY SING
The Strawberry Roan
When the White Roses
Bloom in Red River Valley
The Angel Song
Can't Shake the Sands
of Texas from My Shoes
Texas Sandman
with
GLORIA HENRY · JACK HOLT · DICK JONES · PAT BUTTRAM
Screenplay by Dwight Cummins and Dorothy Yost
Directed by JOHN ENGLISH · Produced by ARMAND SCHAEFER
A Gene Autry Production

Gene and Dick Jones are seen here in this climactic moment from THE STRAWBERRY ROAN. The script called for Dick's character to ride Champion. Gene personally chose Dick for the role because he wanted only an expert horseman on Champ.

Parker, Ted Mapes, Sam Flint, Champion.

Comment: This is Gene's first color picture and first outing with Pat Buttram, albeit in a minor role. But the real star of the film is Gene's horse, Champion, whose beauty and training are nicely highlighted by the Cinecolor camera and the story. This is the story of Champion, a wild horse Gene captures on the range, and of the horse's attempts to escape the wrath of rancher Walt Bailey (Holt), whose son (Dick Jones) was thrown and crippled when he tried to break Champ.

"Cinecolor, a strong story, a great cast. . .plus good songs. . .makes this one a classic. . . ." -JGS

Songs: "The Strawberry Roan," "The Angel Song," "Texas Sandman," and "When the White Roses Bloom (in Red River Valley)."

LOADED PISTOLS (Columbia, 1949) 77 M.

Rating: ***½

Producer, Armand Schaefer; director, John English; screenplay, Dwight Cummins and Dorothy Yost.

Cast: Gene Autry, Barbara Britton, Chill Wills, Jack Holt, Russell Arms, Robert Shayne, Vince Barnett, Leon Weaver, Fred Kohler, Clem Bevans, Sandy Sanders, Champion.

Comment: When a friend of his is murdered, Gene sets out to discover the identity of the murderer and to disprove the faulty conclusion of the sheriff that the killer is young Larry Evans (Russell Arms).

You can be sure that this isn't Gene making the transfer, but it is a typical action scene from the Columbia series. A stunt man was, of course, always used for dangerous sequences. The production company couldn't put the entire film in jeopardy by letting the star risk his neck needlessly.

Songs: "Loaded Pistols," "Pretty Mary," "A Boy from Texas, A Girl from Tennessee," "When the Bloom Is on the Sage," and "Jim Crack Corn."

* * *

THE BIG SOMBRERO (Columbia, 1949) 77 M.

Rating: ***½

Producer, Armand Schaefer; director, Frank McDonald; screenplay, Olive Cooper.

Cast: Gene Autry, Elena Verdugo, Stephen Dunne, George J. Lewis, Vera Marshe, William Edmunds, Martin Garralaga, Gene Stutenroth, Neyle Morrow, Bob Cason, Pierce Lyden, Rian Valente, Antonio Filauri, Champion.

Comment: This feature is Gene's only other color movie. Out of work entertainer Gene Autry is given a job by a former associate in a scheme to move Mexican settlers off The Big Sombrero, a beautiful and vast estate south of the border. Gene, however, turns against his employer and befriends the poor rancheros.

"Delightful... colorful... great songs...." -JGS

Songs: "You Belong To My Heart," "I'm Thankful for Small Favors," "My Adobe Hacienda," "Rancho Pillow," "La Golondrina," "The Trail to Mexico," "Clementine," and "Goodbye to My Old Mexico."

* * *

RIDERS OF THE WHISTLING PINES (Columbia, 1949) 72 M.

Rating: ***

Producer, Armand Schaefer; director, John English; screenplay, Jack Townley.

Cast: Gene Autry, Patricia White, Jimmy Lloyd, Douglas Dumbrille, Damian O'Flynn, Clayton Moore, Harry Cheshire, Leon Weaver, Loie Bridge, Cass County Boys, Jason Robards, Sr., Britt Wood, Len Torrey, Roy Gordon, The Pinafores, Champion.

Comment: Gene gets mixed up with some outlaws in timberland that is under the watchful eye of the Forestry Department. After being framed for a killing and for poisoning cattle, Gene finally captures the real villains, proves his innocence, and saves the woodland from potential destruction at the hands of the baddies.

"... well-produced... good songs help...." -JGS

Songs: "It's My Lazy Day," "Let's Go Roamin' Around the Range," "Hair of Gold," "Little Big Dry," "Yellow Rose of Texas," "Every Time I Feel the Spirit," "Toolie, Oolie Dooley."

* * *

RIM OF THE CANYON (Columbia, 1949) 70 M.

Rating: ***

Yes, that's really Gene in the action sequence up to this point. Over the years Gene surprised many people with his willingness to perform the action scenes right up to the point where it was absolutely necessary to bring in the stunt man. After all, it would have been a simple matter to cut to a longer shot before this point in the action and to use a stunt man.

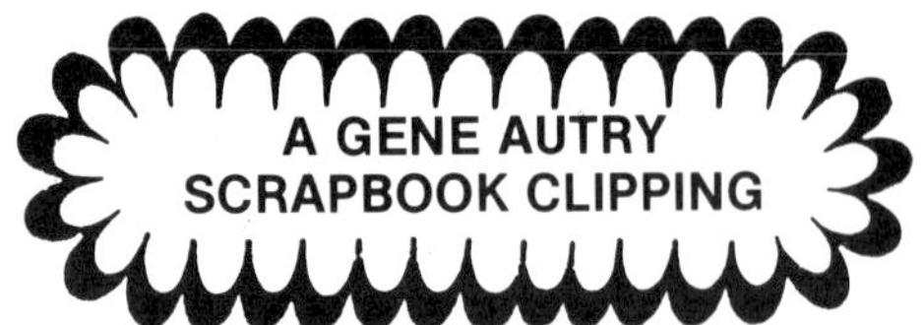

western stars MOVIE preview

rim of the CANYON

Chalk up one more hit for the versatile Autry. In between his radio work, records and rodeos, Gene produces another fast-paced thriller.

■ *Rim of the Canyon* is the seventh picture Gene has made for Columbia, but everyone—including Gene—has long since lost track of how many films he's made altogether in his seventeen years in Hollywood. Gene started working for peanuts, now makes upwards of $200,000 a year between his movies, radio work (he stars on the Wrigley Radio show "Melody Ranch"), his records (Columbia Records says he stays on top of their popularity poll, and his "Silver-Haired Daddy of Mine" has sold over 500,000 copies), his rodeo and his other enterprises. He's the idol of the kids and once turned down an offer of a huge hunk of dough for endorsing a leading brand of cigarettes. Why? Because he thought "his gang" (as he calls his fans) might start smoking at too tender an age! The scope of his influence is terrific. He is a one-man corporation, with chunks of income deriving from such diverse sources as comic magazines, records, radio stations and kids' clothing! Most frequently asked question in Autry fan letters is, "Do you still ride the original Champion?" Answer to that one is no. This is Champion the second. The original one who, as you may remember, was the first horse in history to fly from coast to coast (in a plane, natch) died at the age of seventeen. The new one hails from Oklahoma (from a town named, of all things, Gene Autry), and he flies too, as does his air-minded master. Gene's a good-natured guy. Ask the people who work with him. Better still, ask the gal who owns one. Pretty, dark-haired Ina Mae Autry married Gene in 1932, expects to be married to him still in 1992. Says the fellow in the big hat is an angel in spurs. *Rim of the Canyon* was adapted from Joseph Chadwich's story, "Phantom .45's Talk Loud," and it's done in Columbia's exciting new process called Monochrome. Leading lady is cute newcomer Nan Leslie whose first movie offer came after she'd appeared on the cover of Liberty magazine when she was seventeen. It's solid entertainment and solid action—Gene's movies generally are—and it's Gene at his best, which is very, very good indeed.

1. In 1929, Jake Fargo and Charlie Lewis, held up a stagecoach and made off with Tim Hanlon's $30,000.

2. Marshal Steve Autry takes up the chase and succeeds in tracking down the outlaws, in a lair near town.

3. Fargo and Lewis (who have been joined by pal Reagan) must be tricked if Autry is to get the drop.

4. & 4a. Succeeding in his ruse, the marshal lets the outlaws relax, then pounces suddenly and captures them.

While Gene tries to win the stagecoach race, an enemy of his late father breaks out of jail and steals his horse.

rim of the canyon, continued

6. *Twenty years later:* Gene (Steve's son) returns to town for stagecoach race.

7. Old outlaw trio break jail, steals Champion, two other horses, for getaway.

8. His coach capsized, Gene hikes to Mourner's Flat, now a ghost town.

9. & 9a. He finds schoolteacher Ruth Lambert talking to Big Tim's ghost.

10. Gene and Ruth are interrupted by old prospector Loco John who tells them that Fargo's gang beat him up—and that Champion is being tortured with a spade bit.

11. Ruth disappears, then suddenly returns, transformed by evening gown she says is a gift of Big Tim—whose funeral had been held 20 years before.

14. The battle is an ugly one, Fargo using every dirty trick he knows to subdue Gene. Desperate, the outlaw gets set to brain Gene with a pistol butt.

15. Gun in hand, Big Tim—no ghost at all—pitches into the fracas and the crooked trio, in panic, turn tail. Gene goes after them, with the two older men.

18. Old prospector Loco John attempts to steal a gun for Gene, but Lewis, catching him at it, kills him. Gene gets Lewis but the others make their escape.

19. Receiving his horse, Champion, Gene trails Fargo and Reagan, overtakes them, and—like his father—gets set to capture them single-handed.

12. Fargo and his men burst in, guns drawn, menacing the couple. Failing to find the $30,000 he had hidden there 20 years back, Fargo blames Autry.

13. In his fury, Fargo slugs Gene and then begins a tremendous battle with all five men in the tangle. Unarmed as he is, Gene cannot hold out singlehanded against the other three indefinitely, but Gene himself gives Reagan a wicked going over.

16. Meanwhile Tim Hanlon explains that another man was buried in his place while he fled to Mexico. Now he has returned to recover the hidden $30,000.

21. Back in the saddle again, Gene takes Reagan off to jail. Now that the Fargo gang has been destroyed, Big Tim Hanlon leaves for Mexico with his money. Gene, who gained $2000 for recapturing the outlaws, turns his attention to more pleasant matters: Ruth.

20. Gene man-handles Reagan and captures him but finds himself facing Fargo unarmed. Then Champion recognizing his tormentor, tramples Fargo to death.

17. Trapped in the old hotel, Gene, Big Tim and Loco John find that Fargo has set fire to the building. The outlaw, knowing that this will drive them out, waits to snare Gene and the others, and to get back the $30,000 which he is certain they now possess.

(THE RIM OF THE CANYON pictorial summary publicity release originally appeared in *Western Stars*, Volume 1, No. 3, October-December 1949.)

Producer, Armand Schaefer; director, John English; screenplay, John K. Butler from a story by Joseph Chadwick.

Cast: Gene Autry, Nan Leslie, Thurston Hall, Clem Bevans, Walter Sande, Jock O'Mahoney, Francis McDonald, Alan Hale, Jr., Amelita Ward, John R. McKee, Champion.

Comment: See Scrapbook Clipping for plot to *RIM OF THE CANYON.*

"A different, underrated film." -TE

"Liked the double role Gene played." -CR

Songs: "Rim of the Canyon," and "You're the Only Star in My Blue Heaven."

* * *

THE COWBOY AND THE INDIANS (Columbia 1949) 68 M.

Rating: ***

Producer, Armand Schaefer; director, John English; screenplay, Dwight Cummins and Dorothy Yost.

Cast: Gene Autry, Sheila Ryan, Frank Richards, Hank Patterson, Jay Silverheels, Claudia Drake, George Nokes, Charles Stevens, Alex Fraser, Clayton Moore, Frank Lackteen, Chief Yowlachie, Lee Roberts, Nolan Leary, Maudie Prickett, Harry Mackin, Charles Quigley, Champion.

Comment: This feature deals with the plight of a reservation of poor Indians when a crooked Indian agent takes advantage of their vulnerability. Autry and female doctor Shelia Ryan help the starving Indians.

". . . handsomely mounted. . . ." -JGS

Songs: "Here Comes Santa Claus," "America," "One Little Indian Boy," and "Silent Night."

* * *

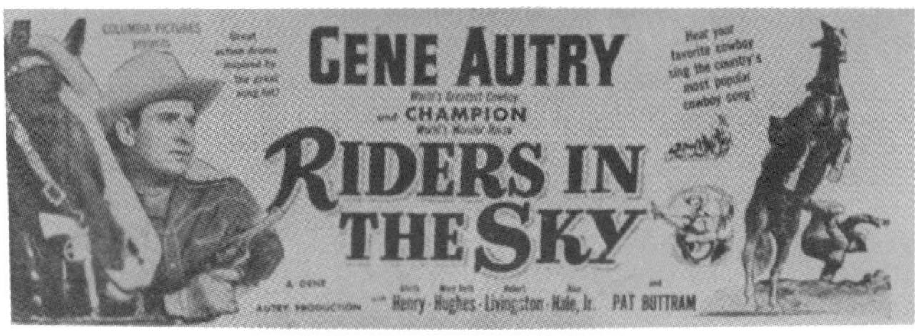

RIDERS IN THE SKY (Columbia, 1949) 69 M.

Rating: ***

Producer, Armand Schaefer; director, John English; screenplay, Gerald Geraghty from a story by Herbert A. Woodbury.

Cast: Gene Autry, Gloria Henry, Pat Buttram, Mary Beth Hughes, Robert Livingston, Steve Darrell, Alan Hale, Jr., Tom London, Hank Patterson, Ben Welden, Dennis Moore, Joe Forte, Kenne Duncan, Frank Jaquet, Roy Gordon, Loie Bridge, Champion.

Comment: The story is one about the town that is run by a slick gambler. Gene arrives to help his rancher friend, who has been thrown in the clink on a murder charge. Gene gets the goods on the gambler and wraps it all up.

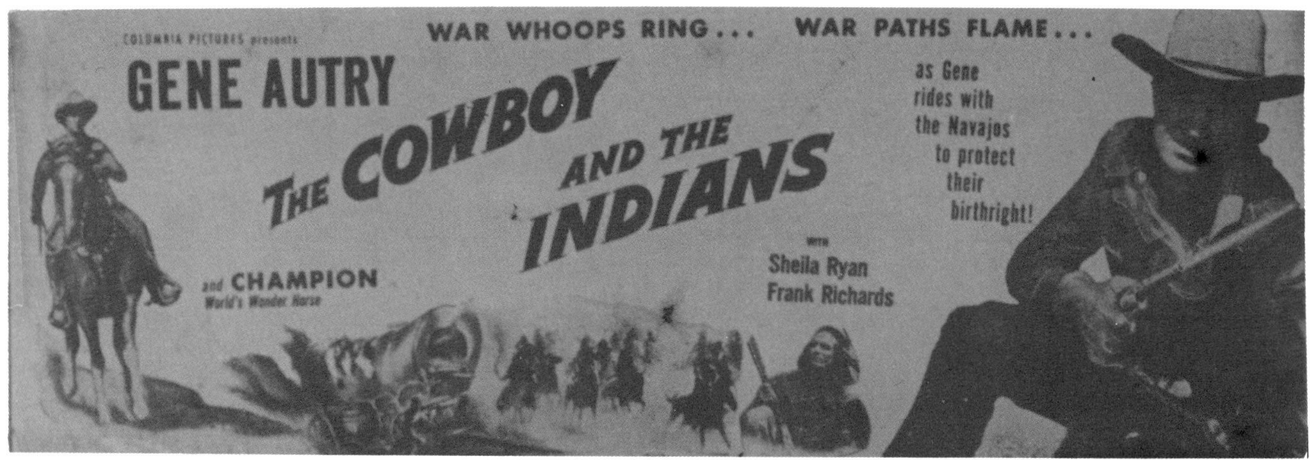

WAR WHOOPS RING...
WAR PATHS FLAME...
as Gene rides with the Navajos to protect their birthright!
COLUMBIA PICTURES presents
GENE AUTRY
World's Greatest Cowboy
and CHAMPION World's Wonder Horse
THE COWBOY AND THE INDIANS
with
SHEILA RYAN
FRANK RICHARDS
HANK PATTERSON
Written by
Dwight Cummins and Dorothy Yost
Directed by JOHN ENGLISH
Produced by ARMAND SCHAEFER
A GENE AUTRY PRODUCTION

Gene stops villain Robert Livingston in this lobby card scene from RIDERS IN THE SKY. Interestingly, there is no such scene in the film.

"Very loosely constructed plot. . . ." -JGS

Songs: "Riders in the Sky," "It Makes No Difference Now," and "The Streets of Laredo."

* * *

SONS OF NEW MEXICO (Columbia, 1950) 70 M.

Rating: ***

Producer, Armand Schaefer; director, John English; screenplay, Paul Gangelin.

Cast: Gene Autry, Gail Davis, Robert Armstrong, Dick Jones, Frankie Darro, Irving Bacon, Russell Arms, Marie Blake, Clayton Moore, Sandy Sanders, Roy Gordon, Frank Marvin, Paul Raymond, Pierce Lyden, Kenne Duncan, Champion.

Comment: This Autry feature is about the singing cowboy's efforts to save juvenile delinquent Dick Jones from the evil enticements of gambler Robert Armstrong. Gail Davis makes her first appearance here in an Autry film.

"More in the standard Gene Autry category . . . well-directed. . . ." -JGS

Songs: "Can't Shake the Sands of Texas from My Shoes," "Rainbow on the Rio Colorado," "The Honey Song," and "The New Mexico Military Institute March."

* * *

MULE TRAIN (Columbia, 1950) 69 M.

Rating: ***

Producer, Armand Schaefer; director, John English; screenplay, Gerald Geraghty from a story by Alan James.

Cast: Gene Autry, Pat Buttram, Sheila Ryan, Robert Livingston, Frank Jaquet, Vince Barnett, Syd Saylor, Sandy Sanders, Gregg Barton, Kenne Duncan, Roy Gordon, Stanley Andrews, Robert Hilton, Bob Wilke, John Miljan, Robert Carson, Pat O'Malley, Champion.

Comment: U.S. Marshal Autry comes to the aid of an old friend who is about to have his natural cement claim jumped by villainous contractor and freight shipper, Robert Livingtson.

"Beautifully photographed but with a vague story. . . could have starred anyone. . . not tailor-made Gene Autry stuff. . . ." -JGS

Songs: "Mule Train," "Room Full of Roses," and "The Old Chisholm Trail."

* * *

COW TOWN (Columbia, 1950) 70 M.

Rating: **½

Producer, Armand Schaefer; director, John English; screenplay, Gerald Geraghty.

Cast: Gene Autry, Gail Davis, Harry Shannon, Jock O'Mahoney, Clark "Buddy" Burroughs, Harry Harvey, Steve Darrell, Sandy Sanders, Ralph Sanford, Bud Osborne, Robert Hilton, Ted Mapes, Charles Robertson, House Peters, Jr., Champion.

Comment: COW TOWN raises the question of whether cattle ranches should be fenced in with barbed wire or remain open.

"Good wardrobe." -CR

". . . not the sort of stuff which made Gene Autry great." -JGS

Songs: "Down in the Valley," "Powder Your Face

With Sunshine," "Bury Me Not on the Lone Prairie," and "Buffalo Gals."

* * *

BEYOND THE PURPLE HILLS (Columbia, 1950) 69 M.

Rating: ***

Producer, Armand Schaefer; director, John English; screenplay, Norman S. Hall.

Cast: Gene Autry, Pat Buttram, Jo Dennison, Don Beddoe, James Millican, Don Reynolds, Hugh O'Brian, Roy Gordon, Harry Harvey, Gregg Barton, Bob Wilke, Ralph Peters, Frank Ellis, John Cliff, Sandy Sanders, Champion.

Comment: In this film there is the treat of Champion and newcomer Little Champ showing off their bag of tricks for the delight of youngsters. Gene is appointed sheriff after the former lawman is killed in a robbery. Soon evidence causes Gene to arrest Jack Beaumont (O'Brian) for the murder of his father, Judge Beaumont, even though Gene is sure Jack didn't do it. Jack escapes and soon it is learned that the town banker and the local saloon owner are behind all the nefarious business.

Songs: "Beyond the Purple Hills" and "Dear Hearts and Gentle People."

* * *

INDIAN TERRITORY (Columbia, 1950) 70 M.

Rating: ***

Producer, Armand Schaefer; director, John English; screenplay, Norman S. Hall.

Cast: Gene Autry, Pat Buttram, Gail Davis, Kirby Grant, James Griffith, Philip Van Zandt, Pat Collins, Roy Gordon, Charles Stevens, Robert Carson, Champion.

Comment: This feature takes place in the old west just after the Civil War. Autry, an Indian agent working undercover in the Union Army, is assigned the task of getting to the bottom of some Indian uprisings that have been taking place in the territory.

"A good one of its type. . . with great photography. . . ." -JGS

Songs: "When the Campfire Is Low on the Prairie" and "Chattanooga Shoe Shine Boy."

* * *

THE BLAZING SUN (Columbia, 1950) 69 M.

Rating: ***½

Producer, Armand Schaefer; director, John English; screenplay, Jack Townley.

Cast: Gene Autry, Pat Buttram, Lynne Roberts, Anne Gwynne, Edward Norris, Kenne Duncan, Alan Hale, Jr., Gregg Barton, Steve Darrell, Tom London, Sandy Sanders, Frankie Marvin, Champion.

Comment: Gene is in the modern West this time on the trail of a couple of bank robbers. They use all sorts of modern devices—short wave radios,

"Beyond the Purple Hills"

Cast of Characters

GENE AUTRY

Rawley	PAT BUTTRAM	Mollie	JO DENNISON
Amos Rayburn	DON BEDDOE	Morgan	JAMES MILLICAN
Chip	DON REYNOLDS	Jack	HUGH O'BRIAN

Judge Beaumont........ROY GORDON

A Republic Picture

Produced by Armand Schaefer; directed by John English; screenplay by Norman S. Hall

1 Autry is called from his ranch to try to talk some sense into his friend, Jack Beaumont, son of the town judge. Jack brandishes his six-gun wildly after a few extra drinks at the saloon of Rocky Morgan, who is a sly crook.

2 Unable to reason with Jack, Gene takes his gun by force. They are unaware that the town bank is being held up and sheriff Whiteside killed by bandits working for Rocky Morgan.

3 Gene recovers the money and returns it to Mollie, Jack's fiancee, and to her uncle, Amos Rayburn, who runs the bank. The Judge makes Gene sheriff.

4 Autry is called in by Amos, who finds the Judge's body following an argument between Jack and his father. Amos asks for Jack's arrest.

5 Amos tells Gene that the Judge planned to write a new will that night, cutting off his son, Jack, without a cent. Gene agrees it looks bad.

6 Seeking Jack at Morgan's bar, Gene is attacked by Morgan's gunmen. A wandering cowboy, Mike Rawley, helps Gene fight them off. Autry then makes Mike a deputy.

7 At the Beaumont ranch, Gene finds Jack packing to leave because of the argument. Gene tells him the judge was murdered. He finds a shot was fired from Jack's gun.

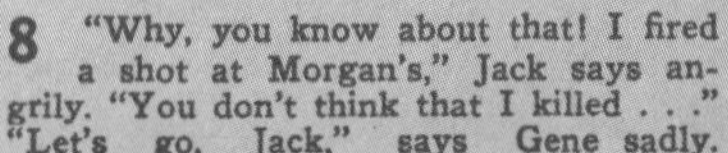

8 "Why, you know about that! I fired a shot at Morgan's," Jack says angrily. "You don't think that I killed . . ." "Let's go, Jack," says Gene sadly.

9 Jack manages to escape, but Autry overtakes him. "I'll never shoot you, Jack Beaumont, but I'll beat the everlasting whey out of you, if you give me any more trouble," the sheriff threatens.

10 Although Gene sets up comfortable quarters for his friend in jail, Jack's young brother, Chip, turns against Gene because of Jack's arrest. He even ignores his favorite pony, Little Champ.

11 During a Fourth of July celebration, Gene promises Mollie that he'll help Jack. He asks her about Amos and learns that her uncle has been spending her money without accounting for it.

12 Seeing Mollie with Gene, Chip thinks Jack is being double-crossed. "Autry's gonna hang you, so he can get your girl."

13 Morgan incites the town to lynch Jack. At the jail, they find he's escaped. Gene alibis that he moved Jack to another jail.

14 Gene and Rawley find Jack's hideout. Gene tells Amos where Jack is. Then he overhears Amos sending Morgan to kill him.

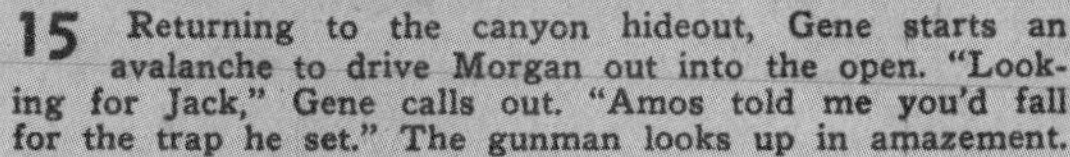

15 Returning to the canyon hideout, Gene starts an avalanche to drive Morgan out into the open. "Looking for Jack," Gene calls out. "Amos told me you'd fall for the trap he set." The gunman looks up in amazement.

16 "That doublecrosser," snarls Morgan. "Did he also tell you he hired me to shoot the Judge and my men to rob his bank . . . or that he's been robbing his niece and the Judge for years?"

17 "You have no evidence against me, other than this crook's word," Amos shouts, as Gene puts him and Morgan in jail. "When your niece and Rawley get here with your records, I'll have plenty of evidence," answers Gene. "I'm sure it will interest a jury, too, Rayburn."

19 With Mollie and Jack reconciled and the real killers behind bars, Chip and Gene again become firm friends. In the corral, they put Champ and Little Champ through their paces. "Little Champ's finally got the hang of it," grins Gene.

18 In his office, Gene is told to "reach". Jack, unaware of the recent arrests, still believes Gene is doublecrossing him. Just then, Mollie and Rawley rush in with the records and explain the frame-up to Jack. Beaumont apologizes to Gene.

(The BEYOND THE PURPLE HILLS pictorial summary publicity release originally appeared in *Western Hollywood Pictorial,* Volume 1, No. 5, September 1950.)

cars, and trains—in their attempts to outwit him.

"Good acting!" -CR

"One of the best of his last films." -TE

Songs: "Brush Those Tears from Your Eyes" and "Along the Navajo Trail."

* * *

GENE AUTRY AND THE MOUNTIES (Columbia, 1951) 70 M.

Rating: ***

Producer, Armand Schaefer; director, John English; screenplay, Norman S. Hall.

Cast: Gene Autry, Pat Buttram, Elena Verdugo, Carlton Young, Richard Emory, Herbert Rawlinson, Trevor Bardette, Francis McDonald, Jim Frasher, Gregg Barton, House Peters, Jr., Jody Gilbert, Nolan Leary, Champion.

Comment: Gene is a U.S. Marshal operating near the Montana-Canada border in pursuit of a bank robber and his gang. When the outlaws cross over into Canada, Gene enlists the help of the Mounties in his quest for justice.

"It is uplifting, as a top-notch Gene Autry film ought to be." -JGS

Songs: "Blue Canadian Rockies" and "Onteora."

* * *

TEXANS NEVER CRY (Columbia, 1951) 66 M.

Rating: ***

Producer, Armand Schaefer; director, Frank McDonald; screenplay, Norman S. Hall.

Cast: Gene Autry, Pat Buttram, Mary Castle, Russ Hayden, Gail Davis, Richard Powers, Don Harvey, Roy Gordon, Michael Reagan, Frank Fenton, Sandy Sanders, John R. McKee, Harry Mackin, Harry Tyler, Minerva Urecal, Richard Flato, I. Stanford Jolley, Duke York, Roy Butler, Champion.

Comment: Gene, a Texas Ranger, saves a family from eviction. It seems they have been swindled by shrewd crooks selling counterfeit lottery tickets.

". . . vague plot which could have been handled in 55 minutes in lieu of 66." -JGS

Songs: "Texans Never Cry" and "Ride, Ranger, Ride."

* * *

WHIRLWIND (Columbia, 1951) 70 M.

Rating: ****

Producer, Armand Schaefer; director, John English; screenplay, Norman S. Hall.

Cast: Gene Autry, Smiley Burnette, Gail Davis, Thurston Hall, Harry Lauter, Dick Curtis, Harry Harvey, Gregg Barton, Tommy Ivo, Kenne Duncan, Al Wyatt, Gary Goodwin, Champion.

Comment: Gene's a postal inspector out to break up a frontier mafia. Smiley Burnette reteams with Gene for this feature.

"The very best Columbia film Autry ever made." -GP

"One of Gene's better movies." -CR

"An excellent, impressive film. One of the best of his last films." -JGS

Songs: "Whirlwind," "Tweedle-O-Twill," and "As Long As I Have My Horse."

* * *

SILVER CANYON (Columbia, 1951) 71 M,

Rating: **½

Producer, Armand Schaefer; director, John English; screenplay, Gerald Geraghty based on a story by Alan James.

Cast: Gene Autry, Pat Buttram, Gail Davis, Jim Davis, Bob Steele, Edgar Dearing, Richard Alexander, Terry Frost, Peter Mamakos, Duke York, Eugene Borden, Champion.

Comment: The story is about a Utah guerrilla raider during Civil War days. Gene's a federal scout assigned to handling the problem.

"Strong plot elements and nice photography. . . ." -JGS

Songs: "Ridin' Down the Canyon" and "Fort Worth Jail."

* * *

HILLS OF UTAH (Columbia, 1951) 70 M.

Rating: ***

Producer, Armand Schaefer; director, John English; screenplay, Gerald Geraghty based on a story by Les Savage, Jr.

Cast: Gene Autry, Pat Buttram, Elaine Riley, Donna Martell, Onslow Stevens, Denver Pyle, William Fawcett, Harry Lauter, Kenne Duncan, Harry Harvey, Sandy Sanders, Tom London, Champion.

Comment: Gene is a new doctor setting up practice in a Utah town. Because of the conflicts between the copper miners and ranchers, the doctoring business keeps him pretty busy. Presently, Gene's Lawman instincts get the best of him, and he captures the outlaws who are egging on the two factions.

"I just like the movie!" -CR

". . . a story which is told very, very, slowly. . . ." -JGS

Songs: "Utah" and "Peter Cottontail."

* * *

VALLEY OF FIRE (Columbia, 1951) 70 M.

Rating: ***

Producer, Armand Schaefer; director, John English; screenplay, Gerald Geraghty from a story by Earl Snell.

Cast: Gene Autry, Pat Buttram, Gail Davis, Russell Hayden, Christine Larson, Harry Lauter, Terry Frost, Barbara Stanley, Teddy Infuhr, Marjorie Liszt, Riley Hill, Victor Sen Yung, Gregg Barton, Sandy Sanders, Bud Osborne, Fred Sherman, James Magill, Duke York, Champion.

Comment: Gene's the mayor of a frontier village very much lacking in female citizens. He arranges for a wagon train of fine ladies to be shipped out to this mesa metropolis. Unfortunately, villains plan a hijacking of the wagon train of ladies.

". . .so very attractively photographed! The story doesn't match up." -JGS

Songs: "Here's to the Ladies" and "On Top of Old Smoky."

* * *

THE OLD WEST (Columbia, 1952) 61 M.

Rating: ***

Producer, Armand Schaefer; director, George Archainbaud; screenplay, Gerald Geraghty.

Cast: Gene Autry, Pat Buttram, Gail Davis, Lyle Talbot, Louis Jean Heydt, House Peters, Sr., Dick Jones, Kathy Johnson, Don Harvey, Dee Pollock, Raymond L. Morgan, James Craven, Tom London, Frankie Marvin, Champion.

Comment: Gene tames and sells wild horses to the stagecoach line managed by Arlie Williams (Gail Davis). Competitor Doc Lockwood (Lyle Talbot) ambushes and shoots Gene, who is nursed back to health by a wandering peddler. After a rigged stagecoach race and a gunfight, Gene puts an end to Lockwood's evil ways. Gene takes time in the film to display the talents of Champion and Little Champ.

"Uplifting, entertaining, charming. . . this is one of the better Columbia entries. . . ." -JGS

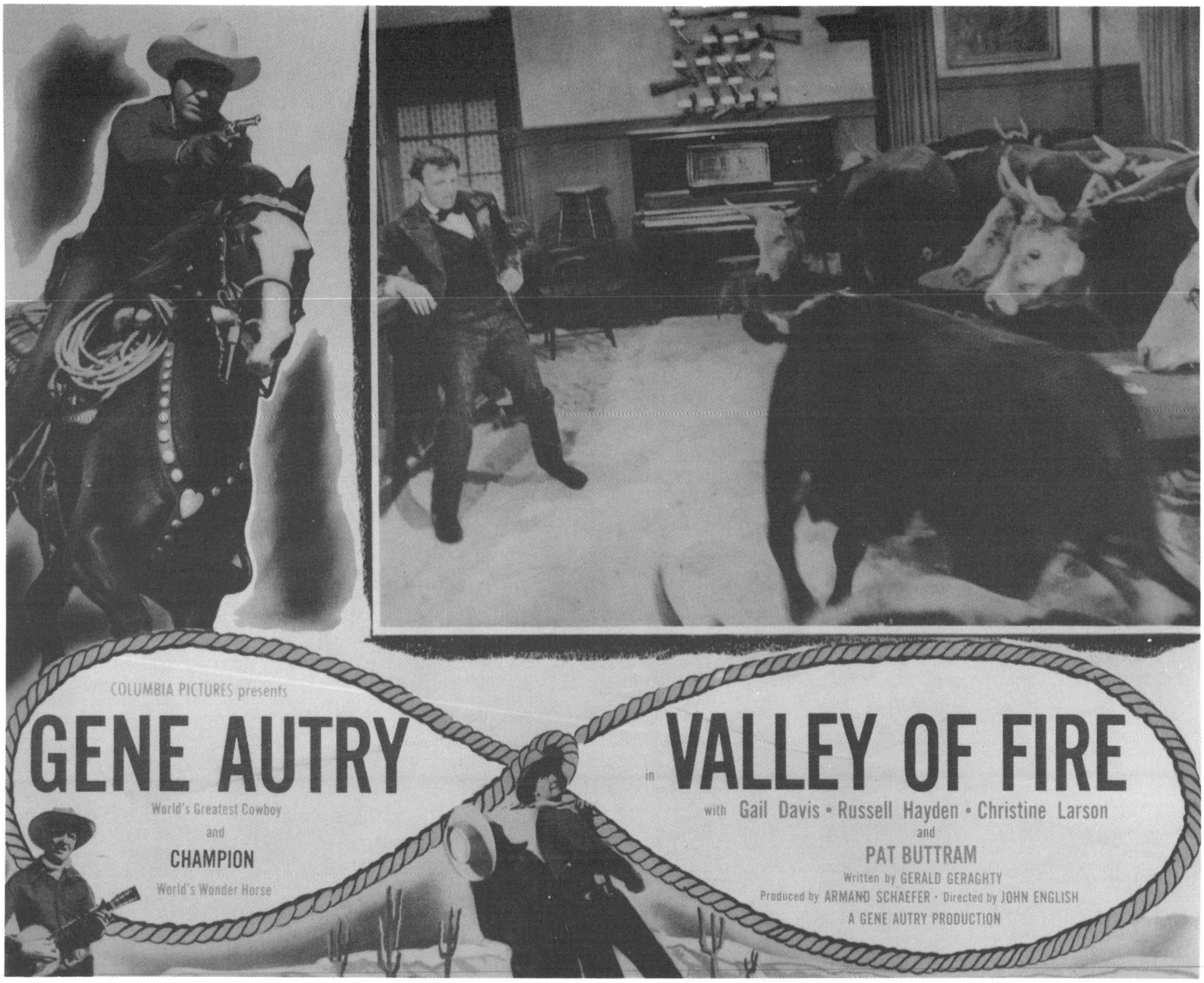

Saloon operator Harry Lauter has acquired some customers he doesn't want in this action scene from VALLEY OF FIRE.

Songs: "Somebody Bigger Than You and I" and "Music by the Angels."

* * *

NIGHT STAGE TO GALVESTON (Columbia, 1952) 62 M.

Rating: ***

Producer, Armand Schaefer; director, George Archainbaud; screenplay, Norman S. Hall.

Cast: Gene Autry, Pat Buttram, Virginia Huston, Thurston Hall, Judy Nugent, Robert Livingston, Harry Cording, Robert Bice, Frank Sully, Clayton Moore, Frank Rawls, Steve Clark, Harry Lauter, Robert Peyton, Lois Austin, Champion.

Comment: We're back in Texas after the days of the Texas Rangers when law is enforced by the state's police—some of whom are corrupt and brutal with the citizens. Gene, a former Texas Ranger, works with some of his buddies to bring

A GENE AUTRY SCRAPBOOK CLIPPING

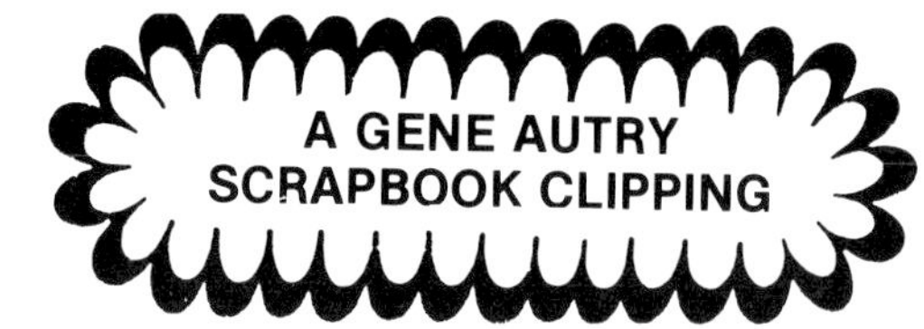

GENE AUTRY

GENE'S MOVIES:

"the old west:" gene again

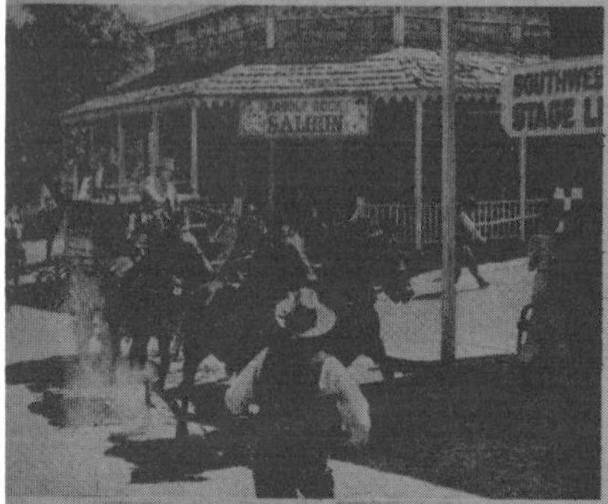

1. Veteran Jeff Bleeker drives the stage to wide-open Saddle Rock so well even his daughter can't realize he is half-blind.

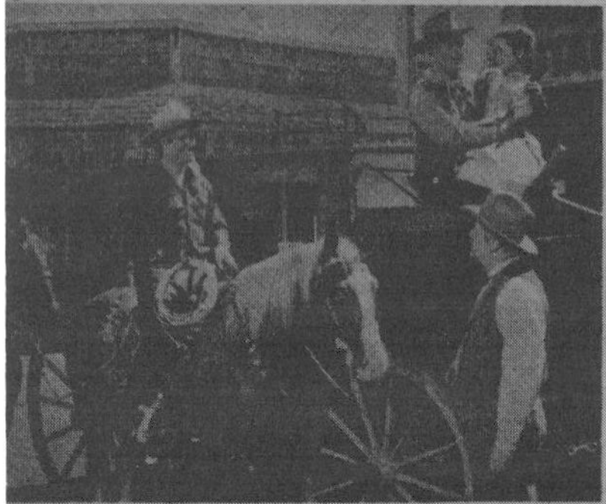

2. Only little Judie and Gene Autry, who hunts wild mustangs for stage teams, are not dominated by horse-breeder Lockwood.

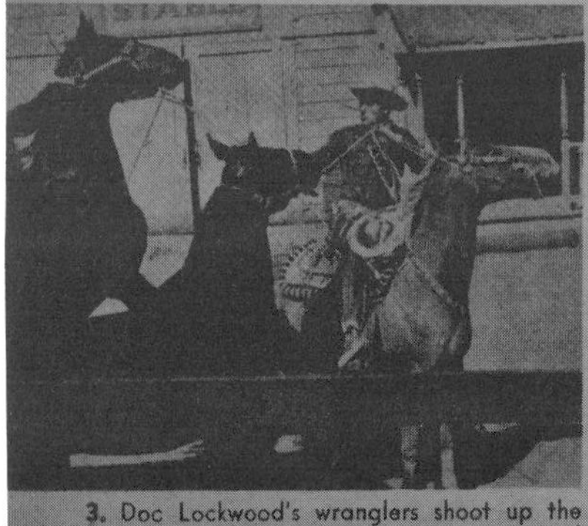

3. Doc Lockwood's wranglers shoot up the town only too often. Gun-happy Pinto and Hod Evers cause Gene's mustangs to bolt.

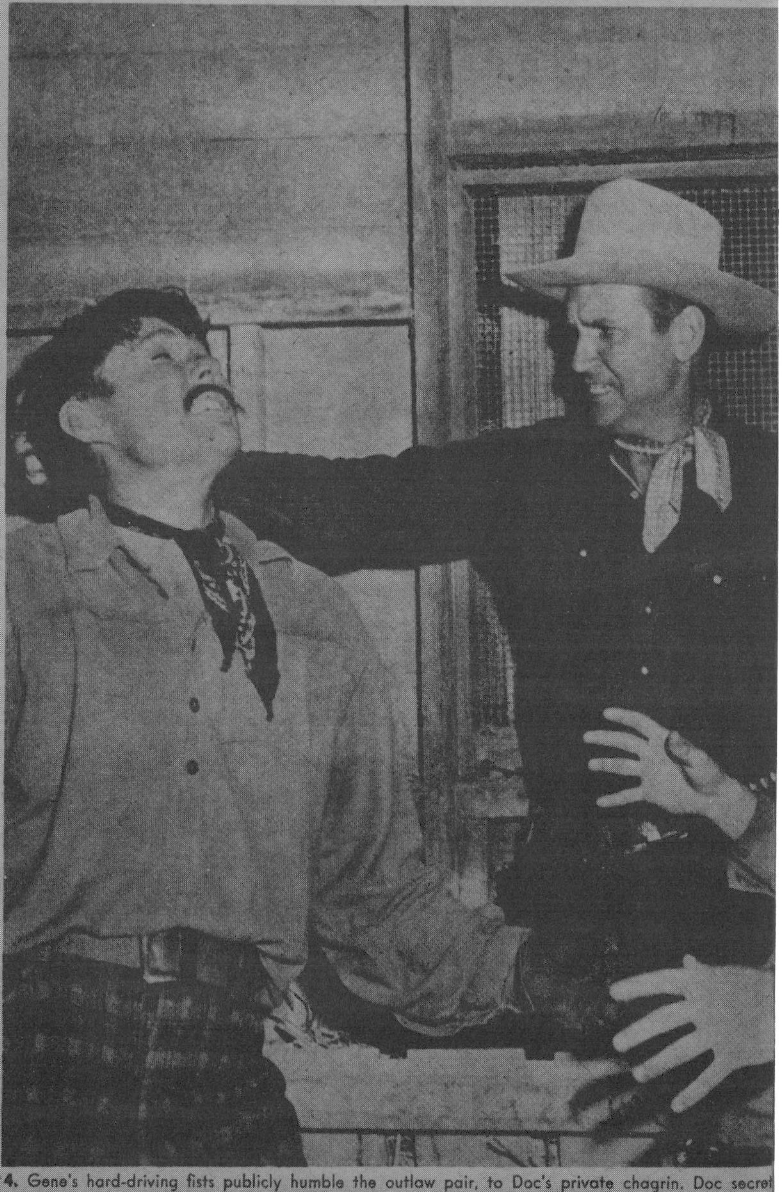

4. Gene's hard-driving fists publicly humble the outlaw pair, to Doc's private chagrin. Doc secre

triumphs over villainy

5. Hod and Pinto ambush Gene in revenge. They leave him unconscious by a trail to his camp, with only Champ to summon aid.

■ First of the singing cowboys who were to change a pattern of Western movie idols set back in silent days by such stalwarts as Tom Mix and William S. Hart, Gene Autry rode a twisting trail to Hollywood. Born the grandson of a Baptist minister, he first used his now-celebrated voice in the church choir in Tioga, Texas. A medicine show gave Gene his earliest taste of theatre business at the tender age of sixteen, but it was on railroading he first set his youthful eyes. He had become a full-fledged dispatcher in Chelsea, Oklahoma, before the time a great man named Will Rogers wandered in to send a telegram and remained to launch the singing career of a tall cowpoke with a guitar. Between Rogers and movie stardom lay several years of hard recording and radio work, and marriage to a pretty schoolteacher named Ina Mae Spivey. Then came a first break in pictures and a skyrocket climb to the top. During World War II, Gene was in uniform for the Air Corps; but returned to yet greater popularity both in films and as the star of the mammoth Madison Square Garden Championship Rodeo. He is owner of the two famous horses Champion and Little Champion. Both of these celebrated animals appear with Autry in his latest Columbia release, *The Old West,* which tells an exciting story of how wild horse hunter Gene conquers evil forces in a cattle town.

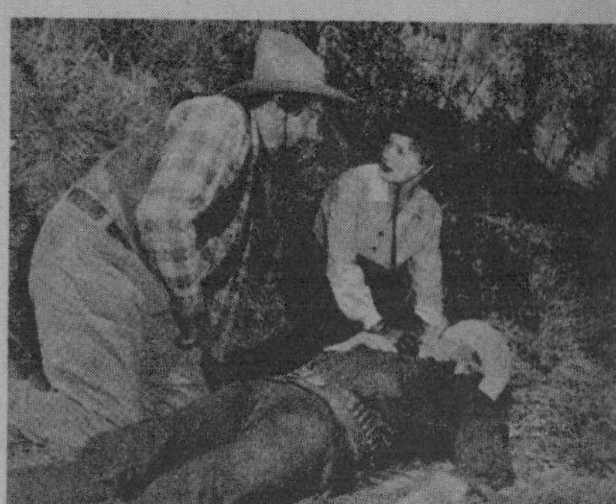

6. Due to the horse, Arlie Williams and a traveling peddler, Panhandle Gibbs, take Gene home. He is nursed by a new Parson.

7. Well again, Gene returns the favor by helping Parson Brooks pass out handbills to a prayer meeting opposed by Lockwood.

CAST:

Gene Autry....................Gene Autry
Panhandle Gibbs..............Pat Buttram
Arlie Williams..................Gail Davis
Doc Lockwood..................Lyle Talbot
Jeff Bleeker.............Louis Jean Heydt
Parson Jonathan Brooks....House Peters, Sr.
Saunders................House Peters, Jr.
Pinto........................Dick Jones

owns all Saddle Rock's saloons.

8. Caught by irate ranchers, the fleeing Hod and Pinto are dragged to Saddle Rock for lynching. Gene rides to rescue them.

more→

9. Only balked briefly by Gene, the ranchers pursue, on a false trail pointed by Judie. Meanwhile, blind Jeff is jolting stage agent Daniels into town on a crazy ride which enrages Daniels.

10. Persuaded by the wily Doc that Gene's wild mustangs are at fault, Daniels is near to awarding Doc the horse contract when Gene rides up to suggest a race between his animals and Doc's.

13. Before the race commences, Judie is found and regains consciousness. In fear of Doc, she refuses to name her attacker—despite Jeff's plea. Jobless, Jeff agrees to drive Doc's entry.

14. Too late to object, and unaware that a repentant Pinto and Hod have surrendered to the law and bared Doc's hold on Saddle Rock vice, Arlie discovers the secret of Jeff's failing sight.

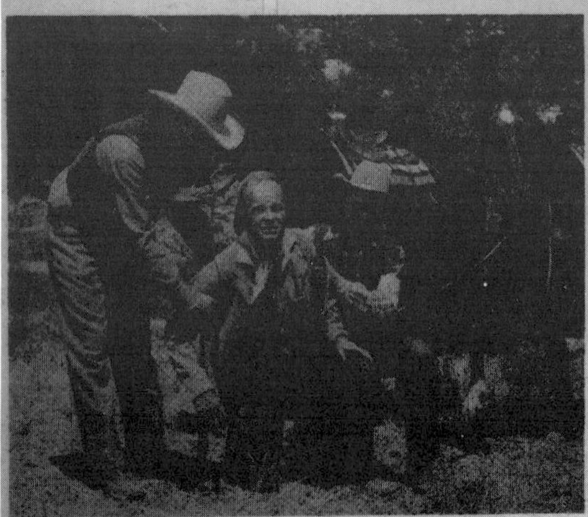

15. A mad race ends in the blinded man's crackup and the wreck of Gene's sabotaged stage. Panhandle is the victor, as friends help Jeff. In town, little Judie has named her two assailants.

16. With Doc's seeming help, Gene arrests the guilty wranglers But, faced with Hod and Pinto, Doc realizes his game is up an makes a break to escape the consequences of his reign of evi

11. Fired by Daniels, Jeff and Judie pack to leave town. But Judie sees two of Doc's wranglers tampering with the stage Gene will drive in the race, and she is beaten up.

12. With the race about to be run, the taunts of excited spectators force Panhandle to enter his ramshackle peddler's wagon. The contract for new stage teams depends on the race's outcome.

THE END. With his friends, Gene outguns the fugitive trio, and Saddle Rock gets religion from Pastor Brooks—while Jeff lands a new assignment he can handle and Gene keeps his old contract to provide the stage mustangs.

(THE OLD WEST pictorial summary publicity release originally appeared in *Who's Who in Western Stars*, Volume 1, No. 1, 1952.)

about a return to proper law enforcement.

". . . above average." -JGS

Songs: "Down in Slumberland," "I've Got a Heart As Big As Texas," and "Eyes of Texas."

* * *

APACHE COUNTRY (Columbia, 1952) 62 M.

Rating: ***

Producer, Armand Schaefer; director, George Archainbaud; screenplay, Norman S. Hall.

Cast: Gene Autry, Pat Buttram, Carolina Cotton, Harry Lauter, Mary Scott, Sydney Mason, Francis X. Bushman, Gregg Barton, Tom London, Byron Fougler, Frank Matts, Mickey Simpson, The Cass County Boys, Tony Whitecloud's Jemez Indians, Champion.

Comment: Cavalry scout Gene Autry is commissioned by the President to break up a frontier ring which uses Indian raids to cover up its bandit activities. Carolina Cotton tries to assist Gene and is also seeking revenge for the murder of her father.

Songs: "Cold, Cold Heart," "Crime Will Never Pay," "I Love to Yodel," and "The Covered Wagon Rolled Right Along."

* * *

BARBED WIRE (Columbia, 1952) 61 M.

Rating: ***½

Producer, Armand Schaefer; director, George Archainbaud; screenplay, Gerald Geraghty.

Cast: Gene Autry, Pat Buttram, Anne James, William Fawcett, Leonard Penn, Michael Vallon,

Gene is seen here with three actors who played sidekicks at one time or another in their careers. Gordon Jones (next to Gene) was Roy Rogers' sidekick in the late 1940s, Pat Buttram (center) was Gene's current one, and Syd Saylor (right) had sidekicked for Bob Steele and John Wayne, among others

Terry Frost, Clayton Moore, Edwin Parker, Sandy Sanders, Frankie Marvin, Cass County Boys, Champion.

Comment: Texas cattlemen and farmers are feuding again, causing a delay in the big cattle drive. Autry, a cattle buyer, gets involved to protect his business interests and ultimately brings peace to the range land once more.

"Good story on the coming of the wire." -CR

Songs: "Mexicali Rose" and "Old Buckaroo."

* * *

WAGON TEAM (Columbia, 1952) 61 M.

Rating: ***

Producer, Armand Schaefer; director, George Archainbaud; screenplay, Gerald Geraghty.

Cast: Gene Autry, Pat Buttram, Gail Davis, Dick Jones, Gordon Jones, Harry Harvey, Henry Rowland, George J. Lewis, John Cason, Cass County Boys, Gregg Barton, Pierce Lyden, Carlo Tricoli, Champion.

Comment: An army payroll has been stolen from a stagecoach by a gang of outlaws. Gene plays a special investigator for the stage line sent to solve the crime. As a cover he takes a job as a singer for a medicine show.

"Livelier pace than many Columbias. . . a good one. . . . " -JGS

Songs: "Back in the Saddle Again," "In and Out of

the Jailhouse," "Howdy, Friends and Neighbors," and "I've Been Invited to a Jubilee."

* * *

BLUE CANADIAN ROCKIES (Columbia, 1952) 62 M.

Rating: ***

Producer, Armand Schaefer; director, George Archainbaud; screenplay, Gerald Geraghty.

Cast: Gene Autry, Pat Buttram, Gail Davis, Carolina Cotton, Ross Ford, Tom London, John Merton, Gene Roth, Don Beddoe, Maurtiz Hugo, David Garcia, Cass County Boys, Champion.

Comment: Gene is sent to Canada by his employer to try to discourage the daughter from marrying a fortune hunter. When Gene arrives he finds she has turned the place into a dude ranch and wild game preserve. There are some mysterious killings going on, and Gene gets to the bottom of them.

"Very, very good story!" -CR

". . . songs aplenty. . .more humor here, too, than in most of the Columbia entries. Carolina Cotton is delightful in her role." -JGS

Songs: "Any Time," "Mama Don't Allow No Music Played in Here," "Blue Canadian Rockies," "The Old Chisholm Trail," "Froggy Went A-Courtin'," "Yodel, Yodel, Yodel," and "Lovin' Ducky Daddy."

* * *

WINNING OF THE WEST (Columbia, 1953) 57 M.

Rating: ***

Producer, Armand Schaefer; director, George Archainbaud; screenplay, Norman S. Hall.

Cast: Gene Autry, Smiley Burnette, Gail Davis, Richard Crane, Robert Livingtston, House Peters, Jr., Gregg Barton, William Forrest, Ewing Mitchell, Rodd Redwing, George Chesebro, Frank Jocquet, Charles Delaney, Champion.

Comment: The script is a brother-against-brother yarn as Gene discovers that his younger brother is with a gang of outlaws selling "protection" to townspeople and miners.

"Extra-good one, with a quicker pace than usual." -JGS

Songs: "I'm a Cowpoke Pokin' Along," "Fetch Me Down My Trusty .45," "Cowboy Blues," and "Five Minutes Late and a Dollar Short."

* * *

ON TOP OF OLD SMOKY (Columbia, 1953) 59 M.

Rating: ***

Producer, Armand Schaefer; director, George Archainbaud; screenplay, Gerald Geraghty.

Cast: Gene Autry, Smiley Burnette, Gail Davis, Grandon Rhodes, Sheila Ryan, Kenne Duncan, Robert Bice, Zon Murray, Cass County Boys, Champion.

Comment: Gene and the Cass County Boys, traveling troubadours, find themselves impersonating Texas Rangers to help Gail Davis protect her valuable property from mineral poachers.

"This one is great fun. It has an impromptu look, as though Gene and Smiley suddenly decided to

make a movie together, improvising along the way. -JGS

Songs: "If It Wasn't for the Rain," "On Top of Old Smoky," "I Hang My Head and Cry," "I Saw Her First," and "The Trail of Mexico."

* * *

GOLDTOWN GHOST RIDERS (Columbia, 1953) 57 M.

Rating: ***½

Producer, Armand Schaefer; director, George Archainbaud; screenplay, Gerald Geraghty.

Cast: Gene Autry, Smiley Burnette, Gail Davis, Kirk Riley, Carleton Young, Neyle Morrow, Denver Pyle, Steve Conte, John Doucette, Champion.

Comment: Gene is a circuit judge trying an accused murderer in a mining town out West. The twist is that the accused claims that he can't be tried for the crime since he already has served his prison sentence for the killing. It seems that years before the accused murderer had thought he killed his partner (a fellow swindler in a gold rush fraud), was tried and sent to prison. In reality the victim lived and assumed a new identity. Now, ten years later and released from prison, the convicted man discovers his old victim and this time does him in for good.

". . . the most complicated story of any Gene Autry movie, but it is worked out well and is very succinct. . . ." -JGS

Songs: "A Gold Mine in Your Heart," "Pancho's Widow," and "The Thieving Burro."

* * *

PACK TRAIN (Columbia, 1953) 56 M.

Rating: ***½

Producer, Armand Schaefer; director, George Archainbaud; screenplay, Norman S. Hall.

Cast: Gene Autry, Smiley Burnette, Gail Davis, Kenne Duncan, Sheila Ryan, Tom London, Harry Lauter, Melinda Plowman, B.G. Norman, Champion.

Comment: When Sunshine Valley Settlers face disaster because of a food and medicine shortage, Gene and Dan Coleman (Tom London) purchase supplies in Trail's End. Additional supplies promised by the operators of the town's only store are not forthcoming, forcing Gene to take action.

"A somber story, but with good characterizations from a fine cast and with cohesive action. . . this is one of Gene's best Columbia features." -JGS

Songs: "God's Little Candles," "Wagon Train," and "Hominy Grits."

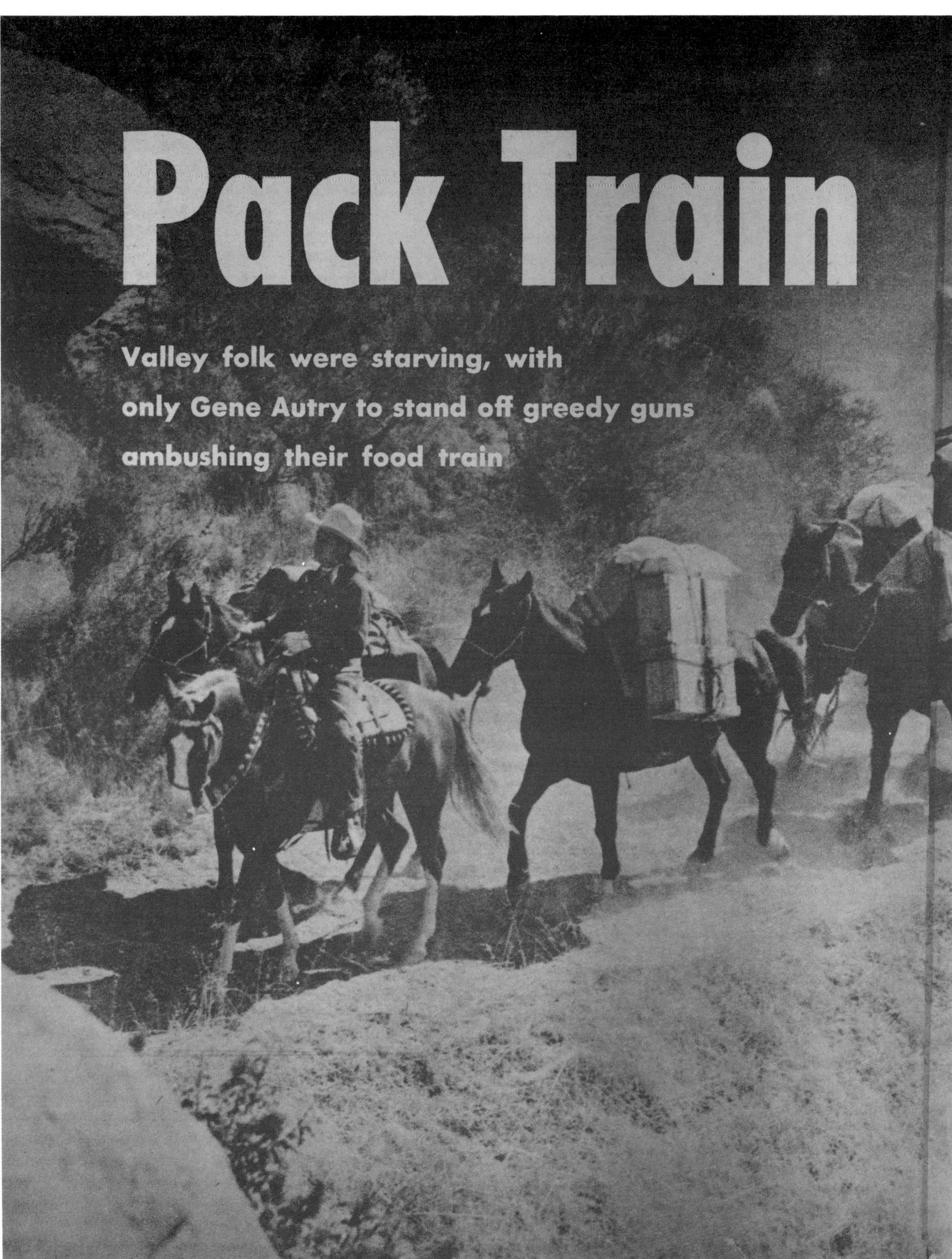
Pack Train
Valley folk were starving, with
only Gene Autry to stand off greedy guns
ambushing their food train

1. Gene looked from one girl to the other, instantly sensing the hostility which had flared between shopkeeper Lola Riker (right) and old Dan Coleman's daughter from Sunshine Valley.

■ Gene guides Dan Coleman and his pretty daughter, Jennifer, into the town of Trail's End. They seek badly needed supplies for a new settlement at Sunshine Valley—and find the only store is run by Lola Riker and her crafty sweetheart, Ross McLain. Lola dislikes Jennifer, but makes up to Gene when she hears he carries five thousand dollars in settler money. She takes him to see McLain, who utters some snide remarks about Jennifer. Gene subdues him before the saloon crowd, loads what few goods Lola has on hand into the Coleman wagon. He pays for delivery of more within a week, then heads back for the Valley. They take along his old pal, Smiley Burnette, who now is driving for the Riker-McLain combine. The lone wagon is ambushed at its first camp by McLain and two hirelings—out to kill the party and keep the settler money. McLain and one man escape. But Gene outstalks the other and, after a fight, has him at his mercy. He spares this man, Wade, and thus wins himself a friend. Settlers at the new and needy community cheer the wagon's arrival, but are downcast at the few supplies aboard. Smiley returns to town and Gene waits with the others. The meager stores dwindle. When it is obvious McLain will not deliver as promised, Gene rides again for Trail's End. He finds that gold has been discovered nearby and supply prices are soaring. Lola has sold the Sunshine Valley supplies over again. McLain refuses to make good, until Gene forces them at gun's point to turn over what was paid for. He and Smiley start a loaded wagon train to the Valley, well aware that an angry McLain will spare no effort to recapture his merchandise. McLain does not disappoint them. He dynamites a cliff under which the wagons are rolling, wrecking most of them. Gene sends back the wounded in the remaining wagons, reloads the supplies onto the horses,

Beset by every bushwhacking trick at McLain's command, Gene

2. Goaded at last by Ross McLain's snide comments about Jennifer, Gene beat the brash boss of Trail's End unmercifully before an astonished gallery that included beautiful, unscrupulous Lola.

3. When McLain's gunmen sprang an ambush on the night camp of the lone wagon rushing stop-gap relief to Sunshine Valley, Gene and Jennifer took fast cover and returned the blistering fire.

6. Bent on recapturing the merchandise, McLain blew up a cliff to destroy Gene's wagons; making it necessary for the supplies to be reloaded onto the wagon teams in a makeshift pack train.

7. Even then the McLain gang did not give up—and man after man in the convoy was cut down, until only Gene's gun and that of his loyal pal Smiley Burnette still held off the ambushers.

pack train, continued

and heads his improvised pack train on toward Sunshine Valley. From every vantage point, McLain men molest them. One by one, the few remaining riders are picked off—or desert. At last, only Gene and Smiley are left to keep the horses plodding forward. But still Gene does not give up. He knows how desperately his friends need food and medicine. McLain's last desperate raid is beaten off within sight of the Valley, but only because sturdy Dan Coleman leads the settlers in a rescue ride. Despite all hazards, Gene has brought through his pack train. But the score between Sunshine Valley and McLain stands unsettled. A child has died for lack of medicine which would have come in time save for McLain's delaying. Back to Trail's End on a third errand rides Gene; this time with Dan Coleman keeping him company. They search the town for McLain, gradually realizing he has been warned of their coming and taken cover. In an alley, first drawing a gun for self-protection, a grateful Wade tells Gene that his erstwhile boss is even now holding up the eastbound train. He aims to get far away across the Badlands, ahead of Gene's vengeance guns. Spurring Champion for the rail-head, Gene intercepts the train. There follows a battle royal with the ruthless McLain, as Gene and a now-frightened profiteer slug it out along the swaying car roofs and in the caboose. Gene is victorious; McLain is dragged back to jail. The sheriff names Smiley

herded the vital supplies on the trail to Sunshine Settlement

4. Gene and the Colemans rolled the scantily filled wagon safe to the Valley. But its stores fast used up, Gene had to head for Trail's End and the fresh supplies McLain had not shipped.

5. Money-mad partners Lola and McLain were re-selling Sunshine Valley purchases to gold rush miners for big profits—so only Gene's gun won him grudging delivery of the disputed goods he needed.

8. The supplies at last safe in Sunshine Valley, Gene returned to Trail's End to face McLain; but heard from a gunman he once had spared that the crook was fleeing aboard a hijacked train.

9. Pursuing McLain, Gene cornered him in a hand-to-hand battle atop the racing engine—and later could bring the Valley back news that the new settlement's foe would trouble them no more.

to serve as acting manager of the supply business—left without managers now that both McLain and his sultry partner Lola will be facing prison sentences for their heartless efforts to create a rich monopoly for their own profit. It is obvious to all the settlers that, from today on, with Smiley in charge of things, they need fear no further discrimination against the fair prices offered for necessary goods by Coleman and his fellow homesteaders. Never again will greed and evil demand such a useless toll as the death of a sick and helpless child. The infant community in the Valley seems destined to prosper until it becomes the fruitful Eden envisaged by its settlers.

THE CAST

Gene Autry.................................. himself
Smiley Burnette.................................. himself
Jennifer Coleman.................................. Gail Davis
Ross McLain.................................. Kenne Duncan
Lola Riker.................................. Sheila Ryan
Dan Coleman.................................. Tom London
Roy Wade.................................. Harry Lauter
Judy.................................. Melinda Plowman
Ted.................................. B. G. Norman
1st McLain man.................................. Frank Marvin
2nd McLain man.................................. Norman Westcoatt

Adapted from the Columbia Picture

(The preceding publicity release originally appeared in *Who's Who in Western Stars*, Vol. 1, No. 3, 1953.)

Gene's fists pounded Webb, the bogu
redman, into submission in a vicious brawl

Ranger Captain Gene Autry plays a deadly game with a brace of cool killers

Saginaw Trail

■ In 1827, the Saginaw Trail is beginning to be used by settlers pouring into the wild Great Lakes region. Game flees before them, and traders like ambitious Jules Brissac feel the pinch as fur profits dwindle. Brissac, though, has effective help from Miller Webb, ruthless frontier adventurer who in makeup can pass as an Indian. Suddenly, settler wagons begin to be attacked by renegade redmen. Webb and his malcontent braves are out to halt the influx, and Brissac secretly pays the bill. Two incoming settlers killed by Webb are the parents of young Randy Lane. But the boy is left alive. Gene Autry, captain in the famous scout outfit known as Hamilton's Rangers, finds him with his horse, Cloudy, and takes him to the supposed safety of Brissac's fur post. Here, Brissac and Webb hide their concern that a Ranger is investigating the recent raids. Randy meets Brissac's son Phillip, and ward—pretty Flora Tourney—and seemingly is among friends. Gene has his helper, Smiley Burnette, planted among the bearded trappers selling to Brissac, hoping to get some clue to the outrages. Brissac tries to shoot Gene "accidentally," while showing him a pair of duelling pistols, but the attempt fails. Gene soon discovers that a white man in disguise leads the marauders. Webb also tries to kill him, and fails. Gene summons the chiefs of three nearby tribes—the Miamis, the Fox and the Huron—to a council. They deny any knowledge of the raids. By now, both Gene and Smiley are more than suspicious of Brissac. But an arrest is out of the question, for they have not a shred of evidence. Meanwhile, in their shy young way, Randy and Flora are becoming fond of each other. This enrages spoiled Phillip, who always has planned to marry his father's ward—and her fortune—when they grew up. Searching the post, Gene finds a secret passage from Brissac's study to Miller Webb's

1. Meeting young Randy Lane alone on the Saginaw Trail after the slaying of his parents by renegade Indians, Gene brought the bewildered youth to the shelter of the Brissac fur post.

2. The arrival of a Ranger in their valley was alarming news for trader Jules Brissac and his paid murderer, Miller Webb, who led the renegade sorties disguised as an Indian warrior.

3. Working to unmask the Indian killers, Autry held a pow-wow with a trio of friendly chiefs and realized that none of the local tribes was making war on settlers along the old Trail.

Settlers heading west were doomed by crafty murderers

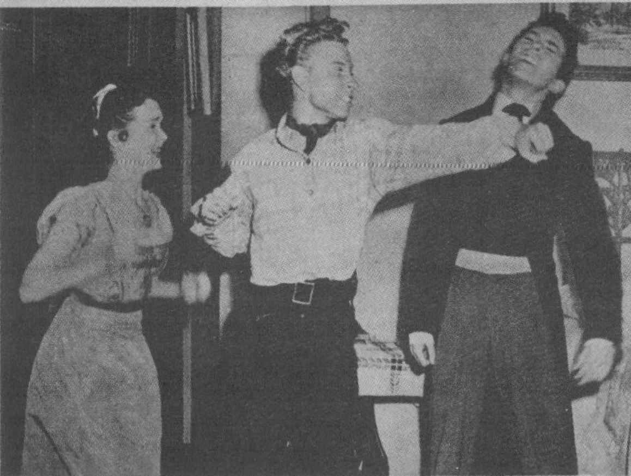

4. When snide Phillip Brissac sought to keep Randy and Flora from rushing proof of Webb's guilt to Gene, Randy fought him off with the courage of a young panther, while Flora watched.

5. Forgetting that he had been detailed by Autry to police the two unsavory Brissacs, Smiley led the fur trappers in a wild ride down the old Trail to help break up the ambush awaiting the new wagons.

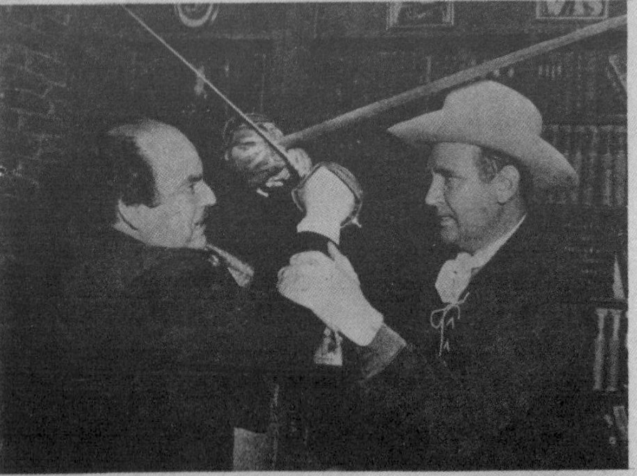

6. At the post where Brissac once dreamed of setting himself up like a French aristocrat, Gene at last subdued the crafty trader in a slashing sword duel that ended his rule forever.

THE CAST

Gene Autry	himself
Smiley Burnette	himself
Flora Tourney	Connie Marshall
Jules Brissac	Eugene Borden
Randy Lane	Ralph Reed
Phillip Brissac	Henry Blair
Miller Webb	Myron Healey
Jean Leblanc	Mickey Simpson
Red Bird	John War Eagle
The Huron	Rod Red Wing
The Fox	Billy Wilkerson
Lin Oakes	Gregg Barton
Walt Curry	John Parrish

saginaw trail continued

quarters, and knows the two are linked in the crimes. He is caught by Webb while searching the latter's room. A wild fight results, from which Gene escapes just before Brissac's arrival. Since Gene was masked during the encounter, neither of his enemies recognizes him. Word reaches Brissac that new settlers are coming in. Smiley sees the Indian messenger departing, and informs Gene. While they give chase, young Randy decides to complete the search of Webb's room for Gene. He and Flora discover a towel in one drawer, stained with Indian war paint. Phillip, however, interrupts the hunt and tries to take over the evidence. He and Randy tangle like wildcats, and later Phillip shoots Cloudy. Now Gene has proof that Webb is the white "Indian". But Webb already has lit out, with his renegade Delawares, to stop the new wagons. While Smiley remains behind to guard the Brissacs, Gene and a determined Randy ride the Trail to overtake the killers. Near the ambush, they proceed afoot. Gene silently picks off one after another of the waiting redmen. Just as the ambush is sprung, he jumps Webb himself. They tangle in mortal combat. The fight is still on when Smiley arrives, leading the trappers—who guard the wagons the rest of their way. Realizing the Brissacs are no longer guarded, Gene spurs back to the post just in time to find them preparing to escape. They are dragging with them an unwilling Flora. Brissac snatches one of a pair of swords from his wall, and Gene siezes the other. They battle until Gene corners and disarms the trader. Randy has meanwhile subdued young Phillip. The Saginaw Trail is at last safe for all the hopeful hearts that will follow it westward toward a new land; and there is every indication that, when they are both a trifle older, the romance that has budded so shyly between Flora and the brave young son of the martyred pioneers will culminate in a happy marriage. Scout Gene Autry has once again check-mated evil.

(The preceding publicity release originally appeared in *Who's Who in Western Stars*, Vol. 1, No. 3, 1953.)

GENE AUTRY
AND
CHAMPION
WORLD'S WONDER HORSE
IN ONE GREAT
COLUMBIA
ACTION PICTURE
AFTER ANOTHER!
"BLUE CANADIAN ROCKIES"
"WINNING OF THE WEST"
"ON TOP OF OLD SMOKY"
"GOLDTOWN GHOST RIDERS"
"PACK TRAIN"
"SAGINAW TRAIL"
"LAST OF THE PONY RIDERS"
GENE AUTRY PRODUCTIONS
EXECUTIVE PRODUCER ARMAND SCHAEFER

SAGINAW TRAIL (Columbia, 1953) 56 M.

Rating: **

Producer, Armand Schaefer; director, George Archainbaud; screenplay, Dorothy Yost and Dwight Cummins.

Cast: Gene Autry, Smiley Burnette, Connie Marshall, Eugene Borden, Ralph Reed, Henry Blair, Myron Healey, Mickey Simpson, John War Eagle, Rodd Redwing, Billy Wilkerson, Gregg Barton, John Parrish, Champion.

Comment: We are in northern Michigan in 1827. Gene, a captain in Hamilton's Rangers, is called upon to stop Indian raiding parties that are driving away settlers from the area. The renegades are led by a French fur trapper who fears that the settlers will drive the wild game away.

"I liked the Story." -CR

"My personal favorite Columbia feature. . . the earliest period setting of any Gene Autry film (1827) with Gene, Smiley, and even Champion decked out in period gear. . . atmospheric. . .offbeat. . .charming!" -JGS

Songs: "Beautiful Dreamer," "When It's Prayer Meetin' Time in the Hollow," and "Mam'selle."

* * *

LAST OF THE PONY RIDERS (Columbia, 1953) 58 M.

Rating: ***½

Dick Jones, one of the pony riders, is in big trouble in this scene. Don't worry, Dickie, Gene is on the way!

Producer, Armand Schaefer; director, George Archainbaud; screenplay, Ruth Woodman.

Cast: Gene Autry, Smiley Burnette, Kathleen Case, Dick Jones, John Downey, Howard Wright, Arthur Space, Gregg Barton, Buzz Henry, Harry Mackin, Harry Hines, Champion.

Comment: The story concerns the transition period in the old West from Pony Express to stagecoach and telegraph. Gene's setting up a stage line and wants to keep the mail franchise he had with the Pony Express. The local banker tries to undermine Gene's success.

"Great action, great acting, very good story." -CR

"Gene and Smiley ended their series with one of the very finest films they ever made. In many ways this looks like the beginning of a new series rather than the end of an old one. . . a very fitting ending for a beautiful era which lives on in memory." -JGS

Songs: "Sing Me a Song of the Saddle" and "Sugar Babe."

CHAPTER 7
COLLECTING GENE AUTRY MEMORABILIA

Everybody Was a Cowboy — Once Upon a Time

During those years
When heroes were real
And horses had a flash of fire and wildness in their eyes
A boy could go there—to that land of make-believe
And ride the trails
And wear the guns
And right the wrongs
And ride those mighty steeds with grace and ease.

And every now and then, in times of quiet reverie
A man looks back and slips through time
And travels through a maze of memories
And hums a long-forgotten cowboy tune—and smiles.

NR

A show business celebrity's name and face have always had a magical effect on the public. The products the stars use and/or endorse are generally sought after by their loyal band of fans. Whether their likeness is baked onto a T shirt or seen in a magazine touting the latest vitamin-enriched, energy-packed cereal, those stars who have that elusive ability to move products off shelves and into the homes of the country are sought after by the moguls of Madison Avenue—the marketplace of the world. The practice of celebrity endorsements started long before Gene Autry came onto the show business scene, but he was quick to see the benefits to be derived. It was good business!

The first Gene Autry endorsed product was the "Official Gene Autry Guitar." It was offered in the early 1930s while Gene was still at WLS radio in Chicago. When Gene ventured to Hollywood in 1934 and proceeded to get his name on movie marquees across the country and then the world, his wholesome reputation as a cowboy singer and movie star stood him in good stead with parents whose little tykes wanted the latest Gene Autry cap pistol, blue jeans, suspenders—whatever. By the late 1930s Gene Autry endorsed and licensed products (such as comic books, sweatshirts, games, spurs, chaps, cowboy outfits, holsters, and cap pistols) were earning the popular cowboy star approximately twenty-five thousand dollars a year.

Ten years later in the late 1940s the royalties from Gene Autry endorsed merchandise had jumped to approximately one hundred thousand dollars a year. The Dell Company was publishing a million *Gene Autry Comics* each year. Gene Autry wristwatches, bicycles, Whitman novels, kerchiefs, lunch boxes, coloring books, billfolds, and horseshoe nail rings—just to name a few items—were fast-moving merchandise in the department stores across the United States and in other countries where the Gene Autry films and personal appearances played to packed houses.

During the late 1950s Gene's show business career was winding down and so was the merchandising of his products. Years passed and the Autry fans matured into adulthood. Suddenly, yesteryear's playthings—those toys, clothes, and printed products with Gene's name and face emblazoned on them—had a new name: memorabilia.

By the 1970s nostalgia for a less frenetic time was sweeping the country. Many middle-aged youngsters found comfort in the memories of an era when Gene rode Champion across the silver screen and routed the easily-identifiable bad guys with the black hats. The memorabilia from that happier, more carefree time suddenly became highly sought after. Locating one of Gene's old cap pistols or discovering a 1946 Gene Autry comic in the attic of your parent's home was like finding a piece of lost youth. The floodgates of memory were suddenly thrown open, and there you were, that front-row Saturday matinee buckaroo once again.

These nostalgic items are scarce, of course, and become more so with the passing of each year. The collectors of such memorabilia are reluctant to part with their treasures. Several years ago when I was browsing through some collectibles in an antique store, the proprietor asked if I had found anything I couldn't live without. And that seems to be the bottom line for collecting memorabilia. If the item represents a moment from your past too precious to ignore, you make the purchase of "a piece of time."

In recent years Gene Autry memorabilia has become highly sought after. As a result, the prices for such desirable items have risen dramatically. Dealers who sell memorabilia are businessmen who seek a profit for these "antiques" of not-so-long-ago. As with most antiques, a "fair market price" is what the market will bear. During the preparation of this Chapter I discussed current values of Gene Autry memorabilia with three Western memorabilia dealers. In some cases there was a wide variance in the value that each dealer placed on an item, but mostly they were in general agreement with only a few dollars separating their estimates.

Availability and the condition of the memorabilia are the two main criteria for arriving at a value. On a poor, fair, good, excellent, mint condition scale, the prices stated in this chapter would be applicable to an excellent-to-mint condition item in its original box or container (if that applied).

There is no reason to assume that these prices will remain stable. In ten years it is likely that the values of many items will double, triple, or even quadruple as, indeed, many rare Gene Autry memorabilia items have during the past decade.

I am most grateful to the dealers who assisted me in compiling the information for this chapter. They are as follows:

Cowboy Trading Co.
Bill Lane, owner
3416 Hull Street
Richmond, Virginia 23225

Mountain Empire Comics
John Stone
Route 2—Box 445
Bristol, Tennessee 37620

Collector's Dream World
Art Thomas
Rt. 4, Box 155 Parkway
Sevierville, Tennessee 37862

Many of the photos in this chapter were provided by Jimmy Glover, whose Autry collection is one of the most extensive in the country.

The Gene Autry Official Cowboy Spurs (circa late 1940s) are now valued at $75-$100 in the original box.

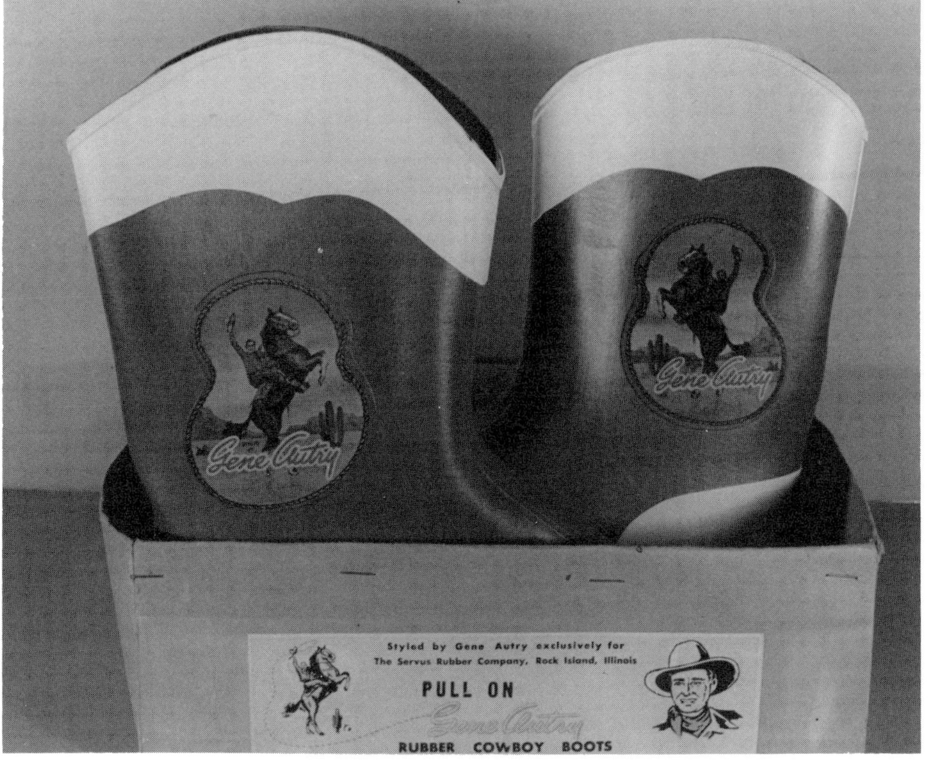

These Gene Autry Rubber Cowboy Boots were really fancy galoshes (circa 1950). Mothers loved them because previously they could never get their children to wear galoshes on a rainy day. Today they would cost mom between $75 and $90.

Gene's Horseshoe Nail Ring was produced by Albin Enterprises of Beverly Hills, no less. Engraved on the band was the Flying A logo and Gene's autograph. The value today is $35-$45 (circa 1950). The backside of the card has the following message: *Hi there! This little horseshoe nail ring from Champion and me has a special spot in my affections because when I was a little lad in Oklahoma, an Indian Chief once gave me one of these rings. I can remember well what he told me. He said: "Horseshoe nail ring better than gold, bring you much luck." I still have my old horseshoe ring, and that's why I thought you might like to have one.*

Always your pal,
Gene Autry

These two billfolds from the 1940s and early 1950s are valued between $25 and $45, depending on condition and whether they are in their original boxes.

The Gene Autry Melody Ranch Lunch Box and Thermos were manufactured in the late 1940s by Landers, Frary & Clark of New Britain, Conn. The lunchbox and Thermos together are valued at $75-$90. Many times the items are sold separately because the dealer does not have both together. The value is in the $35 range if lunchbox and Thermos are sold separately.

The Gene Autry Guitar with Automatic Chord Player and a book of songs was made by Emenee Musical Toys, advertised in *Life*, and commended by *Parents' Magazine.* The guitar was plastic with raised figures on the front of Gene, a holster and gun, spurs, and several other Western items. Current value in box: $150-$200. (circa 1950)

The very rare Gene Autry Monark Bicycle is truly a collector's item since there are so few in existance today. The dealers I surveyed placed a value of $1,500 to $2,000 on the bike. (circa 1950)

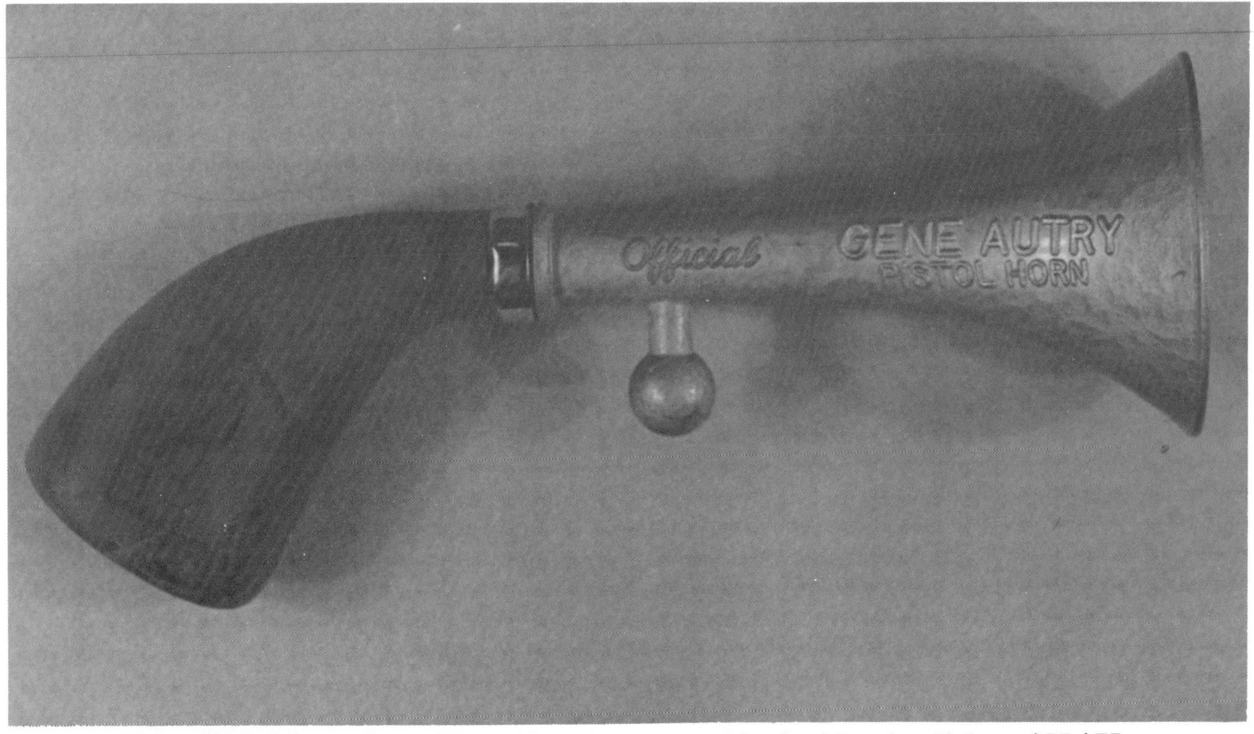

This official Gene Autry Pistol Horn is mounted in the bicycle. Value: $55-$75.

The value of the Gene Autry cap pistols has risen sharply during the past ten years. In 1976 you could purchase one in an original box for approximately $8-$10. Today the above cap pistols would each range from $75-$150 in the original box and in mint condition. Without the box the value for each would be reduced to between $35 and $60. The pictured cap pistols are only three of many that were issued from the late 1930s through the 1950s.

The Gene Autry Wristwatch was manufactured by the Wilane Watch Company in 1948. It came in the above box and sold for $6.95. Today (boxed and in mint condition) it is valued at $175-$225. Without the box and in less than mint condition, it can be purchased for $75-$150.

Gene Autry Souvenir Programs from his yearly personal appearance tours are popular among collectors. Depending upon condition, of course, the programs usually sell for $30-$45. The program on the left was issued in the 1950s. The program on the right is from the 1940s.

The Gene Autry Chaps and Vest Outfit (circa early 1940s) is very hard to find today, and, thus, the value has gone up greatly. In the original box the outfit would be valued today at $125-$150. Without the box the value would drop to $70-$120.

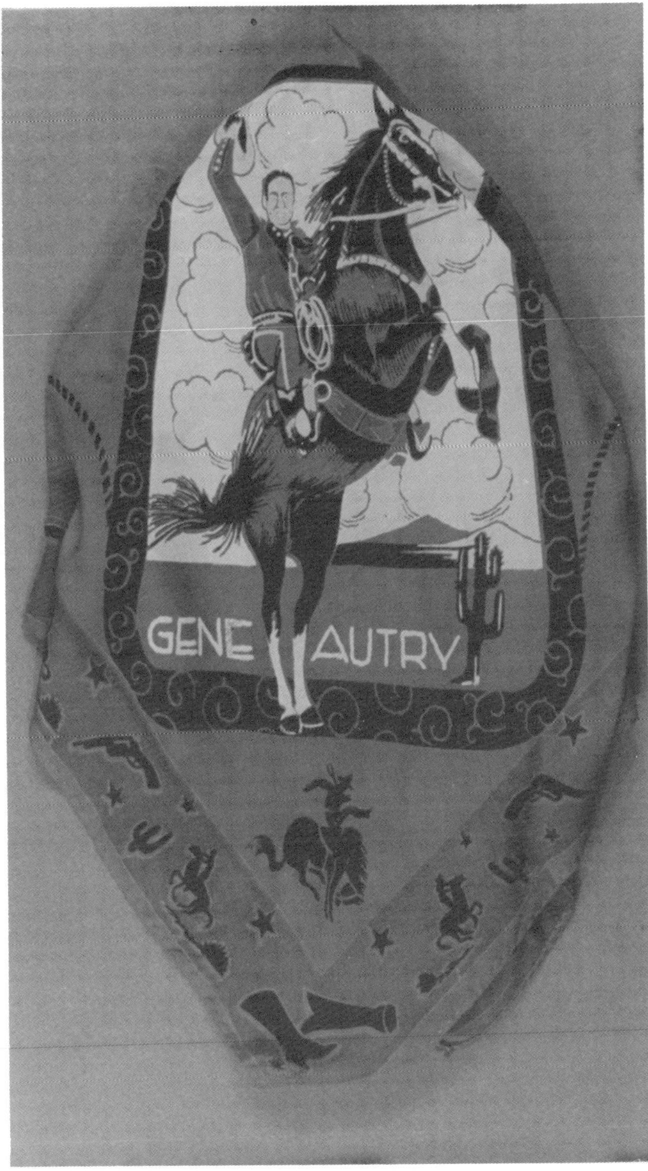

The Gene Autry satin-rayon neckerchief received a wide range of values from the dealers I talked with. The low was $20-$25. The high was $75-$125. The higher price range was based upon the scarcity of the item.

The Gene Autry authentic belt received a wide range of values depending on condition and if the cardboard attachment were included. The belt by itself: $25-$30. With the card: $75-$90. (circa 1950)

The Gene Autry Jeans are valued at $75-$125 because they are almost impossible to find in new condition. (circa 1949)

The Gene Autry Bandit Trail Game was produced in the 1940s. The game is rarely seen today by collectors and dealers. Consequently, it has a rather high value of $85-$90.

Gene Autry's Dude Ranch Game (circa 1950) was manufactured later than the Bandit Trail Game, but it also is not easily located. Values range from $40 to $90.

The above poster is called a one sheet and was originally used in movie theaters to advertise current and upcoming films. In the movie memorabilia trade the one sheet would be referred to as an example of "movie paper."

A Short Treatise on "Movie Paper" for the Novice

"Movie paper," as it is often called, refers to any artwork, photographs, or printed information that is prepared by a studio to publicize a movie. These items generally include one sheets (27x41-inch posters,) inserts (14x36-inch posters), half sheets (22x28-inch posters), lobby cards (11x14-inch posters, usually in sets of eight with one being a title card and the others called scene cards), pressbooks (publicity releases and photos designed for movie exhibitor use), and stills (8x10-inch black & white and color glossy photos).

The value of movie paper is primarily based upon condition, age, availability, and the popularity of the individual movie and/or star. For example, the value of the original one sheet from TUMBLING TUMBLEWEEDS (1935) would be considerably greater than the one sheet for LAST OF THE PONY RIDERS (1953) for most of the above reasons. The same rules apply for the other types of publicity materials.

The buyers of movie paper should be cautious when making a purchase of vintage material. Using the Autry movies as a case in point, many of the films were re-released at various times over the years. With each re-release new publicity materials were produced. These reissue posters are, of course, worth much less than posters from an original release. The buyer should examine posters for a studio notice that indicates a re-release of the film and, thus, a reissue of the publicity materials.

Gene Autry movie paper of all kinds has shown a considerable increase in value in recent years. In 1973 I purchased two original one sheet posters from Gene Autry films of 1940 and 1941 for $8 each. I recently saw comparable 1940 original one sheets advertised by a reputable dealer for over $200 each. Autry inserts and half sheets range from as low as $20 to over $100, again depending on the criteria stated above. Lobby cards vary greatly in price. A title lobby card may run from $10 to $100, depending upon the usual conditions. Scene cards are less expensive unless they contain an especially good shot of the star. Scene cards, with rare exceptions, usually range from $3 to $25. Pressbooks generally range from $20 to $50. Black & white 8x10 stills are reproduced by the thousands, so the prices are low at $1.50-$2. Color 8x10 photos range from $3-$5.

One final comment to the prospective buyer of movie paper: Remember that "what the market will bear" usually dictates price. The values stated for Gene Autry movie paper, as for most movie paper, fluctuate greatly, and the reader should interpret stated values as only "ballpark" prices.

The above scene lobby card would be priced relatively low ($3-$6) because Gene is not in the scene and because the card is from a later film in the series.

A DELL 10¢ MAGAZINE
MAY-JUNE
Gene Autry
COMICS

The first Gene Autry comic book was published on December 31, 1941, by the Fawcett Company. Issue No. 1 is very rare and valued at $500 in mint condition. The Dell four-color series followed and has values ranging from $140 for an early issue to $85 for No. 93, the last issue before Dell started *Gene Autry Comics* in May-June of 1946. Issue No. 1 (pictured on previous page) is valued at $140. There are 121 issues in the Dell series, running to January-March, 1959. In August 1955, the title was changed to *Gene Autry and Champion.* Issue No. 121 has a mint value of about $6. Most issues had photo covers of Gene.

A series of Gene Autry "Better Little Books" was published starting in the late 1930s and continuing through the mid '40s. Values vary widely, but most of the books can be purchased for $20-$25.

The Gene Autry New Better Little Books were published in the late '40s. They are valued at $15-$20.

The two books pictured here are British imports that were published by Purnell & Sons, Ltd. in the late '50s. Both books featured adventure stories with frequent cartoon drawings. The Gene Autry book contained no writing credit; the drawings were by R. Wilson. Value: $25-$40. The *Champion the Wonder Horse* book was based on the "Champion" television series. The adventure stories were written by Arthur Groom and the illustrations were by John Pollack. Value: $20-$35.

There were many Gene Autry coloring books published throughout his career. The two on this page and the one on the first page of this chapter are representative of the '40s era. When purchasing a Gene Autry coloring book, the collector should check copyright dates to be certain when the book was *actually* published. At least two coloring books were reissued in 1975. They look almost exactly like the original issues of 1950 and 1953. The coloring books of the 1940s are valued at $35-$45. Those of the 1950s are worth $7-$12. The reissues should be worth little more than the 39 cents printed on the cover.

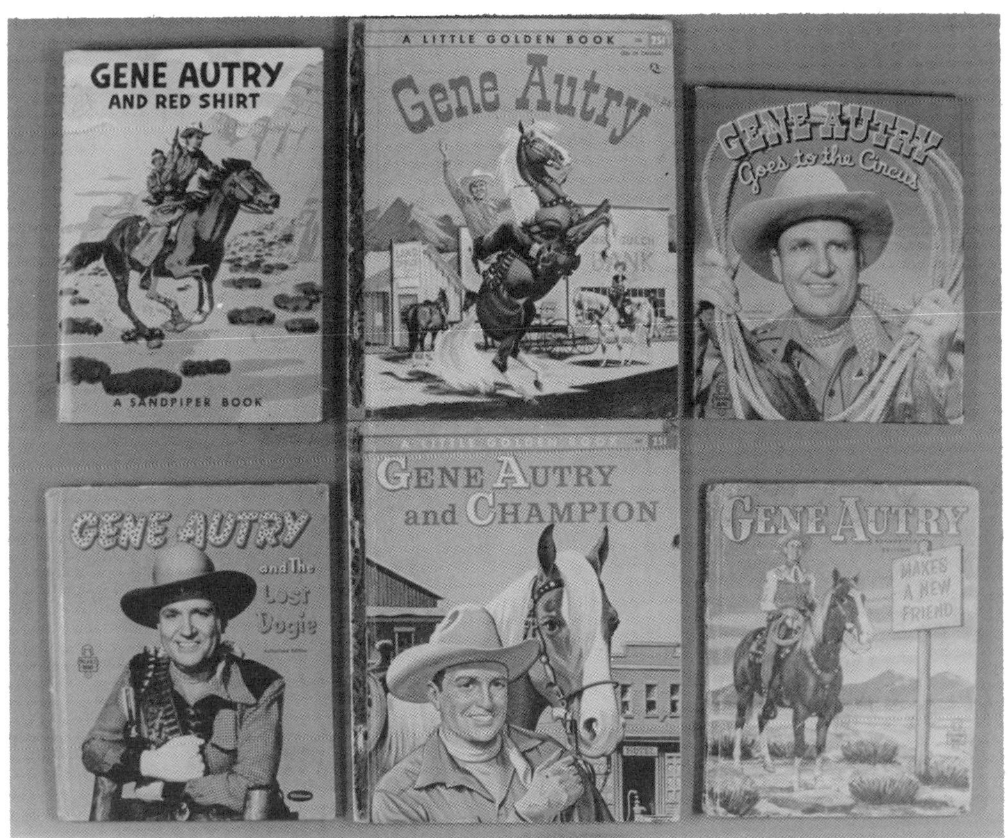

The Gene Autry "Little Golden Books" and "Tell-A-Tale" books were popular during the 1950s. The Sandpiper book entitled *Gene Autry and Red Shirt* is a novel with cartoon drawings. The books are valued at $7-$12 these days.

The Gene Autry novels published by Whitman were very popular during the 1940s and 1950s. The eight published were the following:

Thief River Outlaws (1944)
The Redwood Pirates (1946)
Golden Ladder Gang (1950)
Badmen of Broken Bow (1951)
Big Valley Grab (1952)
The Golden Stallion (1954)
The Ghost Riders (1955)
Arapaho War Drums (1957)

The value of the Whitman novels has remained comparatively low because so many were published and remain available. With a dust jacket the value is $10-$12.

Fan magazines which feature articles about Gene vary in value depending on the extent of the article. This issue of *Western Stars* is priced at $25-$35.

Gene's autobiography was published in 1978 by Doubleday. It sold for $8.95. A dealer with 50 copies of this book would have a very good investment for future years.

In 1982 The Art Merchant issued a limited edition art work entitled "America's Favorite Cowboy, Gene Autry," each of which was personally autographed by Gene. There were a total of 1600 copies autographed. The buyer receives a certificate of authenticity with the purchase of the print. Each copy sells for $100.

The Art Merchant is located in Hollywood, California.

In 1984 Nostalgia Collectibles and Gene Autry issued a 25,000 limited edition of a collector's plate entitled "Gene Autry, America's Favorite Cowboy." The 9½ inch in diameter, full-color plate sells for $45.

The company has also issued an 8 inch limited edition musicial figurine of Gene on Champion (not pictured). The figurine features Gene singing five of his famous songs. The figurine costs $135. This item is also limited to 25,000 copies.

Nostalgia Collectibles is located in Northbrook, IL.

CHAPTER 8

BACK IN THE SADDLE AGAIN— 91 MORE TIMES THE TELEVISION YEARS

Gene Autry was the first movie star to make a regular series for television. His decision to enter television with a half-hour filmed series in 1950 did not endear him to movie exhibitors or even Columbia Pictures, his own releasing company for his feature films. Gene, however, could see that the trail dust was settling for the B Westerns in movie theaters and that the new and, perhaps, last outlet for such entertainment fare was what the movie industry was still considering the enemy — television.

When I interviewed Gene for *The Singing Cowboys,* he told me of the turmoil of that time and of a Theatre Owners of America convention he addressed shortly after he announced his intention to enter television with a regular series.

> *Gene Autry:* I caught all kinds of hell from theatre owners, exhibitors, and even from Columbia Pictures—they were all over me for making this first series, which was released over the CBS network. Mr. Wrigley bought them.
>
> About that time there was a Theatre Owners of America convention held in Chicago, I think it was. I made a speech before them and said, "Look, you fellows are hollering about progress. Whether you like it or not, television is coming in and you might as well get ready to face the fact. I remember when radio first came in you said that it was going to ruin the theatres. Instead of that it developed a lot of stars for you fellows in the theatres. Look at Bing Crosby; he's a radio artist. Also, look at Bob Hope; he was first in radio and then came into pictures. Radio has developed some very fine talent for you. I think television is going to do the same thing and the time will come when all of you producers in Hollywood are going to be making television pictures. And you'll probably wind up selling your old product to television." And it all came true.

Gene's television series, "The Gene Autry Show," went on the air Sunday, July 23, 1950, over the CBS Television Network. The time was 7:00 P.M. Long-time associate Armand Schaefer was producer for the series with Louis Gray acting as associate producer. Carl Cotner was musicial director; the photography was handled by William Bradford who was a regular in Gene's feature productions. Gene selected Pat Buttram as his regular sidekick in the television series. This whole team was still around in 1955 when episode ninety-one, the last one, was shot by Gene's Flying A Productions.

In my preparation of the television series log I wanted in some way to determine outstanding episodes from the series. It was with this thought in mind that I went back to the six Gene Autry authorities and film collectors who had rated the Autry feature films. I asked them if they would indicate their five favorite episodes from "The Gene Autry Show" television series. Upon receiving my request, they expressed some frustration with the task, since five episodes represented such a small portion of the ninety-one episode series. They good-naturally acceded to my request, however, and their selections and comments are noted in the TV log. My thanks again to Truman L. Evitt, Jimmy Glover, Gary Parmenter, Charlie Rhine, Sr., Jesse Rush, and Jon Guyot Smith.

Special thanks are due Truman Evitt and Jon Guyot Smith for detailed additional information which they provided me for the TV log. Both gentlemen had been working independently on such a log when my letter requesting assistance arrived. It was at this time that I first learned of the elaborate research they had been doing on the television log. (I had originally intended to provide only episode titles and release dates because a detailed log was not known to exist.) They both graciously offered to make their research available to me for this book.

It is interesting and a little ironic that both men had been pursuing their research totally unaware of the other's work until they offered to share it with me. Instead of being chagrined by the knowledge of their similar endeavors, each expressed a desire to see what the other man had uncovered in his research. Such, I have found, is the nature of the Gene Autryphile, to coin a new term.

The Gene Autry Show TV Log

Head for Texas (July 23, 1950) Author's note: The date indicates when the program was first telecast.)

Director, Frank McDonald; screenplay, Dwight Cummins.

Cast: Gene Autry, Pat Buttram, Barbara Stanley, Jim Frasher, George J. Lewis, House Peters, Jr., Ben Weldon, Ray Bennett.

Song: "Sing Me a Song of the Saddle"

Plot: Gene befriends an ex-jockey who helps him arrest some cattle thieves.

* * *

**Gold Dust Charlie* (July 30, 1950)

Director, Frank McDonald; screenplay, Jack Townley.

Cast: Gene Autry, Pat Buttram, Sheila Ryan, Steve Darrell, Ralph Sanford, Alan Hale, Jr., Tom London, Gregg Barton, Sam Flint, Frankie Marvin, Bob Woodward, and The Cass County Boys (Fred S. Martin, Bert Dodson, Jerry Scoggins).

Songs: "Mexicali Rose," "Cowboy Blues," "Home on the Range," and "Great Grandad."

Plot: Gene is arrested as a homicide suspect in his attempt to register a land claim.

* * *

The Silver Arrow (August 6, 1950)

Director, Frank McDonald; screenplay, Elizabeth Beecher.

Cast: Gene Autry, Pat Buttram, Ray Bennett, George J. Lewis, Gregg Barton, Ben Weldon, Robert Livingston, Jim Frasher, Sandy Sanders.

Song: "Can't Shake the Sands of Texas from My Shoes"

Plot: Gene clears the name of young Randy Edwards (Jim Frasher), falsely convicted of one crime and now framed on a new murder charge in which a former witness is killed with a silver arrow—Randy's "sign."

* * *

The Doodle Bug (August 13, 1950)

Director, Frank McDonald; screenplay, Polly James.

Cast: Gene Autry, Pat Buttram, Sheila Ryan, Steve Darrell, Minerva Urecal, Gregg Barton, Alan Hale, Jr., Tommy Ivo, Tom London.

Song: Ridin' Down the Canyon"

Plot: Stageline superintendent Gene Autry goes to Dentoville to investigate a series of gold shipment robberies.

* * *

**The Star Toter* (August 20, 1950)

Director, Frank McDonald; screenplay, Jack Townley.

Cast: Gene Autry, Pat Buttram, Barbara Stanley, Billy Gray, George J. Lewis, House Peters, Jr., Robert Livingston, Wes Hudman, Frankie Marvin, Beatrice Gray.

Song: "Back in the Saddle Again"

Plot: Gene befriends a twelve-year-old son of a hardened criminal and teaches him respect for the law.

Comment: "I believe this is the second best TV Autry show made. It has a good message, too." -GP

* * *

The Double Switch (August 27, 1950)

Director, Frank McDonald; screenplay, Earle Snell.

Cast: Gene Autry, Pat Buttram, Steve Darrell, Sam Flint, Tom London, Alan Hale, Jr., Gregg Barton, Frankie Marvin.

Song: "When the Bloom Is on the Sage"

*Author's note: The number of stars before an episode title indicates how many of the six Gene Autry TV series raters voted the episode one of their five favorites.

Plot: Gene sets a trap to capture a gang of clever stagecoach robbers.

* * *

Blackwater Valley Feud (September 3, 1950)

Director, George Archainbaud; screenplay, Paul Gangelin.

Cast: Gene Autry, Pat Buttram, Gail Davis, William Haade, Stanley Andrews, Francis McDonald, Harry Lauter, Jack Ingram.

Song: "That's My Home"

Plot: Gene matches wits with—and ultimately defeats—a crafty land-grabber.

* * *

Doublecross Valley (September 10, 1950)

Director, George Archainbaud; screenplay, J. Benton Cheney.

Cast: Gene Autry, Pat Buttram, Gail Davis, Stanley Andrews, Harry Lauter, William Haade, Francis McDonald, Michael Ragan, Wade Crosby, Bob Cason, Frankie Marvin, Charles Lyon.

Song: "Texans Never Cry"

Plot: Gene uncovers a rich gold cache as he helps a friend defend his ranch.

* * *

The Posse (September 17, 1950)

Director, Geroge Archainbaud; screenplay, Betty Burbridge.

Cast: Gene Autry, Pat Buttram, Wendy Waldron, Francis Ford, John Doucette, Bud Osborne, Bob Wilke, Bob Cason, Bob Woodward, Frankie Marvin.

Song: "Pretty Mary"

Plot: Gene temporarily turns his ranch over to an old man who wants to impress his visiting daughter.

* * *

The Devil's Band (September 24, 1950)

Director, George Archainbaud; screenplay, Elizabeth Beecher.

Cast: Gene Autry, Pat Buttram, Wendy Waldron, Gail Davis, John Doucette, Bud Osborne, Bob Cason, Francis Ford, Bob Wilke, George Lloyd, Wes Hudman.

Song: "Along the Navajo Trail"

Plot: Gene tracks down a bandit gang working under protective political influence and puts an end to their activities.

* * *

Six Shooter Sweepstakes (October 1, 1950)

Director, Frank McDonald; screenplay, Norman S. Hall.

Cast: Gene Autry, Pat Buttram, James Frazier, Virginia Merrick, Harry Harvey, Kenne Duncan, Zon Murray, Tom Neal, Wes Hudman, Louis Morphy, Frankie Marvin.

Song: "Rainbow on the Rio Colorado"

Plot: Champion loses a race, but causes Gene to apprehend some bank robbers.

Comment: A slight change in credits started with this episode. From this point on Louis Gray was listed as producer instead of associate producer, and Armand Schaefer was listed as executive in charge of production rather than producer.

* * *

The Poisoned Waterhole (October 8, 1950)

Director, Frank McDonald; screenplay, Polly James.

Cast: Gene Autry, Pat Buttram, Sheila Ryan, Bill Henry, Leonard Penn, Chief Thundercloud, Don C. Harvey, Tom London, Frankie Marvin, Wes Hudman.

Song: "Mellow Mountain Moon"

Plot: Gene's Indian friends are accused of poisoning a waterhole.

* * *

The Lost Chance (October 15, 1950)

Director, Frank McDonald; screenplay, Paul Gangelin.

Cast: Gene Autry, Pat Buttram, Don Pietro, Zon Murray, Kenne Duncan, Harry Harvey, Sr., Tom Neal, Wes Hudman, Frankie Marvin, Louis Morphy, George Steele, Ken Cooper.

Song: "Goodbye to My Old Mexico"

Plot: Rockbottom's Cattlemen's Association fund is $40,000 short, and its treasurer will go to any extreme to keep this fact a secret. Gene finds out.

* * *

The Black Rider (October 22, 1950)

Director, Frank McDonald; screenplay, Elizabeth Beecher.

Cast: Gene Autry, Pat Buttram, Sheila Ryan, Tom London, Don C. Harvey, Bill Henry, Wes Hudman, Leonard Penn, Frank Downing, Frank Urton, Bob Woodward.

Song: "Night Time in Nevada"

Plot: Rocky Dexter is hanged for a crime in the town of Gold Flat. His sister assumes the identity of "The Black Rider," seeking revenge against the sheriff, judge, witnesses, and members of the jury. Former Texas Ranger Gene Autry is summoned to help put an end to the mysterious murders.

* * *

Gunpowder Range (October 29, 1950)
(Working Title: *Call of the Long Trail)*

In this rare photo Gene is pictured with his two stars of "The Range Rider" television series, Dick Jones (pointing) and Jock Mahoney. Gene's Flying A Productions produced the series in the early 1950s. Dick Jones also starred in the "Buffalo Bill, Jr." Autry-produced series and made many guest appearances in Gene's own series.

Director, George Archainbaud; screenplay, Kenneth Perkins.

Cast: Gene Autry, Pat Buttram, Dick Jones, Gail Davis, George J. Lewis, Kenneth MacDonald, Dick Alexander, Lee Phelps, Chuck Roberson, Wes Hudman, Frank Matts, Rand Brooks, B. Naylor, Frankie Marvin.

Song: "Cool Water"

Plot: Milly Parker (Gail Davis), a cafe proprietor, is worried about her younger brother Tim (Dick Jones) who has a desire to join the Red Wolf Bunch and ride the "long trail" as an outlaw. She sends for Gene Autry, who poses as a bad man in order to persuade Tim to abandon his wild ways.

* * *

**The Breakup* (November 5, 1950)

Director, George Archainbaud; screenplay, Sherman Lowe.

Cast: Gene Autry, Pat Buttram, Rand Brooks, Lynne Roberts, Jim Bannon, Paul Campbell, Alan Hale, Jr., I. Stanford Jolley, Wes Hudman, Ed Dearing, Bob Woodward, Beatrice Gray, Carl Sepulveda.

Songs: "Painted Desert" and "Broomstick Buckaroo"

Plot: A young couple are split by the bride's father's stubborn nature.

* * *

Twisted Trails (November 12, 1950)

Director, George Archainbaud; screenplay, Dwight Cummins.

Cast: Gene Autry, Pat Buttram, Lynne Roberts, Jim Bannon, Billy Gray, Paul Campbell, Ed Dearing, Alan Hale, Jr., Rand Brooks, Wes Hudman, I. Stanford Jolley, Boyd Stockman, Carl Sepulveda.

Songs: "Roomful of Roses" and "Back in the Saddle Again"

Plot: A twelve-year-old Eastern lad named Eddie Baker (Billy Gray) journeys West in search of his father, little knowing that the man has turned outlaw.

The Fight at Peaceful Mesa (November 19, 1950)

Director, George Archainbaud; screenplay, Paul Gangelin.

Cast: Gene Autry, Pat Buttram, Gail Davis, Kenneth McDonald, George J. Lewis, Lee Phelps, Dick Alexander, Wes Hudman, Chuck Roberson.

Songs: "Be Honest With Me" and "I'm Beginning to Care"

Plot: The inheritance of valuable ranch property proves to be a motive for bloodshed.

* * *

Hot Lead (November 26, 1950)

Director, George Archainbaud; screenplay, Dwight Cummins.

Cast: Gene Autry, Alan Hale, Jr., Jim Frasher, Don C. Harvey, Harry Lauter, Harry (Pappy) Cheshire, Marshall Reed, Kenne Duncan, Frankie Marvin.

Songs: "The Strawberry Roan" and "Good Old-Fashioned Hoedown"

Plot: The Pioneer Bank is robbed of $30,000 by three thugs. The trio is soon abandoned by the younger brothers of despicable Nat Ellis (Don C. Harvey), who follows his wild stallion (Fury) to Gene Autry's ranch. It is there that the youth and the horse find a new understanding and a better life.

* * *

The Gray Dude (December 3, 1950)

Director, Frank McDonald; screenplay, Elizabeth Beecher.

Cast: Gene Autry, Chill Wills, James Griffith, Reed Howes, Robert Filmer, Kermit Maynard, Art Dillard, Tom Monroe, Sam Flint.

Song: "Red River Valley"

Plot: Dude Devlin (James Griffith), murderer and bank robber, is shielded from justice by his brother, Sheriff Davis (Reed Howes) until their relationship is exposed by lawmen Gene Autry and Chill Wills.

**The Killer Horse* (December 10, 1950)

Director, George Archainbaud; screenplay, Kenneth Perkins.

Cast: Gene Autry, Alan Hale, Jr., Billy Kimbley, Harry Lauter, Don C. Harvey, Kenne Duncan, Harry (Pappy) Cheshire, Hal K. Dawson, Marshall Reed, Frankie Marvin, Bob Woodward.

Song: "Rocky Canyon"

Plot: Town bum "Blowfly" Jones (Hal K. Dawson), who is scorned by everyone except his ten-year-old son, Chuck (Bill Kimbley), has a thoroughbred horse—his sole possession. The animal is suddenly framed in the savage murder of two prospectors.

Comment: ". . . an excellent TV Show. Fourth best in my judgment." -GP

* * *

***The Peacemaker* (December 17, 1950)

Director, Frank McDonald; screenplay, Paul Gangelin.

Cast: Gene Autry, Chill Wills, Peggy Stewart, Russell Hayden, Robert Filmer, Sam Flint, James Griffith, Kermit Maynard, Reed Howes, Art Dillard, George Steele, John Kee, Tom Monroe.

Songs: "I've Got a Heart as Big as Texas" and "Let Me Cry on Your Shoulder"

Plot: A rainmaker becomes involved in a land swindle in which several honest ranchers are implicated. Gene, as investigator, clears up the matter.

Comment: During the filming of this episode, Pat Buttram was seriously injured in a premature cannon blast—a special effect intended as a prop for the "rainmaker." The episode was completed with Chill Wills taking over Buttram's role.

* * *

The Sheriff of Santa Rosa (December 24, 1950)

Director, George Anchainbaud; screenplay, Polly James.

Cast: Gene Autry, Fuzzy Knight, Mira McKinney, Dick Jones, Stanley Andrews, Nan Leslie, Chuck Roberson, Dick Curtis, James Harrison, Boyd Stockman, Al Wyatt.

Songs: "Marquita" and "Tweedle-O-Twill"

Plot: A young man is involved with outlaws and arrested by Gene Autry, who is later persuaded by the boy's mother to help clear him of the charges.

* * *

T.N.T. (December 31, 1950)

Director, George Archainbaud; screenplay, Polly James.

Cast: Gene Autry, Fuzzy Knight, Eileen Janssen, Stanley Andrews, Dick Curtis, Chuck Roberson, James Harrison.

Song: "Tears on My Pillow"

Plot: Gene Autry is being pressured by his new neighbor, Colonel Towne (Stanley Andrews), into selling him water rights. A confrontation comes about only after Gene and Sagebrush (Fuzzy Knight) have the misfortune to meet the former military man's brattish young daughter, whose all-too-prophetic initials are "T.N.T."

* * *

**The Raiders* (April 14, 1951)

Director, John English; screenplay, Betty Burbridge.

Cast: Gene Autry, Fuzzy Knight, Raymond Hatton, Nan Leslie, George Cooper, Reed Howes, Gregg Barton, Bill Kennedy, Jack Ingram, Michael Ragan Wes Hudman, Boyd Stockman.

Song: "The Angel Song"

Plot: Gene and Sagebrush (Fuzzy Knight) are out to apprehend a bandit named "Buckeye" (George Cooper), who has robbed a construction company payroll.

Comment: This episode was filmed in color.

* * *

***Double Barrelled Vengeance* (April 21, 1951)

Director, John English; screenplay, Sue Dwiggins and Vy Russell.

Cast: Gene Autry, Fuzzy Knight, Raymond Hatton,

Nan Leslie, Jack Ingram, Gregg Barton, Bob Cason, Bill Kennedy, Michael Ragan.

Song: "I Wish I Had Never Met Sunshine"

Plot: Undercover investigator Gene Autry encounters trouble when he tries to recover an old Bandit's loot and is impeded by the town sheriff, a former outlaw.

Comment: This episode was filmed in color. "I feel that this is the best Autry TV show." -GP

* * *

Ghost Town Raiders (October 6, 1951)

Director, Frank McDonald; screenplay, John K. Butler.

Cast: Gene Autry, Pat Buttram, William Fawcett, Wendy Waldron, Sam Flint, George J. Lewis, Raphael Bennett, Reed Howes, Kermit Maynard, Art Dillard, Bob Woodward.

Song: "As Long As I Have My Horse"

Plot: As special agent for a mining company, Gene risks his life to track down some bandits.

* * *

Frontier Guard (October 13, 1951)

Director, George Archainbaud; screenplay, Fred Myton.

Cast: Gene Autry, Pat Buttram, James Craven, Donna Martell, Francis McDonald, Ewing Mitchell, Denver Pyle, Gregg Barton, Riley Hill, Tom Monroe.

Song: "Let's Go Roamin' Around the Range"

Plot: As a member of the Border Patrol, Gene helps a rancher who is being terrorized.

* * *

Silver Dollars (October 20, 1951)

Director, Frank McDonald; screenplay, Elizabeth Beecher.

Cast: Gene Autry, Pat Buttram, Wendy Waldron, William Fawcett, Louise Lorimer, Ray Bennett, George J. Lewis, Art Dillard, Kermit Maynard.

Song: "I Want to Be Sure"

Plot: Gene Autry is on the trail of a clever band of counterfeiters.

* * *

Killer's Trail (October 27, 1951)

Director, George Archainbaud; screenplay, Oliver Drake.

Cast: Gene Autry, Pat Buttram, Donna Martell, Francis McDonald, James Craven, Denver Pyle, Ewing Mithcell, Tom Monroe, Gregg Barton, Riley Hill, Bob Woodward.

Song: "Under Fiesta Stars"

Plot: Gene and Pat set out after a mysterious bandit chief.

* * *

Frame for Trouble (November 3, 1951)

Director, David R. Lederman; screenplay, Joe Richardson.

Cast: Gene Autry, Pat Buttram, Gail Davis, Dick Curtis, Dennis Moore, John Halloran, Don C. Harvey, Marshall Reed.

Song: "Ridin' Down the Canyon"

Plot: Gene Autry is falsely charged with murder when he keeps a captured gunslinger's secret rendezvous.

* * *

Warning! Danger! (November 10, 1951)

Director, George Archainbaud; screenplay, Dwight Cummins.

Cast: Gene Autry, Pat Buttram, Dick Jones, Gloria Winters, Teddy Infuhr, Gordon Jones, Harry Lauter, Leonard Penn, Bill Kennedy.

Song: "Down in the Valley"

Plot: Gene befriends two young orphans whose older brother is involved with the outlaw gang.

* * *

Revenge Trail (November 17, 1951)

Director, David R. Lederman; screenplay, Paul Gangelin.

Cast: Gene Autry, Pat Buttram, Gail Davis, Dick Curtis, John Halloran, Don C. Harvey, Dennis Moore, Marshall Reed, Bob Woodward.

Song: "Silver Spurs"

Plot: Hypnotism assists in the capture of a desperate criminal now posing as a medicine show entrepreneur.

* * *

Bandits of Boulder Bluff (November 24, 1951)

Director, George Archainbaud; screenplay, Howard J. Green.

This horse was the third Champion Gene used in films. He rode the horse throughout his "Gene Autry Show" television series. Gene even starred the horse in his own series, "The Adventures of Champion." There were twenty-six half-hour episodes in the 1955 series which co-starred humans Barry Curtis and Jim Bannon. Another co-star was the four-legged actor, Rebel the dog.

Cast: Gene Autry, Pat Buttram, Anne O'Neal, Dick Jones, Leonard Penn, Harry Lauter, Bill Kennedy, Gordon Jones.

Song: "Blue Montana Skies"

Plot: Despite the peacemaking efforts of his aunt, young Tom Colby (Dick Jones) refuses to reconcile his differences with his stubborn stepfather, a mine owner. Gene is subsequently forced to arrest Tom for the old man's murder, but he soon uncovers a plot to frame the young man and take over the mine.

* * *

Outlaw Escape (December 1, 1951)

Director, George Archainbaud; screenplay, Earle Snell.

Cast: Gene Autry, Pat Buttram, Gail Davis, James Craven, Ewing Mitchell, Robert Peyton, Ben Weldon, Myron Healy, Lee Morgan.

Song: "Crime Will Never Pay"

Plot: Town boss Brad Bidwell (James Craven) arranges for the election of Pat Buttram as sheriff so that his nefarious schemes may proceed undeterred. Pat contacts his friend Gene Autry to assist him bring the outlaws to justice.

* * *

The Kid Comes West (December 8, 1951)

Director, George Archainbaud; screenplay, Joe Richardson.

Cast: Gene Autry, Pat Buttram, William Fawcett, Sherry Jackson, Steven Pendleton, Keith Richards, Craig Woods, Sandy Sanders.

Song: "On Top of Old Smoky"

Plot: When his daughter dies, an elderly rancher sends for her child, whom he plans to make his heir.

* * *

The Return of Maverick Dan (December 15, 1951)

Director, George Archainbaud; screenplay, Polly James.

Cast: Gene Autry, Pat Buttram, Carole Nugent, James Craven, Ben Weldon, Myron Healy, Ewing Mitchell, Lee Morgan, Robert Peyton.

Song: "The Cowboy's Dream"

Plot: Gene is on the trail of Dan (Robert Peyton), when he comes across the man's sister who believes Dan to be innocent. She asks Gene to investigate.

* * *

Galloping Hoofs (December 22, 1951)

Director, George Archainbaud; screenplay Dwight Cummins.

Cast: Gene Autry, Pat Buttram, Gail Davis, George J. Lewis, Denver Pyle, Harry Harvey, Belle Mitchell.

Songs: "Mexicali Rose" and "Pretty Mary"

Plot: Gene learns that a convicted embezzler has escaped from jail, accusing his partner of the crime.

* * *

Heir to the Lazy L (December 29, 1951)

Director, Wallace Fox; screenplay, Oliver Drake.

Cast: Gene Autry, Pat Buttram, Gail Davis, Alan Hale, Jr., Sandy Sanders, Helen Servis, Hugh Prosser, Terry Frost.

Song: "Ridin' Double"

Plot: Gene inherits half of a ranch from an uncle, but is attacked by masked men on his way to see it.

* * *

Melody Mesa (January 4, 1952)

Director, George Archainbaud; screenplay, Betty Burbridge.

Cast: Gene Autry, Pat Buttram, Gail Davis, Ewing Mitchell, Denver Pyle, Harry Harvey, Belle Mitchell, George J. Lewis, Riley Hill, Jim Brittain.

Songs: "Ages and Ages Ago" and "Back in the Saddle Again"

Plot: Gene Autry poses as a music teacher in

order to entrap a gang of outlaws.

* * *

****Horse Sense* (January 11, 1952)

Director, Wallace Fox; screenplay, Robert Schaefer and Eric Freiwald.

Cast: Gene Autry, Pat Buttram, Gail Davis, Alan Hale, Jr., Dick Jones, Hugh Prosser, Terry Frost, Sandy Sanders, Bob Woodward.

Song: "Cowboy's Heaven"

Plot: Champion's uncanny intelligence proves vital in bringing to justice an evildoer.

Comment: "The episode has a good story and contains one of my favorite songs." -JG

". . . one of my very favorites." -GP

* * *

Rock River Feud (January 18, 1952)

Director, George Archainbaud; screenplay, Earle Snell.

Cast: Gene Autry, Pat Buttram, Sherry Jackson, William Fawcett, Craig Woods, Steve Pendleton, Keith Richards, Sandy Sanders.

Song: "Yellow Rose of Texas"

Plot: Gene and Pat ride into a community and become involved in a longstanding feud which involves Pat's relatives.

* * *

The Lawless Press (January 25, 1952)

Director, George Archainbaud; screenplay, Robert Schaefer and Eric Freiwald.

Cast: Gene Autry, Pat Buttram, Roy Gordon, James Anderson, George Pembroke, Dennis Moore, Gregg Barton, Ed Hinkle, Bruce Norman, Frankie Marvin.

Song: "When You and I Were Young, Maggie"

Plot: Sheriff Gene Autry is up against a crooked newspaperman who prints headlines reporting crimes before they are committed.

The Western Way (February 1, 1952)

Director, George Archainbaud; screenplay, Norman S. Hall

Cast: Gene Autry, Pat Buttram, Mira McKinney, Dick Jones, Steve Clark, Harry Lauter, Bob Wilke, Don C. Harvey.

Song: "Charmin' Billy"

Plot: Gene helps a sweet old lady regain her prodigal son who has been implicated in some criminal activities.

* * *

The Ruthless Renegade (February 8, 1952)

Director, George Archainbaud; screenplay, Elizabeth Beecher.

Cast: Gene Autry, Pat Buttram, Dennis Moore, Roy Gordon, Jane Frazee, James Anderson, Bruce Norman, Ed Hinkle, Gregg Barton, Frankie Marvin.

Song: "Texas Plains"

Plot: A crusading newspaperwoman tries to single-handedly clean up a lawless community, but her idealism is not wholeheartedly embraced by her husband.

* * *

Hot Lead and Old Lace (February 15, 1952)

Director, George Archainbaud; screenplay, Robert Schaefer and Eric Freiwald.

Cast: Gene Autry, Pat Buttram, Mira McKinney, Harry Lauter, Steve Clark, Don Harvey, Bob Wilke, Bob Woodward.

Song: "Home on the Range"

Plot: After rancher Pete Munroe (Steve Clark) is murdered, his two-fisted elderly niece, Maude (Mira McKinney), arrives from the East to take over the ranch. She is inclined to want to sell out, but is persuaded by foreman Gene Autry to keep the property. Gene reasons that old Pete's murderer must have wanted the ranch for unknown reasons.

PHILADELPHIA
TV TIMES
The Handiest Guide to Television Programs
10¢
PROGRAMS
for Week of
FEB. 7TH
GENE AUTRY
America's beloved singing cowboy is a regular Sunday night TV feature at 7:00 P.M. on WCAU-TV (Channel 10).

Blazeaway (February 22, 1952)

Director, George Blair; screenplay, Paul Gangelin.

Cast: Gene Autry, Pat Buttram, Mary Treen, Richard Travis, Pierre Watkin, Kermit Maynard, Bob Bice, Sandy Sanders, Bob Woodward.

Song: none

Plot: The mayor of Blazeaway tries to frame an Indian tribe in a series of tomahawk murders so that the government will move them elsewhere, thereby giving him control of the Indians' land. Sergeant Gene Autry persuades his commanding officer to let him go to Blazeaway as an undercover agent to clear the Indian Tribe.

* * *

Bullets and Bows (March 2, 1952)

Director, George Blair; screenplay, Robert Schaefer and Eric Freiwald.

Cast: Gene Autry, Pat Buttram, Elaine Riley, Denver Pyle, John Doucette, Gregg Barton, Myron Healey, Bob Woodward.

Song: "Rhythm of the Hoofbeats"

Plot: Pat Buttram tries to operate a dry goods store, but is harrassed by a group of outlaws whom Gene must apprehend.

* * *

Trouble at Silver Creek (March 9, 1952)

Director, George Archainbaud; screenplay, Howard Green.

Cast: Gene Autry, Pat Buttram, Barbara Stanley, Francis McDonald, Leonard Penn, Steve Conte, George Pembroke, Tom Tyler, Craig Woods.

Song: none

Plot: Gene must solve the mystery behind a number of knife murders, including that of Pat's late employer.

* * *

Six-Gun Romeo (March 16, 1952)

Director, George Blair; screenplay, Polly James.

Cast: Gene Autry, Pat Buttram, Elaine Riley, Mary Treen, Richard Travis, Kermit Maynard, Pierre Watkin, Bob Bice, Frankie Marvin.

Song: "I'm Beginning to Care"

Plot: Pat Buttram tackles more than is willing to be handled when he gets himself a mail-order sweetheart.

* * *

The Sheriff Is a Lady (March 23, 1952)

Director, George Blair; screenplay, Dwight Cummins.

Cast: Gene Autry, Pat Buttram, Elaine Riley, Denver Pyle, Dick Jones, Myron Healey, John Doucette, Gregg Barton.

Songs: "After Tomorrow" and "Sing Me a Song of the Saddle"

Plot: A headstrong woman sheriff is intent upon arresting Gene Autry, unaware that he is also a lawman.

* * *

Trail of the Witch (March 30, 1952)

Director, George Archainbaud; screenplay, Joe Richardson.

Cast: Gene Autry, Pat Buttram, Almira Sessions, Francis McDonald, Bill George, Leonard Penn, Steve Conte, Tom Tyler, Craig Woods, George Pembroke, Bob Woodward.

Song: none

Plot: Gene and Pat, trailing desperadoes, are led to the shack of an old hag who, as it develops, is hiding the badmen and frightening off those who seek them.

* * *

Thunder Out West (July 14, 1953)

Director, George Archainbaud; screenplay, Dorrell and Stuart McGowan.

Cast: Gene Autry, Pat Buttram, Wendy Waldron, Lyle Talbot, William Fawcett, Lane Chandler, Harry Lauter, Bob Woodward, Tom Tyler, George Slocum, Larry Hudson.

Song: "Old Nevada Moon"

Plot: Sheriff Gene Autry, with the unexpected help of his deputy's telescope, uncovers the identity of a safecracker.

* * *

Outlaw Stage (July 21, 1953)

Director, Wallace Fox; screenplay, Robert Schaefer and Eric Freiwald.

Cast: Gene Autry, Pat Buttram, Don C. Harvey, Edmund Cobb, Frank Jacquet, Harry Mackin, Pierce Lyden, Julian Upton, Steve Conte, Kermit Maynard.

Song: "Rainbow on the Rio Colorado"

Plot: Gene must clear Johnny Peters (Harry Mackin) of a charge that he is in league with outlaws.

* * *

Ghost Mountain (July 28, 1953)

Director, George Archainbaud; screenplay, Dwight Cummins.

Cast: Gene Autry, Pat Buttram, Eileen Janssen, Ross Ford, Clayton Moore, John Doucette, Ewing Brown, Sandy Sanders.

Songs: "I'll Go Ridin' Down That Texas Trail" and "If You'll Let Me Be Your Little Sweetheart"

Plot: Crooks attempt to frighten an archaeologist away from the area where he is digging for an old Spanish treasure. Gene Autry apprehends the criminals during the course of trying to help the man's twelve-year-old daughter.

* * *

The Old Prospector (August 4, 1953)

Director, George Archainbaud; screenplay, Milton J. Raison.

Cast: Gene Autry, Pat Buttram, Lyle Talbot, Myron Healey, Terry Frost, Bernard Szold, Ewing Mitchell, Sandy Sanders.

Song: "I'm a Cowpoke Pokin' Along"

Plot: Gene becomes involved in the capture of criminals who threaten the life of a conniving old prospector.

Narrow Escape (August 11, 1953)

Director, Ross Lederman; screenplay, Virginia M. Cooke.

Cast: Gene Autry, Pat Buttram, Sheila Ryan, David Coleman, Rick Vallin, Bill Henry, George Pembroke, Marshall Reed, Frankie Marvin.

Song: "Love, Burning Love"

Plot: Pat Buttram sends away for a mail-order sweetheart who turns out to be beautiful Marcy Nevers (Sheila Ryan), an Eastern widow with a young son.

* * *

Border Justice (August 18, 1953)

Director, Wallace Fox; screenplay, Robert Schaefer and Eric Freiwald.

Cast: Gene Autry, Pat Buttram, Sheila Ryan, Pierce Lyden, Steve Conte, Don C. Harvey, Edmund Cobb, Julian Upton.

Song: "Guns and Guitars"

Plot: Gene Autry, investigating a smuggling ring operating on the Mexican border, faces unexpected danger when he is nearly blown to shreds by an explosive cupcake!

* * *

Gypsy Wagon (August 25, 1953)

Director, George Archainbaud; screenplay, Virginia M. Cooke.

Cast: Gene Autry, Pat Buttram, Gloria Talbot, Lyle Talbot, Bernard Szold, Myron Healey, Ewing Mitchell, Terry Frost, Sandy Sanders, Herman Hack.

Song: "Onteora"

Plot: Gene tries to befriend and clear of false charges an old gypsy and his beautiful daughter.

* * *

The Bandidos (September 1, 1953)

Director, George Archainbaud; screenplay, Dwight Cummins.

Cast: Gene Autry, Pat Buttram, Wendy Waldron,

Harry Lauter, William Fawcett, Lane Bradford, Tom Tyler, Larry Hudson, Bob Dominquez, Lane Chandler.

Songs: "Back in the Saddle Again" and "Dixie Cannonball"

Plot: Gene tries to protect a visiting dignitary from an attempted assassination.

* * *

Dry Gulch at Devil's Elbow (September 8, 1953)

Director, George Archainbaud; screenplay, William Telaak.

Cast: Gene Autry, Pat Buttram, John Doucette, Clayton Moore, Joe McGuinn, Sandy Sanders, Ross Ford, Ewing Brown.

Song: "Fetch Me Down My Trusty .45"

Plot: Outlaws overhear Pat's boastful tall tales that he has known many desperate criminals and the location of their stolen loot. When Gene and Pat are kidnapped because of these lies, Pat must feign temporary amnesia long enough for Gene to formulate an escape plan.

* * *

Cold Decked (September 15, 1953)

Director, Wallace Fox; screenplay, Elizabeth Beecher.

Cast: Gene Autry, Pat Buttram, Alan Bridge, Stanley Andrews, William Fawcett, Henry Rowland, Gregg Barton, Kenne Duncan, Myron Healey, Ted Mapes, Bob Woodward, Terry Frost.

Song: "The Yellow Rose of Texas" (The same scene was used in *Rock River Feud.)*

Plot: When banker Ben Tansey (Stanley Andrews) fails to show up one morning, the townsfolk fear he has absconded with their hard-earned funds. Fortunately for Ben, Gene Autry refuses to believe his old friend capable of such a crime.

* * *

The Steel Ribbon (September 22, 1953)

Director, William Berke; screenplay, Robert Schaefer and Eric Freiwald.

Cast: Gene Autry, Pat Buttram, Gail Davis, Robert Lowery, Dick Emory, John Hamilton, Terry Frost, Rusty Wescoatt, Tom London, Frankie Marvin, Bob Woodward.

Song: "Gallivantin' Galveston Gal"

Plot: Crooked depot agent Dan Parker (John Hamilton) and his henchmen are hijacking payroll shipments from the railroad. Investigators Gene Autry and Pat Buttram uncover the plot with the help of feisty mine operator Billie Carter (Gail Davis) and her crew.

* * *

Rio Renegades (September 29, 1953)

Director, George Archainbaud; screenplay Elizabeth Beecher.

Cast: Gene Autry, Pat Buttram, Stanley Andrews, Effie Laird, Sheila Ryan, Myron Healey, Lee Van Cleef, Harry Harvey.

Song: "Rocky Canyon"

Plot: Corinne Sheldon (Sheila Ryan), hairdresser in the town of Rio Vista, learns from the townswomen where their husbands keep their valuables, and she instructs her two hired gunmen as to the most effective method of staging robberies.

* * *

Ransom Cross (October 6, 1953)

Director, William Berke; screenplay, Robert Schaefer and Eric Freiwald.

Cast: Gene Autry, Pat Buttram, Gail Davis, John Hamilton, Robert Lowery, Terry Frost, Rusty Wescoatt, Tom London, Frankie Marvin, Bob Woodward.

Song: none

Plot: Archaeologists find a valuable old Spanish cross which an Eastern confidence man plots to steal and hold for ransom.

* * *

Santa Fe Raiders (July 6, 1954)

Director, Ross Lederman; screenplay, Oliver Drake.

Cast: Gene Autry, Pat Buttram, Gloria Saunders,

Dick Jones, Tom London, Henry Rowland, Stanley Andrews, Al Bridge, Myron Healey, Gregg Barton, Kenne Duncan, Terry Frost, Frankie Marvin, Bob Woodward.

Song: "Westward Ho!"

Plot: Gene comes to the aid of a beleagurered old freight line operator and, subsequently, helps the son take over the business after the old man is murdered.

* * *

Johnny Jackaroo (July 13, 1954)

Director, Ross Lederman; screenplay, Robert Schaefer and Eric Freiwald.

Cast: Gene Autry, Pat Buttram, Ann Doran, B.G. Norman, William Fawcett, Harry Lauter, Henry Rowland, Denver Pyle, Gregg Barton.

Song: "Gone with the West"

Plot: Johnny (B.G. Norman), the incorrigible eleven-year-old nephew of Gene and Pat's boss, ranch owner Lynne Moore (Ann Doran), so irritates Pat that he plans a make-believe stage holdup to frighten some sense into the boy. Two disgruntled ranch hands intervene, however, and carry out a real robbery in the guise of Pat and Gene.

* * *

The Holdup (July 20, 1954)

Director, Ross Lederman; screenplay, Norman S. Hall.

Cast: Gene Autry, Pat Buttram, William Fawcett, Arthur Space, Rochelle Stanton, Rory Mallinson, James Best, Forrest Taylor, Gregg Barton, Red Morgan, Frankie Marvin.

Song: "I Only Want a Buddy Not a Friend"

Plot: A crooked oil man tries to defraud a rancher out of his valuable property, but the man's foreman (Gene Autry) has the foresight to telegraph a few lawmen to check the promoter's references.

* * *

Prize Winner (July 27, 1954)

Director, Ross Lederman; screenplay, Virginia M. Cooke.

Cast: Gene Autry, Pat Buttram, Sheila Ryan, George Pembroke, Louise Lorimer, Ferris Taylor, Rick Vallin, Marshall Reed, Edgar Dearing, Bob Woodward, Frankie Marvin.

Song: "God's Little Candles"

Plot: Pat Buttram has a prize chicken which he plans to enter in a contest. When two crooks steal a wealthy couple's diamond collection, they hide it in Pat's chicken feed and later attempt to recover the ill-gotten goods.

* * *

The Sharpshooter (August 3, 1954)

Director, Frank McDonald; screenplay, Robert Schaefer and Eric Freiwald.

Cast: Gene Autry, Pat Buttram, Dick Jones.

Margaret Field, Stanley Andrews, Henry Rowland, Denver Pyle, Tex Terry, Frankie Marvin.

Song: "Crime Will Never Pay"

Plot: Randy Barker (Dick Jones) has been framed by an outlaw who killed a sheriff. When the young man escapes from prison, he depends upon Gene Autry to clear his name.

* * *

Talking Guns (August 10, 1954)

Director, Ross Lederman; screenplay, Dwight Cummins.

Cast: Gene Autry, Pat Buttram, William Fawcett, Dee Pollock, Jim Bannon, Harry Lauter, I. Stanford Jolley, Pierce Lyden, Emmett Lynn.

Song: "The Cowboy's Trademarks"

Plot: Old miner Grandpa Decker (William Fawcett) has not been in his right mind since an accident befell him, so he unwittingly uses his property as a hideout for a trio of outlaws. In attempting to help the old man's grandsons, Gene flushes the badmen into the open and ultimately restores Grandpa Decker to his senses.

* * *

Hoodoo Canyon (August 17, 1954)

Director, Ross Lederman; screenplay, Fred Myton.

Cast: Gene Autry, Pat Buttram, James Best, Arthur Space, Rochelle Stanton, Forrest Taylor, William Fawcett, Rory Mallinson, Gregg Barton.

Song: "Hillbilly Wedding in June"

Plot: Ray Saunders (James Best) is a fresh young man in the process of rebelling against his father. Gene attempts to help the two men bridge the generation gap.

* * *

The Carnival Comes West (August 24, 1954)

Director, Ross Lederman; screenplay, Buckley Angell.

Cast: Gene Autry, Pat Buttram, Ann Doran, Clayton Moore, William Fawcett, Denver Pyle, Henry Rowland, Harry Lauter, Gregg Barton, Pat Mitchell.

Songs: "Ridin' All Day" and "Silver Spurs"

Plot: A former circus performer, now a respectable ranch owner, desperately strives to conceal her past by refusing to allow the carnival in which she once starred to play a local engagement.

* * *

Battle Axe (August 31, 1954)

Director, George Archainbaud; screenplay Virginia M. Cooke.

Cast: Gene Autry, Pat Buttram, Mira McKinney, Francis McDonald, Rick Vallin, Peter Votrian, Kenne Duncan, Gregg Barton, Terry Frost, Wes Hudman, Frankie Marvin, and The Cass County Boys.

Song: "What's Gonna' Happen to Me?"

Plot: A stubborn woman sheriff rules impulsively, but fails to employ logic and common sense. As a result, she is deceived by a smooth-talking confidence man despite the warnings of the former sheriff and Gene Autry.

* * *

The Outlaw of Blue Mesa (September 7, 1954)

Director, Frank McDonald; screenplay, Oliver Drake.

Cast: Gene Autry, Pat Buttram, Denver Pyle, Claire Carleton, Dick Jones, Margaret Field, Hank Patterson, Henry Rowland, Tex Terry.

Song: "When the Bloom Is on the Sage"

Plot: Gene and Pat are insurance investigators trying to put an end to a series of bank shipment robberies.

* * *

Civil War at Deadwood (September 14, 1954)

Director, Ross Lederman; screenplay Shelby Gordon.

Cast: Gene Autry, Pat Buttram, William Fawcett, Emmett Lynn, Gail Davis, Jim Bannon, Stanley Andrews, Harry Lauter, I. Stanford Jolley, Pierce Lyden, Frankie Marvin.

Song: none

Plot: Gene and Pat happen upon two old codgers who are still fighting the Civil War. Their heated quarrel is taken advantage of by crooked men in the nearby town.

* * *

Boots and Ballots (September 25, 1954)

Director, George Archainbaud; screenplay, Robert Schaefer and Eric Freiwald.

Cast: Gene Autry, Pat Buttram, Kenne Duncan, Mira McKinney, Rick Vallin, Terry Frost, Gregg Barton, Howard McNeely, Frankie Marvin, Bob Woodward.

Song: "Mama Don't Allow No Music Played in Here"

Plot: A heated political campaign is interrrupted when a lady mayoral candidate's adopted son is kidnapped by members of the opposing party.

* * *

Outlaw Warning (October 2, 1954)

Director, George Archainbaud; screenplay, Robert Schaefer and Eric Freiwald.

Cast: Gene Autry, Pat Buttram, Sheila Ryan, Stanley Andrews, Myron Healey, Lee Van Cleef, Gregg Barton, Mickey Little, Melinda Plowman, Francis McDonald, Harry Harvey, Budd Buster, Bob Woodward.

Song: "I've Got a Heart as Big as Texas"

Plot: Pat Buttram is the witness whose testimony enables a judge to send an outlaw to prison. When the outlaw later escapes, he seeks revenge on both the judge and the hapless Pat.

Comment: The plot called for Pat Buttram to don a suit of armor. The comedian sustained injuries while wearing the awkward costume.

* * *

***The Million Dollar Fiddle* (October 1, 1955)

Director, Ray Nazarro; screenplay, Maurice Geraghty.

Cast: Gene Autry, Pat Buttram, Nestor Paiva, Peter Votrian, Jean Howell, Larry Lauter, Joe Besser, Frank Jenks, Mike Ragan.

Songs: "The Yellow Rose of Texas" and "Back in the Saddle Again"

Plot: Ten-year-old world famous violin prodigy Reginald Redaldo (Peter Votrian) dreams of visiting Gene Autry and Champion. When his train passes through Autryville, the unhappy youngster runs away for a vacation at the Flying A Ranch, unaware that a dishonest ranch hand will steal his priceless Stradivarius.

Comment: This episode was filmed in color. "The episode has a strong quality of 'niceness' about it. The concept of 'love thy neighbor' was never better illustrated than in Gene Autry films such as this one." -JGS

* * *

The Stage to San Dimas (October 8, 1955)

Director, George Archainbaud; screenplay, John K. Butler.

Cast: Gene Autry, Pat Buttram, Barbara Knudson, Keith Richards, George J. Lewis, Myron Healey, Steve Conte, Jack Daly, Edward Clark, Jacquelyn Park, Frankie Marvin.

Songs: "Sing Me a Song of the Saddle" and "Mellow Mountain Moon"

Plot: Gene provides protection for the stagecoach to San Dimas, which rolls through outlaw and hostile Indian territory.

Comment: This episode was filmed in color.

* * *

The Portrait of White Cloud (October 15, 1955)

Director, Robert G. Walker; screenplay, John K. Butler.

Cast: Gene Autry, Pat Buttram, Glenn Strange, Jack Daly, Dick Rich, John Close, Steve Raines, Terry Frost, Joseph Michaels, The Cass County Boys.

Songs: "It's My Lazy Day"

Plot: A portrait painter plans crimes while sketching his models. All of the models are conveniently chosen to help the crafty artist gain financial reward dishonestly.

A GENE AUTRY SCRAPBOOK CLIPPING

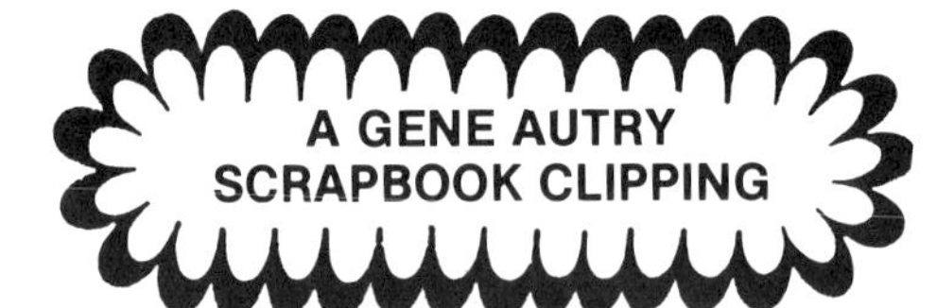

GENE AUTRY

WHENEVER the subject of the western film arises, it wouldn't take long before the magic name of Gene Autry pops up. Like many of the western heroes, the name of Gene Autry has become a legend.

Older filmgoers will remember Gene as their dashing western hero. Youngsters still have the opportunity of seeing him riding the range even today. His old films have been shown constantly at children's matinee shows, though they must appear a little dated today with the advent of the adult western film in more recent times.

Let it also be said that Gene set the precedent for the popularity of the western on television. Eleven years ago he was the first star and the only cowboy to make films especially written and produced for use on television. He made his films at a place called Pioneertown (an apt name), situated

Gene with his two horses, Champion and Little Champion

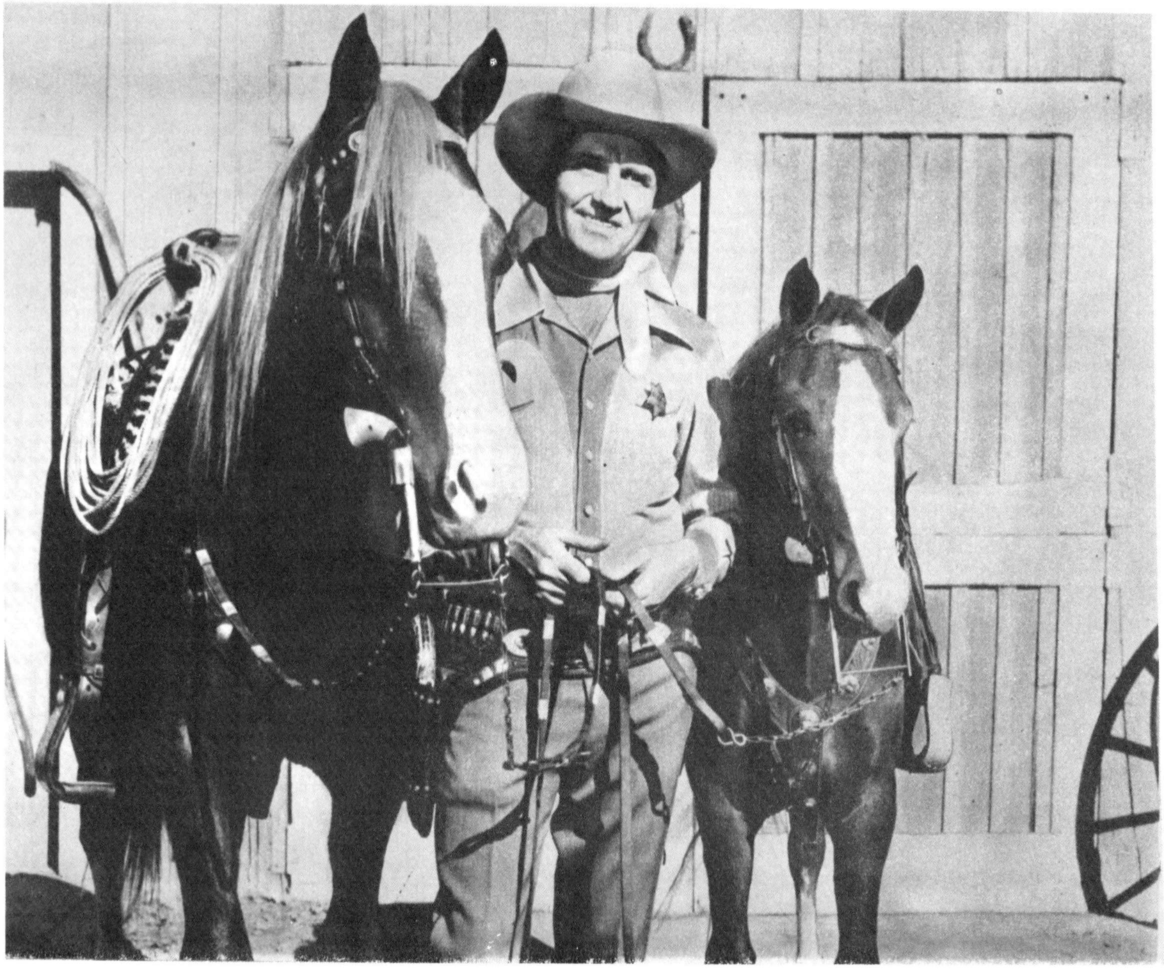

Gene pictured with a group of Jemez Indians

in the Californian desert about fifty miles from Palm Springs. He made two half-hour films a week.

His tight-working schedule was copied by his later contemporaries, who were quick to realise the potential of the western on television.

" We used to shoot two pictures at the same time," smiled Gene. " While we were making these, the director was planning two more. Filming two films at once, the director always looked for the possibilities of switching a shot so it could be used in two films. If, for instance, the camera filmed a rider coming down the side of a mountain, it might also re-shoot him going up the mountain for another film ! "

Gene was also quick to realise that when making a western for television, scenes of doubles doing the more dangerous work for the leading stars looked very phony indeed, because of the close range covered by the TV camera for smaller screens. So it became necessary for the stars to perform the stunts themselves. Many of the western stars you see on TV today do their own dangerous stunts.

Gene always did, from the time he first started to make westerns in 1935.

His first film appearance was in a Ken Maynard western titled *In Old Santa Fe*, in which Gene's part consisted of a musical try-out. He sang two songs, and the public response was good enough for producers to give him another break. Gene was then starred in a western serial titled *Phantom Empire*.

Soon he became one of the world's most popular screen cowboys.

Today he is a millionaire and lives on the lavishly decorated Melody Ranch.

Even today Gene loves being a cowboy, and he wears cowboy clothes all the time. His wife once said, " Gene really dresses for the children, though. They like to see him in colourful clothes. He even comes down to breakfast fully dressed in a cowboy suit, with tie and boots."

His wardrobe is full of the most expensive cowboy outfits in the world. His suits are said to cost about £70 each! He has over a hundred and fifty colourful embroidered shirts, which cost about £20 each. One of them has the national emblem embroidered across it.

It is said that Gene has never owned a pair of shoes since he became a western star. He always wears Texas-made leather boots and has over fifty pairs of these, all in different colours. When he walks down a street he

Gene loves buying cowboy shirts. His extensive wardrobe proves it!

Just a few of Gene's cowboy boots

always wears his trousers on the outside of his boots, knowing that only range hands would tuck their trousers inside.

He always wears a big, ten-gallon white hat. He has about fifty to a hundred of these, and when he orders new ones he orders them by the dozen.

Gene is still one of the most colourful personalities in the film capital. He owns several companies which, he says, keep him as young as ever.

Gene Autry has certainly carved a niche for his name in the world of the western film.

(The preceding publicity release originally appeared in *The Boy's Western Television and Film Annual.* Edited by Ken and Sylvia Ferguson, Purnell & Sons Ltd., Great Britain, 1963.)

Comment: This episode was filmed in color.

* * *

Law Comes to Scorpion (October 22, 1955)

Director, George Archainbaud; screenplay, Maurice Tembragel.

Cast: Gene Autry, Pat Buttram, Arthur Space, Sidney Mason, Myron Healy, Lisa Montell, Richard Avonde, Earle Hodgins, Bob Cason.

Songs: "Somebody Bigger Than You and I" and "I Wish I Had Never Met Sunshine"

Plot: Gene helps a parson and his daughter convert the people in the sin-ridden town of Scorpion.

Comment: This episode was filmed in color.

* * *

****The Golden Chariot* (October 29, 1955)

Director, Ray Nazarro; screenplay, Maurice Geraghty.

Cast: Gene Autry, Pat Buttram, Junius Matthews, Jean Howell, Harry Lauter, Ralph Sanford, Elizabeth Harrower, Bob Woodward, Frankie Marvin, Byron Foulger.

Song: "Good Old Fashioned Hoedown"

Plot: The community is collecting funds to erect a new school. Gene is against gambling, but when his bumbling friend Pat secretly bets the school fund and loses it in a crooked chariot race at a carnival, he steps in and saves the day.

Comment: This episode was filmed in color.

"Its delightful story and memorable characters make it one of my special favorites." -JGS

". . . prettiest scenery of all the television shows." -JG

* * *

**Guns Below the Border* (November 5, 1955)

Director, George Archainbaud; screenplay, John K. Butler.

Cast: Gene Autry, Pat Buttram, Myron Healy, Keith Richards, Lane Bradford, George J. Lewis, David Leonard, Eugenia Paul, Steve Conte, David Saber.

Songs: "Marquita" and "Under Fiesta Stars"

Plot: Border Patrolman Gene Autry works with his Mexican counterpart to stop a band of smugglers who are moving rifles across the border.

Comment: This episode was filmed in color. "This is the famous film in which Gene was unable to remember the long speech about the priest and the mission bell. In his autobiography Gene mistakenly attributes the incident to BELLS OF CAPISTRANO." -JGS

* * *

****Ghost Ranch* (November 12, 1955)

Director, George Archainbaud; screenplay, Maurice Geraghty.

Cast: Gene Autry, Pat Buttram, Sally Fraser, Harry Harvey, Maxine Gates, Bob Woodward, The Cass County Boys.

Song: "You're the Only Good Thing (That's Happened to Me)"

Plot: The Jingle Bell Ranch has been inherited by headstrong Torrey Palmer (Sally Fraser), a recent graduate of a business college. To put the ranch on a paying basis, Torrey plans to sell all of the "non-essential" livestock. When she learns that foreman Gene Autry personally owns Champion, she decides to merely sell Little Champ to the highest bidder.

Comment: This episode was filmed in color. "Excellent story." -JG

". . . a marvelous episode in which Gene combats no crooks at all, but is pitted against a strong-willed lady boss. . . one of his best performances. . . ." -JGS

* * *

***Go West, Young Lady* (November 19, 1955)

Director, Robert Walker; screenplay, John K. Butler.

Cast: Gene Autry, Pat Buttram, Nan Leslie, John Close, Dick Rich, Jack Daly, Muriel Landers, Isabelle Dwan, Terry Frost, The Cass County

Boys.

Songs: "Back in the Saddle Again," "When the Bloom Is on the Sage," and "Back in the Doghouse Again" (parody)

Plot: Gene's ranch cook, Pat Buttram, places an ad for a wife in a lonely hearts column, unaware that hundreds of women will be sending hard-earned money to the dishonest club operators for the privilege of supposedly wedding Gene!

Comment: This episode was filmed in color. "Excellent! I rank this show as the third best." -GP

* * *

***Feuding Friends* (November 26, 1955)

Director, George Archainbaud; screenplay, Robert Blane.

Cast: Gene Autry, Pat Buttram, Arthur Space, Myron Healy, Sydney Mason Richard Avonde, Dennis Moore, Reed Howes, Brad Morrow, Bob Cason.

Song: "Crime Will Never Pay"

Plot: In a plot to uncover a counterfeiting ring, Gene and Pat pretend to be bitter enemies.

Comment: This episode was filmed in color.

* * *

****Saddle Up* (December 3, 1955)
(This is the first chapter of a trilogy entitled *Code of the Flying A.)*

Director, George Archainbaud; screenplay, John K. Butler.

Cast: Gene Autry, Pat Buttram, Sally Mansfield, Leonard Penn, Sammy Ogg, Gregg Barton, Will Crandall, The Cass County Boys.

Songs: "Gallivantin' Galveston Gal" and "Pretty Mary"

Plot: The late Mamie Weston has willed her ranch to be a home for underprivileged children with Gene Autry as administrator. However, if Gene should fail to make the ranch a safe and satisfactory home for the kids, the property reverts to Mrs. Weston's only son, the notorious "Big Jim" Weston. Gene faces a stiff challenge when a seemingly incorrigible youngster arrives at the Flying A and, coincidentially, uncovers a rustling scheme perpetrated by two disgruntled ranch hands.

Comment: This episode was filmed in color. "I rank the whole trilogy as the fifth best of his shows." -GP

"At the top of my list is the trilogy. . . " -JGS

* * *

****Ride, Ranchero!* (December 10, 1955)
(This is the second chapter of the trilogy, *Code of the Flying A.)*

Director, George Archainbaud; screenplay, John K. Butler.

Cast: Gene Autry, Pat Buttram, Sally Mansfield, Emile Meyer, Leonard Penn, Peter Votrian, Sammy Ogg, Kenne Duncan, Gregg Barton, Will Crandall, Bob Woodward, the Cass County Boys.

Song: "Ridin' Down the Canyon"

Plot: Gene decides to secure parole for Big Jim Weston (Emile Meyer), so that he may have a "second chance" at the Flying A Ranch, now a successful home for boys. Big Jim, however, schemes to make Gene's work fail so that he may inherit the property himself.

Comment: This episode was filmed in color. "It is a charming story which gives Gene an opportunity to outdo himself in terms of the 'kindliness' aspect of his famous characterization. The script is a thorough delight." -JGS

* * *

****The Rangerette* (December 17, 1955)
(This is the third chapter of the trilogy, *Code of the Flying A.)*

Director, George Archainbaud; screenplay, John K. Butler.

Cast: Gene Autry, Pat Buttram, Emile Meyer, Sally Mansfield, Nancy Gilbert, Leonard Penn, Sammy Ogg, Peter Votrian, Kenne Duncan, Gregg Barton, Will Crandall, The Cass County Boys.

Songs: "Blue Montana Skies" and "Old MacDonald Had a Farm"

Plot: Gene's old friend, Father O'Toole, sends him a child from a Chicago orphanage. Gene little dreams that Gerrie Wentworth is a girl and the daughter of Big Jim Weston, who is now on his way back to prison for life. It is further revealed that Lawyer Martin Pickett (Leonard Penn), executor of the Weston estate, is also a dishonest individual seeking to gain the Flying A Ranch for himself. With the help of Big Jim, who is reformed by his little daughter, Gene finally rounds up all of the evildoers and resumes running the Flying A as a home for youngsters who need a second chance to become solid citizens.

Comment: This episode was filmed in color. "Gene's singing of "Blue Montana Skies" is beautiful." -GP

"The story unfolds in the manner of a serial, yet human-interest values and good characterizations replace Western physical action to some extent. It is the quintessential Gene Autry. . . " -JGS

****Dynamite* (December 24, 1955)

Director, George Archainbaud; screenplay, Maurice Geraghty.

Cast: Gene Autry, Pat Buttram, Francis McDonald, Sally Fraser, Glenn Strange, Robert Bice, Harry Harvey, Sr., John Boutwell, Bob Woodward, The Cass County Boys.

Song: "Sierra Nevada"

Plot: A mining engineer once accused of a wrongdoing has an opportunity to clear his name when he helps apprehend some crooks and then saves the life of Pat Buttram, who is imprisoned in a mine shaft.

Comment: This episode was filmed in color and was the last original episode of "The Gene Autry Show" to be telecast.

The camera once more captures the classic image of Gene rescuing the heroine. He had now done the deed in ninety feature films, ninety-one television episodes, and countless radio adventures. It was time for other cowboys to carry on the tradition.

CHAPTER 9
GENE AUTRY ON TOUR

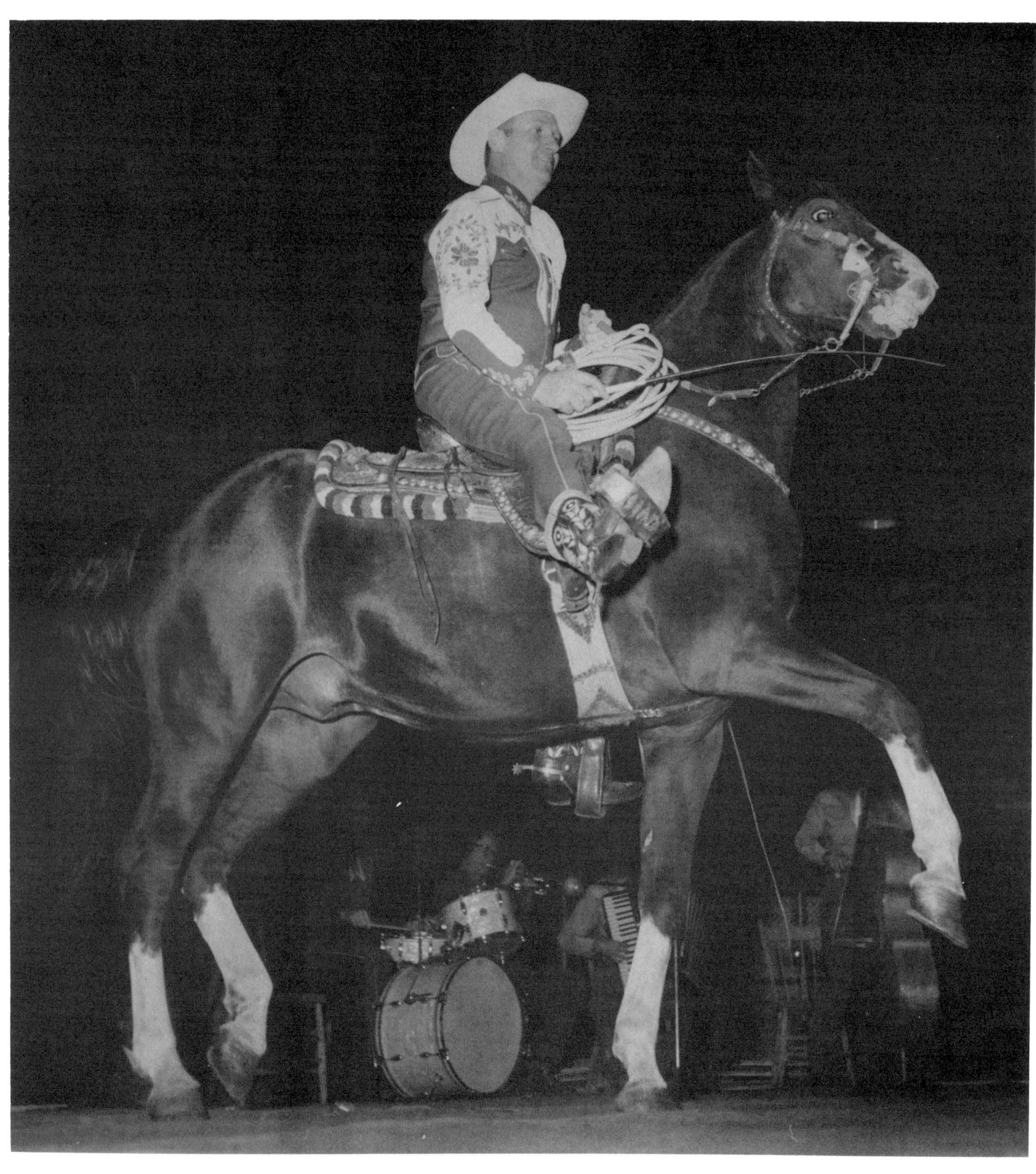

Gene Autry loved to tour. His long-time sidekick Pat Buttram has mentioned that even in recent years—long after his performing career—Gene has commented rather wistfully, "Let's go on a tour again, just one more time."

Gene's fascination with touring goes back to the beginning of his career in Chicago. When not performing on the WLS "National Barn Dance" program, he was constantly making personal appearances throughout the mid West. After his film career began in the 1930s, Gene would always hit the road during a filming hiatus to promote the film in current release and to make extra money—his movie salary never did compare with his tour income.

The tours over the years came in all kinds of packages. It might be a small stage show tour with just a few performers (The Cass County Boys, Frankie Marvin, Johnny Bond, Smiley Burnette or Pat Buttram, Carl Cotner, and Champion) to a full-fledged troupe of performers (all of the above with a pick-up orchestra, the entire radio cast, Tony White Cloud and his Jemez Indians, and additional guest stars such as Rufe Davis, Merle Travis, Gail Davis—TV's Annie Oakley, Jock Mahoney and Dick Jones of the "Range Rider" series. Gene and his troupe appeared in concert, with rodeos, at state and county fairs—in just about any setting which could hold an audience.

The Cass County Boys (Bert Dodson, Jerry Scoggins, and Fred Martin) joined Gene Autry in November of 1945, shortly after Gene was discharged from service in World War II. They had been a very popular threesome in Dallas, Texas, on WFAA radio, a clear-channel, 50,000 watt station. During part of the war Gene was stationed at Love Field in Dallas. It was while there that he

Gene has a stage full of performers for this appearance in Burlington, Vermont. That's Pat Buttram and Smiley Burnette beside Gene during the curtain call. Tony White Cloud and his Jemez Indians are to the right. The Cass County Boys are behind the Indians. The others are featured performers in the personal appearance.

"the things that can

■ Champion has a way of telling me when there's something on his mind. This morning, for example, he kept nosing me over toward his travelling van, which I keep parked at the side of the corral. That could mean only one thing. He's started longing for the applause of an audience again. You might think, after just getting over a 47-day whirlwind tour of playing one-nighters, he might enjoy being turned out to pasture for a while. But not Champ.

For that matter, I'm also beginning to look forward to September when we put our travelling show back on the road. I guess we're what the circus folks call "born troupers." Actually, on a slightly smaller scale, life in our show is very much like that of a circus. We travel by night, arriving in some new town at the crack of dawn—and always have the thrill of new faces and new adventures waiting for us. We live like one big family, sharing each other's successes, disappointments and personal problems. And when something goes wrong, we all pitch in together for the good of the show.

THE UPSET

I remember an incident that happened in Hazleton, Pennsylvania, last February 25, on our winter tour. We had arrived in town just an hour or so before the matinee was scheduled to go on. The local sponsors of the show had erected an eight-foot ramp leading up to the makeshift stage where Champion was to perform. The timbers looked strong enough, so we didn't bother to replace it with the reinforced ramp which we carry with us.

But that's where we made our big mistake. Just as Champ was reaching the top of the ramp, there was a terrifying sound of splintering timbers. Before any of us knew what was happening, one of the big cross beams completely gave way, sending Champ hurtling over the side. By the time I could reach him, he had landed on his side, with one leg still pinned above him in the sagging wreckage.

Everyone in the troupe was frozen in his tracks with horror. Only Champ seemed to know instinctively what to do. He lay there completely still, not moving a muscle, which is all that kept him from ripping a big gash in his leg —or maybe even breaking it. I dropped to my knees by his side and started talking to him in as reassuring a tone of voice as I could muster. "Steady, boy," I pleaded. "Everything's going to be all right. Just don't move."

THE TEARS

That encouragement was all he needed. Rolling his head over in my lap, while I continued to stroke him, he stayed perfectly calm and relaxed until the rest of the company could pry the timbers apart and free his leg. Thank Heaven, his only injury was a minor cut, so, after dabbing a little iodine on it, we decided to go on with the show. The makeshift ramp was pulled aside and our own moved into place. Within five minutes the show was on.

As I waited for Champ at the top of the ramp, I could see that the rest of the company was looking pretty skitterish. They were afraid he'd be too nervous to go through his acts. Even I felt a little leary about it. But that's where we all underestimated him. The minute Champ heard that applause he sprung into action like the real trouper that he is. He made a wide circle of the stage, tossing his head in the air, and finally came to a halt in center stage to take his customary bow. As I looked out into the wings, I could see my grisly old pal, Pat Buttram, applauding as wildly as anyone in the audience. And unless my eyes deceived me, there were a couple of tears running down his face.

THE SET-UP

During that last tour, we travelled a little over 12,000 miles, playing in 13 states, the District of Columbia and parts of Canada. In the 47 days we were on the road, we put on a total of 91 performances, not to mention more than 50 visits to children's and veterans' hospitals.

Champ and Little Champ ride in their own Deisel-powered van, which is cork-lined to protect them against bad jolts. Most of the rest of the company travels in a huge bus. I usually fly my own plane—a two-engine Beechcraft, with my booker, Herb Greene, doubling as co-pilot. When the weather is too bad to get the plane off the ground, I ride with Champ and Little Champ in the van.

Right from the start of this year's Spring tour, it looked like we were destined to be jinxed by the weather. We opened on January 14 at the Forum in Wichita, Kansas, feeling ourselves mighty lucky to have mild breezes blowing across the denuded winter plains. But by the time the evening show broke, about 1 o'clock, those gentle breezes had begun to howl. As I opened the stage door, a whirling blast of wind and snow struck me full in the face, blowing my best white Stetson half way across the stage.

I checked the airport. "Not much chance you'll be taking off from here tonight," was the report from the weather observer. We were due in Omaha, Nebraska, 315 miles away, for a matinee performance the next day. So I sent the bus on ahead and asked Jay Barry, driver of the van, to remain behind with me until we could see if there was any chance for the storm to break. By a little after midnight, it was obvious that we were in for a long siege of it, so I decided to leave the plane behind. Crawling in with Champ and Little Champ, we finally took off at 2 o'clock in one of the most blinding blizzards I've ever run up against. All night the storm raged. Ice formed on the roads and the snow blocked out practically all visibility.

THE CHEERS

When we finally arrived in Omaha, barely half an hour before the show was due to start, we heard the bad news that the city was caught in the grip of one of the worst flu epidemics in many years. More than 40 per cent of the elementary pupils were out of school, and there was talk that the schools might have to be shut down completely.

Nevertheless, we found a big crowd of loyal fans waiting in the auditorium. The Cass County Boys, Smiley Burnette and the rest of the cast kept the crowds entertained while we got Champ and Little Champ unloaded, and the show went off on schedule.

For the next six days, through Iowa, Missouri and back into Kansas, the storm continued to plague us. In Des Moines and Sioux City, some of our own troupe began to come down with the flu. Travelling as we were in such close quarters, it spread through the cast like a tumbleweed racing across the windswept prairies. By the time we

happen on tour" by gene autry

"When you're 47 days and nights on the road, covering over 12,000 miles in 13 states, you're lucky if all that hits you is a blizzard, an epidemic, or a mishap to Champ"

more→

"life in our show is very much like a circus, with always the thrill of new faces and adventures waiting for us"

Taking care of a wardrobe that consists of about 50 shirts and pants to match, and 20 pairs of boots is quite a chore on the road. I like to polish my own boots whenever I get the chance.

"the things that can happen on tour," continued

reached Kansas City, almost the entire company was sick. Fortunately, the storm cleared up on January 21, when we reached Davenport, Iowa, and everyone was soon back on his feet.

Herb Greene, meanwhile, had flown back to Wichita, to pick up my plane. So for the rest of the trip, we were able to fly in the Beechcraft. Only once did we have a close call with it. That was in Kingston, Ontario, Canada, where there is only a small, emergency landing field, used by the local air enthusiasts. After playing the Saturday night show in Kingston, I was scheduled to fly to New York to appear on Ed Sullivan's television show the following evening. When we arrived at the airport for my take-off, we found the runways covered with six inches of snow, which had fallen during the late afternoon. To make matters worse, there were no lights of any description on the runway. However, there was no other means of transportation out of Kingston which could get me to New York in time to rehearse for the TV appearance, so I decided to chance it.

Several of the other members of the show, who had come out to the airport to see me off, quickly set about rounding up a half-dozen kerosene lanterns. Then, with lanterns lighted, they strung out along the path of the runway so as to give me some dim idea of my take-off course. I could hear the snow crunching beneath the wheels as I began picking up speed. Looking into the dense blackness of the night, with only an occasional flicker of light from the widely scattered lanterns to guide me, I could only hope that I would clear any obstructions at the end of the field. As the plane finally left the ground and began to soar upwards, I could hear the shouts of Carl Cotner and Smiley Burnette, telling me that I had made it. Fortunately, we had good flying weather all the way into New York, so that I arrived well ahead of schedule.

THE LAUGHTER

I doubt if the rest of the cast will ever let Pat Buttram live down the trouble we had a few days after this, when we were playing in Indianapolis. We were doing the show in the big Coliseum there, which is used as an ice-skating rink during the winter months. A floor covering had been laid over the portion of the ice where the audience was seated. But there was a short strip of about ten feet between the front row and the stage which was still exposed.

Midway through the show, Pat was supposed to come racing up from the back of the audience to present a bouquet of flowers to pretty Gail Davis, our leading lady. Someone had neglected to tell Pat about the strip of ice, so that when he hit it, he was under full steam. Instead of getting up on the stage where Gail and I were standing, he went sailing right underneath, like Kelly coming into home base. The louder the audience laughed, the madder Pat got. And every time he would stagger to his feet, he'd go scooting off in another direction. By the time he finally managed to crawl out on all fours, the whole act was completely broken up, and there was nothing to do but ring down the curtain while the audience roared.

THE JEERS

During the last two days of the tour, I had my first chance to get a look at *Pack Train*, the movie I had finished the night before we took off from Hollywood. A print of the picture had been flown to us in Rochester, where a good-natured theater manager was kind enough to run it off for us.

I've an idea that my old pal Smiley Burnette would have been just as happy if we hadn't seen it, because everybody started ribbing him again about a little incident that happened while the picture was shooting. It so happens that Smiley is a very frugal man who doesn't believe in allowing anything to go to waste. One scene in the picture called for Sheila Ryan to pelt him with a whole bag of tomatoes. That evening, when the set workers moved in to clean up the mess, they discovered that someone had already scraped up the squashed tomatoes and made off with them. Knowing Smiley and his "saving" ways, we immediately suspected that he was the guilty party. And sure enough, when Sheila went over to his trailer to check, there he was cooking up a fine tomato stew.

Nothing quite that funny happened during the filming of *Saginaw Trail* which went before the cameras back in Hollywood, just two days after the tour closed. And I guess it was just as well that it didn't, because I was so busy I couldn't even have spared the time for a good laugh during that picture.

This was a story of French trappers who stalked their prey in the woods of northern Michigan, back in the 1820's. For the first time, I had to fight a duel with sabres. My coach was an old fencing master who's been training swashbuckling stars for as far back as Douglas Fairbanks. During our final workout before the scene was to be shot, he gave me a good piece of advice that not only helped me through the picture, but which I've since adopted as a mighty good motto for living. "So long as you can maintain a good balance, remember the rules of fair play and never take your eye off your aim," he said, "you never have to worry about coming out the winner." Every day I live, I'm more convinced that he was right.

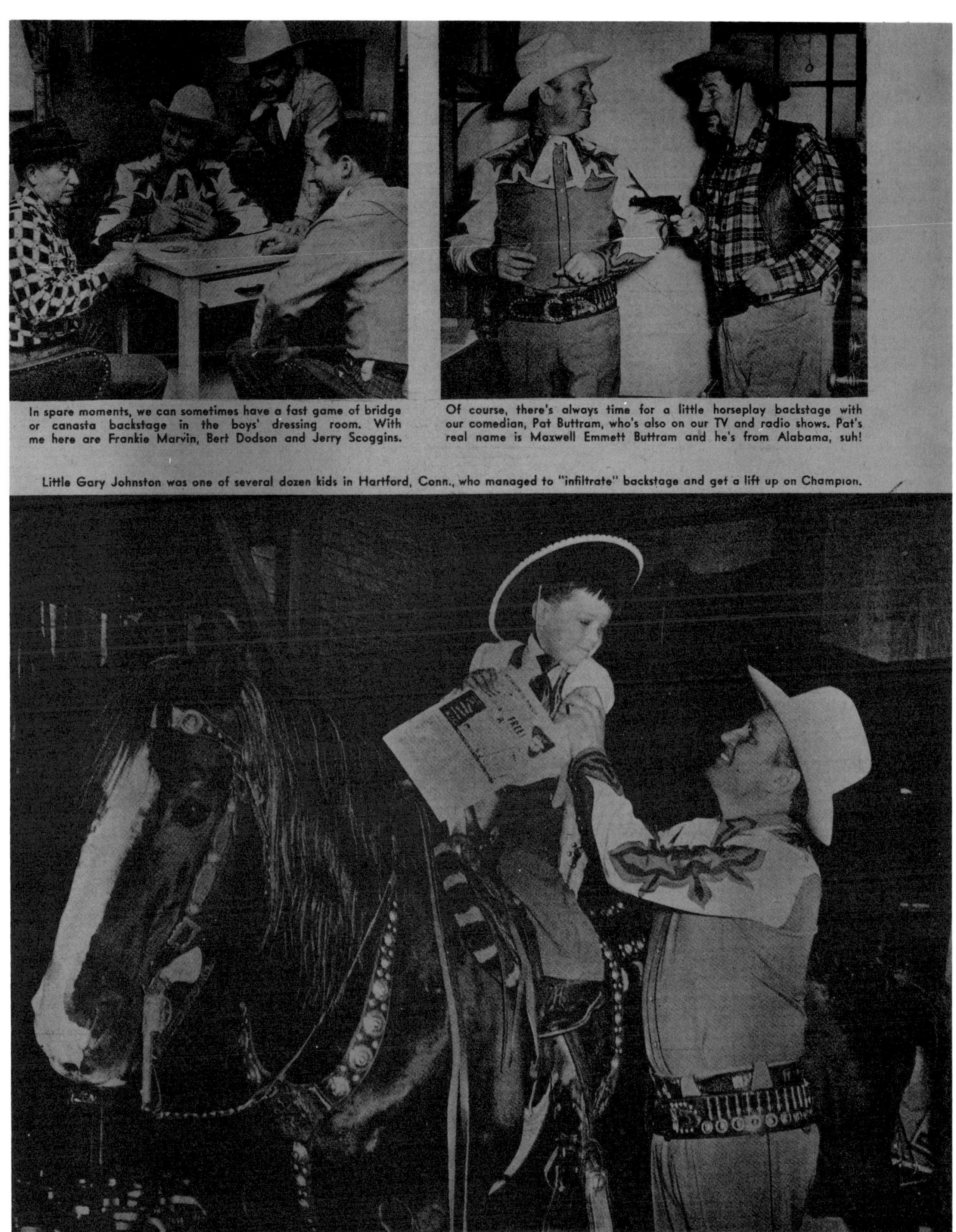

In spare moments, we can sometimes have a fast game of bridge or canasta backstage in the boys' dressing room. With me here are Frankie Marvin, Bert Dodson and Jerry Scoggins.

Of course, there's always time for a little horseplay backstage with our comedian, Pat Buttram, who's also on our TV and radio shows. Pat's real name is Maxwell Emmett Buttram and he's from Alabama, suh!

Little Gary Johnston was one of several dozen kids in Hartford, Conn., who managed to "infiltrate" backstage and get a lift up on Champion.

(The preceding publicity release originally appeared in *Who's Who in Western Stars*, Vol. 1, No. 3, 1953.)

had the opportunity to hear The Boys and also had the chance to perform with them. Their music and voice blend complimented his own voice very nicely, and Gene saw that they would be a fine backup group was well as a solid, appealing musical group in their own right.

While still in the service, Gene promised The Cass County Boys a job when the war was over. He was as good as his word, and they joined him for radio, films, and personal appearance tours and stayed with him for over ten years. The Boys liked radio and films just fine but the tours were

Gene is seen here putting the ever-popular Little Champ through his paces during a tour performance. (Circa 1950)

Champion and Little Champ go through their routine in a simple arena setting. The fellows with the guitars are Jerry Scoggins (of The Cass County Boys) and Johnny Bond. The other two Cass County Boys and a drummer are hidden behind the horses.

another matter. In recent conversations with two of The Cass County Boys, Bert Dodson and Fred Martin, the grueling Autry Tours were discussed in much the way "survivors" recall a great adventure with mixed feelings.

Bert Dodson: We went on tour with Gene shortly after we joined him in late 1945. Believe me, that going to Dubuque, Iowa, in the middle of January was not my idea of something pleasant to do. We almost always did two shows a day and nearly always one-nighters. One of the tours that sticks in my mind as one of the worst was when we did seventy towns in seventy days—ten weeks. That was longer than most. Usually they would run six to eight weeks. Some of those dates were a pretty good jump apart, but we made them all; we never blew a show.

We'd go by bus from town to town. Gene also had a plane, a Cadillac station wagon, and the horse truck. There were four pieces of equipment moving. Gene usually took his plane to the next stop, but if the weather got rough, as often it did, he'd go in the station wagon.

One time we started at Pueblo, Colorado, and worked all the way to New England, then all the way down the East Coast, worked at Tampa, went across the southern part of the United States, played Dallas and other cities, and ended up in Phoenix. The tours were usually in the winter. Gene was either making pictures or doing rodeos the rest of the year, so the January-February time was when he did personals.

When we first started touring with Gene, The Cass County Boys were the stage band. We'd play for the other acts, play our own spot, and play for Gene—play everything in the show. For Gene's spot Carl Cotner, Frankie Marvin, and Johnny Bond were along. We just got to where we were working ourselves to death. We never got off the damned stage from the time the curtain went up until intermission. Usually we didn't have a matinee until 4:00 or 4:30 P.M. because the kids didn't get out of school until then. We'd have a late matinee, and in an hour and a half we'd do the night show. By the time we got through with that, it was 10:30 at night, and we'd have a seven o'clock leave the next morning.

Fred Martin: On the rodeo tours Gene usually had The Cass County Boys, Carl Cotner, Johnny Bond, and Frankie Marvin. We would go from one town to another. Usually a rodeo would last a week to four weeks. We would do a lot of benefits at all the hospitals in whatever town we were playing. We would do two shows a day in most places, and three a day if they sold out. We were busy boys.

During a rodeo the announcer would break

The Cass County Boys look on as Gail Davis pins a Ranger Badge on Gene in this scene from ON TOP OF OLD SMOKY. Left to right, The Cass County Boys are Jerry Scoggins, Fred Martin, and Bert Dodson.

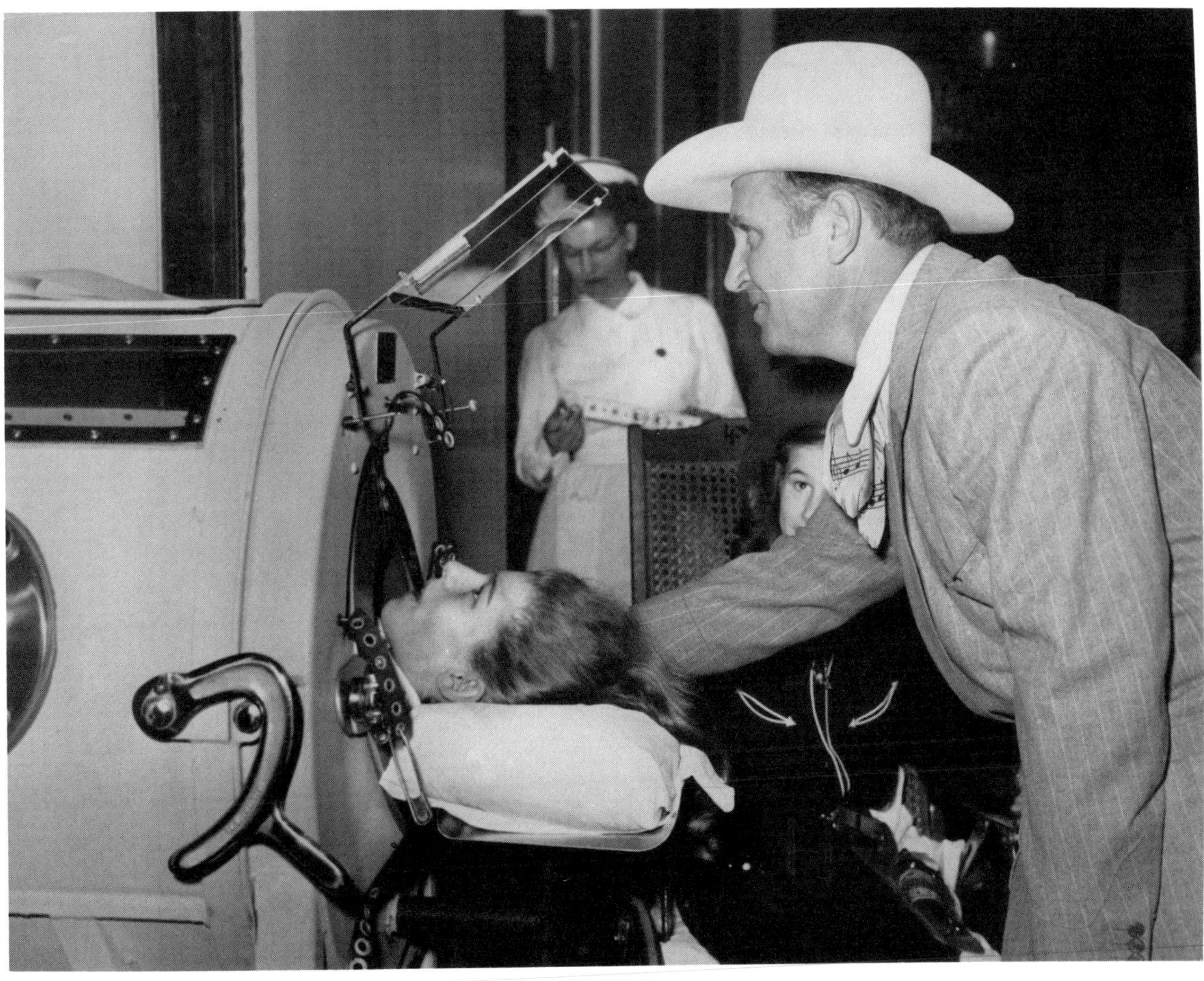

Gene Autry always visited hospitals, children's wards, orphanages, and underprivileged children during his tours across the country.

in and present Gene Autry and his show. As a rule, we six musicians would go to the center of the ring and play "Back in the Saddle Again," and Gene would come out on Champion and do the tricks. We would play that part of it with the rodeo announcer doing the commentary. Then Gene would get off the horse, come over to the microphone, and sing a few songs. He would then introduce the Cass County Boys, Johnny Bond, Frankie Marvin, and Carl Cotner—whoever was on the bill with him. We would each do a few songs. Gene would then come back, and we would do some songs together as an ensemble. That was a typical spot on the rodeo show. They would go back to the rodeo after the Autry show.

It seemed that we were on the road about seven months out of the year. We were playing theaters, too. We played the Oriental in Chicago, the Stanley in Baltimore, and the Riverside in Milwaukee—just to name a few. These would be stage shows in a theater. We often did ten shows a day. Broke attendance records, naturally. They were very short shows, of course. We started at ten o'clock in the morning and finished about one o'clock at night. The show usually consisted of the shortest Gene Autry movie they could find and then the stage show. That was repeated all day long. This was during the late 1940s and early '50s.

We did five shows a day in Boston

because they kept selling the thing out—with over forty thousand seats. We played to a lot of people! We played Chicago; Denver; Pueblo, Colorado; Nampa, Idaho; Madison Square Garden; Cleveland; Birmingham, Alabama. We also played a lot of state fairs—often as part of a rodeo. We played the Iowa State Fair, Alabama State Fair, Louisiana State Fair, Indiana and Ohio fairs, among others.

And could we get from one place to another quickly! We closed one night in Milwaukee and were in Burlington, Vermont, the next evening. Figure that one out! We did the six-hundred-mile drive overnight and all day and pulled in there in time to do a show. The Autry tour was probably one of the best organized shows that has ever been on the road. But I really hated touring. Had I known that there was going to be as much touring as we had, I would never have left Dallas.

Bert Dodson: I'll never forget the time we were in Oklahoma City with Gene for a rodeo benefit. Gene was following the bull riders with his act, entering on Champion. We started into the arena to play Gene's entrance music. When we had just about got to the middle of the arena, the last bull got loose, turned, and started back into the ring. We ran over and climbed the fence while carrying our instruments. You can imagine, I'm going up the fence with one hand, holding my bass by the neck; Scoggins didn't have too much trouble with his guitar; Martin was clawin' pretty good because he had to reach around that accordion. We didn't get hurt; the bull went right under us, just whis-

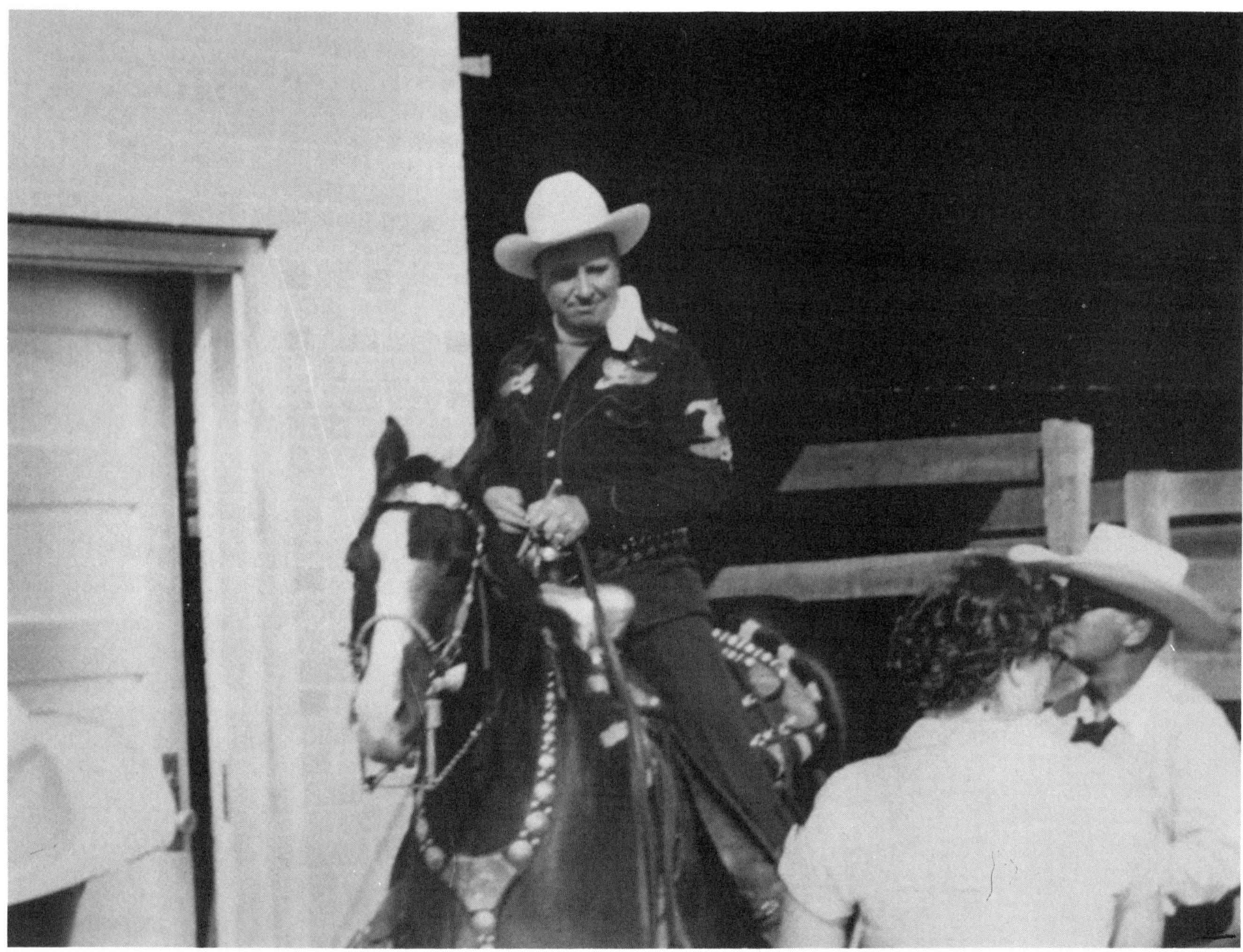

Gene rides from the show ring at the Little Rock, Arkansas, State Fair Grounds after a performance in the summer of 1957.

The singing cowboy meets his fans in Columbus, Ohio.

tling by. We stayed up on the fence until we were sure they got him in.

Fred Martin: How Bert climbed a seven-foot fence with a bass fiddle, holding it by the neck, I'll never know. I climbed the fence with a forty-pound accordion. We were in the center of the ring when the bull got loose. Carrying our musical instruments we outran a Brahma bull! That was one of the highlights of our touring experience.

During January of 1987 I had a chance to talk with Gail "Annie Oakley" Davis in Hollywood. She recalled for me the many tours she made with Gene. Before the "Annie Oakley" television series went on the air, she remembered her tour billing as "Gail of the Golden West." With the arrival of the series, she was "TV's Annie Oakley."

Gail Davis: When I was on tour with Gene as "Gail of the Golden West," I did mostly singing. People forget that I was a singer because I didn't sing in any of Gene's movies or TV shows. I went to London with the Autry show in 1953; that was as "Gail," because we had not yet started the "Annie" series. I did the pilot before we left Los Angeles. Then we went to London with the whole troupe. We did the show at Empress Hall for four weeks. The last week Gene got notice from his production company that the "Annie" pilot had sold. Everyone else went to Paris, Germany, all over the place, while I got on a plane, flew back to New York, met with the Canada Dry people, and signed the original "Annie Oakley" contract. We went into production right after that. That was the last touring show I did with Gene as "Gail of the Golden West." From there on out, any tours we went on it was as "TV's Annie Oakley."

As "Annie" I did a lot of trick shooting on the tours. I had targets set up—like six of them around the arena. When I was introduced, I would first ride around the arena real fast on Target, my "Annie Oakley" horse, and then pull up for a bow. After that, I would take off around the arena again, and with my pistol I'd hit, hopefully, all the targets. I'd then dismount and do several tricks with the rifle.

After the shooting act, I would come back into the arena and sing four or five songs. Then at the end of the show, after Gene had finished his act with songs and the horses, we'd ride around the arena and shake hands with all the kids. It was exhausting, but it was loads of fun.

In towns where we stayed for three or four weeks, it was especially nice because you could settle in. You could check into your hotel room and get your cleaning and other things done. In major cities like New York, Houston, Dallas, or Chicago you would do publicity for the tour on radio and television. You'd meet with the mayor or the governor, whomever, at whatever city you were in. Other times on the bus tours we would be out for, say, seventy one-night stands, doing two shows a day. Now that's tough and fun! The sense of "family" would hold us together. Gene picked his people so carefully that there were few problems.

Gene poses here with a Boy Scout troupe that came to one of his Columbus, Ohio, shows.

Gene visits St. Mary's Home in Dubuque, Iowa, a home for orphaned children. He is greeted by Father Menster, the priest in charge, dressed in Western clothes.

I guess the worst experience I had on tour was when my horse slipped and fell on me. We were playing Chicago at the time. I was riding Champ, Jr. It was the very end of the show when it happened. We had already shook hands with all the kids and were backing out of the arena, saying good-bye to the people, waving, and all of a sudden I disappeared. Champ, Jr. had slipped on some straw and fallen with me. Fortunately, I had gotten out of the stirrup before the fall. The next think I knew I was on a stretcher going to the hospital. Nothing was broken, thank goodness; everything was fine.

I first met Dick Jones at the Charlotte Film Fair in 1983 when I was asked to host a guest star panel on which he was to appear. Because of my familiarity with his Western film roles in Autry features and TV episodes and Dick's two television series, "The Range Rider" and "Buffalo Bill, Jr.," I expected him to be the effervescent, extroverted character he portrayed in most of his acting jobs. Not so. What I found was a soft-spoken, shy, retiring individual who had happy memories of his show business career, but no desire to return to the "rat race." In January of 1987 I met with Dick in a Hollywood restaurant to discuss his years with Gene Autry.

Dick Jones: Gene was a good boss. He was a good man to work for and to work with. I didn't work too many tours with him, but I did work with him real close when we were doing the Madison Square Garden show together. He was the headline attraction and Jock and I were the also-rans. You get pretty close when you are working two-a-day or three-a-day for thirty-one days. I like to consider him a friend and a boss—he was just a regular guy.

I guess my worst experience on tour took place during an appearance at the arena in Cleveland, Ohio. I wasn't on tour with Gene at the time, but Jock and I were on a personal appearance tour for Gene as the stars of "The Range Rider" TV series, which was produced by Gene's Flying A Productions.

This little brown and white horse I had could run backward just about as fast as he could go forward. Part of our "bye-bye" at the end of the show was to run the horse backwards to the exit, tipping our hats to the audience as we went. I was taking my horse out of the arena just as fast as he could go backwards when he suddenly hit the hard terrazzo floor, slipped, and turned over backwards. The cinch broke and I caught the saddle horn in my pelvis bone and I knew I was hurt. As the horse was getting up, I grabbed a hold of the saddle horn and mane, pulling the flank cinch into the horse's flank. He fired both rear legs at me, hitting me in the chest and chin. It caused me to flop and land flat, face down in the arena. And, boy, I was hurting. Jock got off his horse, picked me up, and we walked off together. I can still feel the hurting. That happened around 1954 or '55.

Gene had a lot of fine people working with him on the tours, films, television and radio.

Gail Davis and author David Rothel pose for a picture during their conversation about the Gene Autry tours.

Former child actor Dick Jones started working with Gene in THE STRAWBERRY ROAN in 1948 and continued with the Gene Autry organization in films, television series, and tours through much of the 1950s.

I enjoyed my years with him. It was like a family, one big family.

Jock Mahoney is a gregarious, extroverted fellow whose hearty laughter and conversation are enjoyed frequently these days at Western film festivals. It's hard not to have fun when you're around Jocko. I first met him at the HoustonCon Festival back in the spring of 1977. Through the years I have interviewed him many times, and in the process we have become friends. It was a particular joy a few years back to go horseback riding with him at my home in Sarasota, Florida. We took just a brief, slow ride on the Arabians my wife and I have, but how many people get to horseback ride with a cowboy hero and a rider of Jocko's ability? He told me more about horses and riding in those few minutes than most people probably learn in a lifetime.

Jock's association with Gene Autry goes back to a couple of Columbia features in which he played a heavy and did some stunt work. I talked with Jocko about his years with the Autry organization.

Jock Mahoney: Gene was a good man to work for. I had worked with him on some of his features, and he evidently liked my work as a heavy. In doing fights with Gene, he liked the way I did my actions. When he decided to do "The Range Rider," he called me and Dickie Jones. Our relationship with Gene was always very pleasant, very nice. He was always very helpful, and he was always a gentleman.

As Dick has told you, we didn't tour very much with Gene personally, but we did go out as the stars of "The Range Rider," the series his company produced.

One of the funniest incidents which occurred on a personal appearance with Gene was

Jock Mahoney is seen here as he appeared in "The Range Rider" television series with co-star Dick Jones.

Jock Mahoney and Dick Jones were guest stars at the 1987 Memphis Film Festival. This was the first personal appearance the two performers had made together in many years.

when we were in Los Angeles for the Sheriff's Rodeo at the Coliseum. Gene was introduced by the rodeo announcer. On Gene's entrance his horse Champion did a side-pass, which is beautiful to watch but takes quite a bit of time. Somewhere between the quarter and halfway mark, the announcer apparently decided Gene was taking too much time, and he introduced Dickie and me—The Range Rider and Dick West. Now, you've got to understand that you don't step on your boss's introduction. However, we were introduced and we had to go. So Dick and I do a fast ride up to the quarter mark, wheel our horses, turn, doff our hats to the crowd, and start making our dash to the halfway mark. When we got to Gene, Champion was still doing a side-pass between the quarter and halfway mark in the coliseum. As we went dashing by him, we put our hats over our hearts and said, "Hi, boss!" (laugh) Oh, well, those things happen, I guess. He was a good sport about it; he knew we had to do it.

Alex Gordon has been with Gene Autry for years. As of this writing he is associate producer and research writer for "Melody Ranch Theater," Gene's series on the Nashville Network. Alex is also a noted film historian and is curator of the Gene Autry film collection.

Back in March and April of 1985 Alex wrote a two-part article for *Classic Images* entitled "I Toured with Gene Autry." I found Alex's remembrances of the tours so fascinating that I called him and requested permission to reprint it in this second edition as one of the Gene Autry Scrapbook Clippings. Alex graciously gave his permission and also sent many more rare Gene Autry tour photos for me to include in this chapter.

Advance man Alex Gordon greets Gene upon his arrival in Schenectady, New York, for a personal appearance.

I TOURED WITH GENE AUTRY

by alex gordon

Announcer Charlie Lyons was talking. "And now, here he is — America's Favorite Cowboy, GENE AUTRY!" Handsome and smiling, the screen's original Singing Cowboy stepped out of the wings of New York's CBS Radio Studio into center stage and another *Melody Ranch* broadcast was under way. It was 1950, and my brother Richard and I were sitting in the front row, in the studio audience. Gene Autry was appearing at the Madison Square Garden Rodeo where he holds the all-time attendance record, and during those weeks *Melody Ranch* emanated from the Big Apple. As the show came to an end and the band repeated Gene's theme, "I'm Back in the Saddle Again," the cowboy stepped forward and beckoned to me. Quietly I stood up and, hunched over, approached the stage — "Can you come to my dressing room after the show?" Gene asked. Of course, I said, "Yes."

When I walked in, Gene said he had been reading some of my articles in Autry's Aces, his Fan Club magazine, and asked if I would be interested in handling publicity for his personal appearance tour with the Gene Autry Show in the spring. It meant travelling as advance man for the 85 stop 'one nighters,' two shows in each town or city, then doubling back and covering several places in depth for a week to ten days. Although I had done publicity for movies in England for an independent company, Renown Pictures, I had not travelled in the United States. "Do you think I can do it?" I asked. "I'm not up on plane, train and bus travel in the States." Gene immediately put my fears to rest and told me that his tour manager and co-pilot (of his twin-engined Beechcraft used on tours) Herb Green would call me and send me the itinerary.

During those interim few weeks, my job in New York seemed dull indeed compared to what lay ahead! Travelling with Gene Autry — seeing the Show with all those favorites like Smiley Burnette, Rufe Davis, Gail Davis, Pat Buttram, the Hoosier Hot Shots, the Cass County Boys, Carl Cotner, Frankie Marvin, Champion and Little Champion — visiting virtually every part of the United States — and getting paid for all this — it was a dream come true.

I was assistant to the head booker of Walter Reade Theatres in the East when the call came — I was to join Don Lang, another tour publicist, at the Lord Baltimore Hotel in Baltimore to learn the ropes for a few days before setting off alone to Sioux City, Iowa. As the plane took off and I was on my way for the great adventure, my mind flashed back to World War II London and the events that had led up to all this. It was at the Imperial Cinema on Edgware Road, a small neighborhood house, where I was jammed in a corner seat watching a reissue of Warner Brothers' mammoth Depression Day musical, *Footlight Parade.* The second feature? Gene Autry in *Guns and Guitars.* It was tough to catch a Gene Autry picture in central London — the large circuit houses played them only on Saturday matinees and it was the small cinemas, outlying areas and England's vast industrial areas where the Singing Cowboy was a bigger favorite than Clark Gable and where his films outdrew those of big matinee idols. After *Guns and Guitars*, I would travel for miles by bus whenever an Autry feature was shown, and in 1938 I headed the British Gene Autry Fan Club and published a quarterly magazine, **The Westerner**, with news of Gene's activities. A letter from Gene was the highlight of each issue. The American Club, under Dorothy Crouse, was much larger and published the fine **Autry's Aces**. During the Blitz on London, it was increasingly harder to travel due to bombs and many smaller cinemas being destroyed. I had just gotten out from *South of the Border*, having seen the other feature (Bing Crosby's *East Side of Heaven)* before when that cinema was completely demolished and remember seeing the torn poster fluttering in the wind. The blackout and traffic stoppage from fires meant walking for two hours in the dark to get home after *The Old Barn Dance*. With the paper shortage, it became a problem to continue publishing 5,000 copies of **The Westerner**, and when I went into the Army there was no choice but to stop publication. But one final issue had to come out to explain the situation.

The sergeant at 11th Armored Division stationed at Newmarket prior to going overseas was not sympathetic. All mail was censored because of security regulations, and his staff was not inclined to read 5,000 fan club magazines. In vain I explained that they would have to read only one copy — the others were the same. No way. In desperation, I asked to see the chaplain, always a promising move when problems arose. He took me to a Lieutenant, from where I continued to Captain, Major, Lieutenant-Colonel and finally the Major General in charge of the entire Big Parade. As soon as I saw his Eisenhower-like face as I entered, quaking in my boots I knew I had come to the right place. He understood. Two corporals were assigned to help me mimeograph the copies and stuff them into large envelopes, then to be mailed. "Not snow, nor rain, nor heat, nor gloom of night stays these couriers from the swift completion of their appointed rounds." This famed motto of the United States Postal Service thus applied

Gene is at the controls of his twin-engined Beechcraft which he or his pilot Herb Green flew to personal appearances.

to **The Westerner** magazine, as it would to Gene Autry himself on the road.

"You don't have to join the navy to see the world, just sign up for one of Gene Autry's tours and you'll do plenty of travelling." Pat Buttram may have said it first. Gene was the only Hollywood performer keeping his shows on the road for as long as 85 days without any in-between breaks. Most entertainers figure that 30 days is about all they can take. The Gene Autry Show played everything from the 13,000 seat Coliseum in Indianapolis, the 14,000 at the St. Louis Arena and 15,438 in Toronto, Ontario, to arenas, auditoriums and school gymnasiums with lesser capacity. There was an afternoon and evening show in every location.

Gene Autry and Herb Green would take turns flying the Beechcraft, and several members of the company would take turns flying with Gene. Once I found myself the only passenger, sitting beside him in the cockpit as he finally put the plane on automatic control and moved inside to take a nap. Sequences from all the movie epics I had seen from *Wings to The Dawn Patrol* flashed through my mind as I anxiously waited for his return before another plane, space ship or flying saucer would come rushing towards us from another direction.

When remaining in a town awaiting the show's arrival I would carry a glossy photo of Gene stepping out of his Beechcraft at the local airport for use by the newspaper in time for their deadline. The 'arrival story' would then accompany the picture. In Sioux City, Iowa, one cold January 15th in 1951, eleven-year-old Robert Klingbell had been severely burned in an accident six months earlier and had asked Don Stone, local disc jockey of radio station KSCJ, to see if there was a chance of contacting Gene, as he would be unable to attend the show.

When I heard about it and informed Gene, he immediately agreed to see the boy on arrival; and I handed the arrival picture to the editor of the Sioux City Journal. On the due date, a front page photo showed the Singing Cowboy disembarking from his plane at the airport. In reality, a snow storm had made the flight impossible and Gene drove in from Kansas City, Missouri, just over 300 miles. In addition to visiting Robert, Gene spent time at the home of eight-year-old Celle Weinberg, who was recovering from a blood disease.

A happy ending to the story came a year later when, at Gene's invitation, a fully recovered Robert Klingbell and his family attended the Gene Autry Show as Gene's guests. And so it went in every locality — untiring visits to children's hospitals, or to the homes of crippled kids unable to attend the show — unforgettable memories of faces turning from tears to smiles, of youngsters with a renewed will to live, meeting their hero personally, their dream come true.

"If your youngster has a faith to live by he'll never wander off the trail," Gene would say. "As any cowhand will tell you, it's easier to keep 'em on a well marked trail then to hunt for a maverick once he's wandered away. Even when you find 'em, they don't always want to come back. It's like that with youngsters. Give them a trail to follow — something to guide them when problems come along — and you'll never have a maverick on your hands. Even when the grazing looks greener away from the path, if your kids are sure the path leads to something — even though they can't see the destination — they'll stick to it. It's all in the believing — in having faith. I guess that's the biggest gift any parent can give a child — and it's more valuable than anything money can buy."

Too bad that today's kids, with millions of unhappy runaways, don't have a hero like Gene Autry to look up to.

Many humorous incidents occurred on the Gene Autry tours. These were often due to the weather as the trips were always in late fall and early spring to allow the Singing Cowboy time to film in the summer.

On one occasion Gene piloted his twin-engined Beechcraft into a small airport some distance from his destination. He was grounded there, so he hired an automobile to finish the trip. A blizzard came, and the car was snowbound.

Gene quickly hopped on the only available train of a railroad that touched merely the outskirts of the city in which he was to appear; so he made the last few miles by trolley car. But, he got there, and the show went on as usual.

On another occasion, I met Gene at the airport of Brandon, in Manitoba, Canada, where he arrived piloting his plane, as usual, on the sixth stop of a Canadian tour. After the usual round of hospitals and being welcomed by the mayor, we proceeded to the auditorium, only to find the rest of the cast had not arrived.

By 4:30 there was a packed house of 4,200 people and no cast, no costumes, no music, no props. Suddenly, a telephone call came through the driver of the company bus. It was bogged down on one of Manitoba's muddy roads 100 miles out of Brandon, and the Greyhound bus they had chartered to carry on had also broken down; and even a tractor, hurriedly borrowed from a neighboring farmer, had been stuck in the mud.

Here we had a capacity house and no show! So Herb Green, Gene's co-pilot and tour manager, grabbed a taxi, rushed out to the airport, got Gene's plane out, and flew to the place where the bus had broken down. He picked up members of the cast five at a time and flew them back.

As they trooped wearily into Brandon's arena, they walked directly on stage to 'keep the show rolling.'

Prior to that, for 45 minutes, Gene and Smiley Burnette, who had arrived in his own car/trailer, kept the show going without music or props in impromptu entertainment until the last load arrived!

It was a tremendous task to provide a show for 4,200 fans who otherwise would have been disappointed. It was over at 8:15 instead of 6:30 as scheduled. The evening show was scheduled for 8:30. So, without a break for food and rest, the cast began the next show as soon as the arena had been cleared and the crowds for the evening performance had packed the house once more. And, after that show finished at 11:30, the cast climbed into a chartered bus to proceed for the all night drive to Winnipeg, where they were to perform the next day. "Real troupers, every one of them," Gene commented, never disappointing an audience.

"If it was easy, everyone would be doin' it," was his philosophy. No wonder he has four stars in Hollywood's Walk of Fame, one each for movies, radio, records television. He should have a fifth, for rodeos and personal appearances. No one has matched that record.

I flew from Halifax, Nova Scotia, to Glace Bay, to set up the facilities there, and found myself unable to return due to poor weather at the airport. Rushing by taxi to the train station, I found one about to leave at 9:00 p.m. and asked the clerk at the ticket counter when it would get to Halifax. "At 11," he replied; and I rushed on board, realizing only later that it was a milk train travelling all night, stopping at every little station, and it would not be until 11:00 a.m. the next day when I would be back at my post!

In Washington, D.C. I accompanied Gene to an im-

Gene signs an autograph for a young fan in a children's hospital.

portant rendezvous; he was meeting privately with General Douglas MacArthur. Just before entering the general's quarters, Gene asked me if I would like him to get me the legendary warrior's autograph! He got a signed portrait for himself and one for me, a most unusual event as MacArthur never gave autographs. I have always remembered this with a smile as it was always Gene's autographed photos I treasured, and here he was getting MacArthur!

After more than a year of negotiations, Gene decided to bring his show to England in 1953. I went there three months ahead to coordinate the publicity and other arrangements. The Gene Autry Show was to follow the Sonja Henie Ice Revue for four weeks in the 8000 seat Empress Hall.

It was a real thrill, returning to England for the first time since my emigration in 1947, and Gene Autry received a bigger and more enthusiastic welcome than any other American entertainer before or since. He packed the 8000 seat auditorium twice a day for four weeks whereas most American stars played the 2500 seat London Palladium.

Newspapers and magazines all over the world covered Gene's visit to London, where upon his arrival he was on the "In Town Tonight" program on the BBC. It was his first trip since 1939, when he made his famous record-breaking tour of England, Scotland, and Ireland.

Grace Halsell, special correspondent for several Texas newspapers, flew to London to cover the Gene Autry Show and was a welcome backstage vistor. "When The English Go Wild, It's Either The Queen or Gene Autry" was the headline in the Armarillo Daily News, with a big picture of Gene driving a London taxicab with Little Champion in the back seat, showing him the sights of the city. "Cowboy Gene Autry Wows Kids in London" blazed the Midland Reporter-Telegram, while "Gene Autry and Troupe of Texans Causing Sensation In London" was the word in the Austin Statesman, with a picture of Gene inspecting one of the Queen's guards in front of Buckingham Palace. "Britons Lose Reserve, Cheer Wildly When Gene Autry Arrives In London" headlined the Waco News-Tribune, while "Gene Autry and His Horse, Champion, Take London Along With The Cass County Boys" was the Houston Chronicle's banner line, with a picture of Gene on Champion taking a bow in the ballroom of London's world famous swank Savoy Hotel.

Gene threw a big party for the international press and others at the Savoy Hotel, and 6500 people lined up three hours ahead of time to see Gene ride Champion into the Lobby and then into the ballroom and share sandwiches and champagne at the buffet with the guests.

Representatives from the world's press covered the event, including reporters from Spain, Switzerland and Sweden; and Gene and Mrs. Autry charmed everyone with their friendliness and hospitality. British newspapers referred to them as America's outstanding goodwill ambassadors.

Only three times in London's history has the traffic been stopped on Oxford Street, London's Broadway. The first time was during the first air raid on the world's biggest city, the second time was for the Coronation of the Queen, and the third time was when Gene Autry rode Champion twenty blocks from historic Mable Arch down Oxford Street into Selfridge's, the world's largest department store.

Eighteen thousand people, controlled by police and Scotland Yard, stopped the traffic. Hundreds of buses, taxis, and cars waited while Gene rode along the street amongst them, shaking hands with bus conductors, waving to the cheering crowds, and finally riding into the store into the elevator and up to the third floor where thousands of kids and adults welcomed him to the Gene Autry Corral. There Gene signed 8,759 autographs, books and pictures and posed three hours for countless photographs.

Movie theatres jumped on the bandwagon, and the Rank circuit and other theatres played *Winning of the West*, *Wagon Team*, and other Autry Columbia pictures. The Granada chain revived some of the Republic pictures for their Saturday children's matinees.

Gene entertained 600 kids at a tea party at the Empress Hall and talked to them about making movies; and they were also his guests at the show. At the Children's Hospital in Isleworth, Gene presented a television set to the patients and performed with Champion and Little Champ. Pathe News covered the events. All the kids received comic books. The Gene Autry comic book, three times as thick as the American Dell comic book, was a sensational success in England. Eighty thousand copies were printed for the first edition and sold out within ten days. Many newspapers in England, Scotland and Ireland started running the Gene Autry comic strip. Phillips Records issued the first of a new series of Autry records, with "The Last Round-Up" on one side and "Springtime in the Rockies" on the other.

When Grace Halsell, the young correspondent for the Texas newspapers mentioned earlier in this article, came backstage, she saw the stacks of mail in Gene's dressing room, much of it from the Continent from kids scrawling in French on postal cards that they planned to spend their holidays in England to see their idol.

"I always did want to get some of those French postcards," Gene joked. Gene then told Grace that he and some of the boys in the show were having trouble trying to learn how to use the English money: the shillings, half crown and pounds. "A few of us came over early and were having so much trouble we wondered how the Indians would get along over here. We were really worried about them," Gene said.

Gene pays a visit to the Queen's horse guards during his 1953 British tour.

But Tony White Cloud and his Jemez Indians from New Mexico did better than their paleface brothers. "They keep a sack of nothing but shillings and pay for every bill with just one shilling," Gene told Grace. "One shilling is about 15 cents. Then, when the seller starts screaming, they give him another shilling, and so on until he calms down!"

When I went to the Kensington Palace Hotel to make the room reservations for the show, I was in trouble too. I asked the hotel clerk for a reservation for the Indians, and he told me, "In England, old chap, Indians don't live on reservations!" When I explained that I meant a room reservation and told him that four Indians were coming, he thought I meant Indians from India, maharajas or something, and set aside the hotel's best suites.

The American Indians hardly knew how to act among their lush surroundings; and Chief White Cloud, who makes his own Indian war costumes, lost a button from one suit and called on the hotel phone for a needle. The English hotel clerk thought the Indian was saying 'noodle' and connected with the restaurant. "Noodle," the restaurant man repeated, "you mean soup." The Indian said yes, for his suit. He ended up not with a needle for his suit but with a bowl of noodle soup!

Gene appeared on more radio and television shows than any other American performer of the time. Then there was only one television channel in England and one broadcasting station, with three programs going out over different wavelengths. Gene's one hour show on tv with Champion went over so well that the producer let the show run overtime by half an hour, which was possible only in England where there was no commerical television and, therefore, no sponsor howling if a show ran over. Millions of listeners saw and heard Gene on these programs.

Gene and Mrs. Autry stayed at the Savoy Hotel.

Tony White Cloud and his Jemez Indians accompanied Gene on many of his tours and also appeared with him in the Columbia feature APACHE COUNTRY (1952).

They ran into many American friends there. Ina took the opportunity to see all the famous sights in London: museums, gardens, palaces, and several shows.

Every night after the show, hundreds waited for hours at the stage door of the Empress Hall for Gene, and mobbed him when he entered his taxicab. It nearly always took at least an hour for him to sign all the autographs while he sat in the taxi. Books were passed to him through the window. But, as the fans had come from as far as Scotland and the Continent, he would not disappoint any of them and kept signing until every single one of them was taken care of. Then they would cheer him goodnight.

Now, something about the show itself. As it was not possible, due to the English laws, to present a rodeo in England, as this is considered cruelty to animals, Gene presented the next best thing, the top performers of the rodeo field in a snappy variety show. A twelve piece orchestra in the pit started the program with an overture consisting of a medley of Gene's song hits. Then, to the introduction of "Howdy, Friends and Neighbors," sung by the cast, Gene galloped up a long ramp onto the stage on Champion and introduced the acts.

Barbara Bardo opened the show with her fancy rope tricks, which always won good applause, followed by the Cass County Boys in a medley of their western songs. Then the Indians did their colorful dances, very much appreciated by the English people who had never seen real Indians before.

Pat Buttram then followed with his comedy routines, the Mcquaig Twins sang a popular song medley, Jack and Bobble Knapp did their comedy roping and acrobatics, and then an Italian act, the Cassaveccias, convulsed the crowds with their slapstick comedy in the Keystone Cops style,

Then Gene rode on again, astride Champ, to sing "Back In the Saddle," "Anytime," "Down Yonder," "Mexicali Rose," "Last Roundup," "Cheatin' Heart," "Along the Navajo Trail," "Riders in the Sky," and other hits, having the audience join him in "Rudolph the Rednosed Reindeer," which was as big a hit in England as in the States.

Gene had a cute new routine with this, stopping the song to tell the audience to sing louder, suggesting they would be less shy and bashful if the lights were out. He then called the electrician to douse the lights twice, without avail. Then he drew his gun and shot the four spotlights out. He then said: "All you boys who brought your girl friends can leave me one shilling at the box office when you leave." And after that, the crowd "raised the roof' with their singing!

Finally, Gene sang a selection of Jimmy Kennedy-Michael Carr hits, including "Isle of Capri," "Red Sails In The Sunset," "Harbor Lights," and finishing with a smash rendition of the ever popular "South of the Border."

At this point, Gene usually received many song requests from the audience. One night, a bunch of Texans requested "San Antonio Rose."

Song writer Michael Carr came to see Gene several times, and Gene brought back with him several new songs hits from Carr which he introduced here and recorded.

Following a short intermission, Gene then introduced Carl Cotner, who entertained the audience with his fast fiddling. And the, lovely Gail Davis, who was dressed in her "Annie Oakley" costume from the tv series which was being filmed by Gene's Flying A Productions. Gail sang a medley to great audience response. Rufe Davis then convulsed the crowds with his barnyard noises and songs, and they called him back for many encores.

Then came the high spot of the show. Gene galloped back onto the stage on Champion to present Champ and Little Champ in their many tricks and stunts. The audience loved every minute of it, and at the end of the show, again "raised the roof" when Gene rode Champ right around the arena to shake hands with thousands of kids.

Then he rode back onto the stage, brought back the entire cast for a final bow, and everybody stood while the orchestra played "God Save The Queen," and the British National Anthem.

At first, Gene considered making a tour of the provinces after the London engagement, but it was impossible to find buildings large enough to accommodate the show at such short notice. Therefore, after Herb Green and I flew to Glasgow and visited Birmingham, Edinburgh and other cities to look around, Gene decided to leave the provincial tour for another time.

Also, after the London engagement, there was only a week or so before Gene had to start back for New York and the Madison Square Garden Rodeo. Gene and Mrs. Autry used that week for a visit to several European countries, and had a look-see at France, Spain, Italy, Belgium and Switzerland.

When Gene opened at Madison Square Garden, he received the usual enthusiastic welcome. He always had two appearances at the Rodeo: one with the horses Champion and Little Champion, and one where he sang the songs he made famous, sometimes with colorful lighting and cattle or horse background. On one occasion, the Gene Autry Fan Club presented him with a beautiful gigantic birthday cake, and every member received a piece.

Among the other activities was a special screening of *The Saginaw Trail*, one of Gene's most unusual pictures in which he engages in a sword duel with a French-Canadian villain.

Then it was off to another tour which started in Minneapolis and covered another 85 cities and townships,

Gene and Little Champ entertain a packed house in Burlington, Vermont. Those kids at the footlights are certainly getting a thrill!

for the world's most versatile entertainer. After all, can you think of any other star who was on top for so long in movies, on radio, television, records, rodeos, stage shows, and is active in so many fields?

I think there could be no better finish to this article than to quote you an Editorial which appeared in the Boston Herald of Sunday, August 23, 1953, headed "Ambassador on Horseback."

"One of America's best diplomats is Gene Autry. Through the medium of his radio show, he is doing a great deal to help Great Britain and the United States understand each other. In a very simple way he has helped us to use our own interests to gain understanding. Broadcasting in London, he let our common love of horses bring rodeo lovers and horse show addicts together. For example, the English emphasis is on form, the American on what the horse and rider can do. The English saddle is perfect for a country of hedges and fences which have to be jumped, the American saddle is right for riding the range. Then he let the natural feeling for music bring us together. He presented an English folk song which is an American favorite. Then he sang an American song which was written by two Englishmen who had never left England — "South of the Border." Perhaps Gene Autry, with a guitar and a horse, can do more than pacts and treaties to bring two peoples together."

I'm sure we all agree with the editors of the Boston Sunday Herald. "Ambassador On Horseback" is a good title for Gene Autry — a good will ambassador wherever he goes, whether in a foreign country or in the smallest or largest city in the United States.

He is a man who has worked his way to the top the hard way and a man of whom America will always be proud.

(The preceding article originally appeared in *Classic Images*, March and April, 1985.)

Public recognition for Gene's outstanding work over the years in the area of personal appearance shows came late. It wasn't until April 6, 1987, that the Hollywood Chamber of Commerce honored him with a fifth star on the Hollywood Walk of Fame for his appearances on stage and in rodeos. Gene is the only star to have received five stars on the Walk of Fame. His previous stars were one each for his work in films, radio, television, and recordings.

Gene said at the ceremony, "Well, it means a lot to me. After all, a five-star general is as far as you can go."

Gene and his wife Jackie receive the applause of the audience at the Hollywood Walk of Fame ceremony as Gene is honored with his fifth star.

CHAPTER 10
GENE AUTRY'S
"MELODY RANCH THEATER"

It's "lights, camera, action" on the Cinetel Productions' set for Gene's "Melody Ranch Theater."

In the late summer of 1986 Autry fans everywhere were delightedly surprised to hear that Gene had signed a contract with the Nashville Network to host "Melody Ranch Theater," a ninety-minute weekday series featuring his Republic and Columbia Western films. Who would have guessed that the seventy-nine year old singing cowboy would actively reenter the show business arena! There had been rumors of such a pending deal, but few really expected Gene to get "back in the saddle again."

There were probably several reasons why Gene decided to host the cable TV series. Ground breaking had recently taken place on the Gene Autry Western Heritage Museum, and Gene's added visibility after so many years out of the limelight would perhaps focus and sharpen public interest in the expensive long-range venture. (There were also rumors that proceeds from the series would be used to benefit the museum.) Some people speculated that Gene's competitive juices might have been stimulated because of the popularity of the similar Roy Rogers-Dale Evans series called "Happy Trails Theatre." The most likely reason for Gene's decision to do the series was probably that The Nashville Network "made him an offer he couldn't refuse." It was undoubtedly a good deal from a money standpoint, and Gene has always been receptive to a good deal—after all, he is a businessman par excellence. It could also be guessed that he did it for **all** the above reasons. Whatever, it was a wonderful surprise for fans who had not seen an Autry film on television in decades.

Cinetel Productions of Knoxville, Tennessee, one of the South's largest independent production companies, was contracted to produce the "wrap-arounds." A Cinetel press release announcing the series proudly exclaimed:

AUTRY BACK IN SADDLE AGAIN AT CINETEL

Gene Autry, America's original singing cowboy has returned to television production after a 30-year absence to host "Melody Ranch Theater," a 90-minute program featuring his classic Western movies.

The show will air first on The Nashville Network (TNN) and features openings and closings by Autry who, along with his long-time sidekick, Pat Buttram, shares personal anecdotes about how the films were made, information on co-stars, and significant happenings in Autry's personal life and career.

"Melody Ranch Theater" is produced for TNN by Cinetel Productions in Knoxville, Tenn. All shows are being shot at the Cinetel studios in the Bagwell Communications Center and will be posted in house. Ross K. Bagwell, Jr. directs.

According to Bagwell, "We are delighted to work with Mr. Autry; he is a true professional. We believe the show is significant in that it has been so long since he has been on a regular series, and many features have never been on television before. Mr. Autry's movies are classics; they had a profound impact on all other Western movies."

Cinetel is producing a total of 65 shows featuring such Autry classics as:

-SOUTH OF THE BORDER
-RIDERS IN THE SKY
-THE LAST ROUND-UP
-MULE TRAIN
-SIOUX CITY SUE

During a career which has spanned more than five decades in the entertainment industry, Autry has been the recipient of numerous humanitarian awards. This past January, he was honored by the noted Touchdown Club in Washington, D.C. with the "Hubert T. Humphrey Award," the organization's highest achievement. His career has encompassed all facets of the

David Hall, vice president and general manager of The Nashville Network, and Ross K. Bagwell, Sr., producer of "Melody Ranch Theater," stand on Gene's right and left as he signs the contract for the television series. This photo was taken in Gene's Hollywood office during the summer of 1986.

business—from radio and recording artist to motion picture star, television personality, broadcast executive and major league baseball owner of the California Angels. . . .

The Nashville Network is the entertainment service with a country music emphasis. TNN is now seen in more than 28 million cable television households and is one of the fastest growing network entertainment services. Programming for this 18-hour-a-day, advertiser-supported service is produced by The Nashville Network, a division of Opryland USA, Inc. of Nashville, Tennessee.

Alex Gordon, who has served Gene in several capacities through the years, was assigned the responsibility of associate producer and writer on the "Melody Ranch Theater" series. In an article for *Classic Images* Alex revealed the behind-the-scenes activities for all those involved in the production of the television series:

. . . Can you imagine my feelings when, at promptly 10 AM on Sunday, December 28th, 1986, I sat opposite Gene and his wife Jackie in their twin-engined Hawker-Siddeley jet, with Pat Buttram occupying the fourth seat, heading for Knoxville, Tennesse, where the introductions were to be taped? "The Autry Airline always leaves on time," Jackie Autry had promised. And so it was, with pilot Michael Veta taking off for the smoothest ride I had experienced in years.

. . . Knoxville is hard to reach by commercial airlines as you have to break the flight in Atlanta or Nashville, but the Autry Airlines made it direct. The principals of Cinetel Productions, Ross Bagwell, Sr. and Jr., the latter also the director, were on hand to greet us. Stephen Land, Cinetel's public relations VP, was with them; and a large limousine was to take us to the luxurious Hyatt Regency Hotel.

. . . Our routine was to be as follows: Each morning after an early breakfast we met in the lobby of the hotel at 8:15, to be whisked by limousine and its very able and courteous driver, Joe, to the Bagwell Communications Center, a modern studio complex with two large sound stages and the latest in film and video taping equipment for shooting and editing.

On arrival, some fifteen minutes after leaving the hotel, Gene and Jackie Autry went into their large suite for change of clothing and make-up, while Pat Buttram had his own accommodation complete with a glamorous brunette make-up artist.

. . . Starting promptly, and well before the scheduled 9 AM call, three video cameras would cover the picturesque set, consisting of a ranch house interior with fireplace and large pictures of Gene, Pat Buttram, Smiley Burnette, and other Autry movie cast members on the walls. Gene sat on one chair and Pat Buttram in another. Mostly without cue cards, except for a key name or two per picture, the shooting began.

For the introduction Gene welcomed the viewers to "Melody Ranch Theater," the title of the show, then asked Pat what the picture that day was to be. Pat gave the title, and they discussed the cast and director, after

Gene and Pat Buttram discuss the day's taping schedule with director Ross Bagwell, Jr. (holding papers) as producer Ross Bagwell, Sr. looks on.

Gene and Pat are ready for another day of taping on the "Melody Ranch Theater" set at Cinetel Productions.

which Gene and Pat mentioned a few key points of interest before the picture bagan.

In the middle break, they commented on what had gone before, which prompted stories and reminiscences about players, shooting incidents, locations, action and songs; and, at the finale, they summed up and Gene answered a few questions, time permitting, pertaining to that particular film.

Due to their utter professionalism, Gene and Pat ran through the wraparounds so smoothly that each day they completed many more than originally scheduled, resulting in the final completion of the entire enterprise a full four days earlier than expected.

I had prepared written material for each movie with some reminder information about the casts and credits and stories about the shooting of each picture and other newsworthy events that might provide fodder for the introduction, middle and end breaks. Apart from a few minor cues, there was no need for concern; and Gene's amazing memory conjured up stories that could have provided more than twice the required footage.

. . . The return flight to Los Angeles by Autry Airlines was again a smooth one and very pleasurable. . .

When I phoned Alex Gordon in the fall of 1987 to ask his permission to excerpt the preceding article, he mentioned that plans were well underway for a follow-up twenty-six episodes of "Melody Ranch Theater." Alex said that Autry leading lady, Ann Rutherford, was scheduled to be a guest on one of the programs, as were musician-composer Pee Wee King, director George Sherman, and Roy Rogers. Other guests were still being scheduled for the October taping sesson.

As this book goes to press, The Nashville Network has commercial spots on "Melody Ranch Theater" booked "solid" well into the future. The press and public response has also been positive. Older fans undoubtedly view the shows with a sense of nostalgia; new fans are being created as younger generations discover the singing cowboy for the first time. The Autry magic just keeps rolling along.

CHAPTER 11

THE GENE AUTRY WESTERN HERITAGE MUSEUM

Frederic Remington, "The Cheyenne," Bronze. 1901

PHOTO COURTESY
THEODORE ROOSEVELT COLLECTION
HARVARD COLLEGE LIBRARY

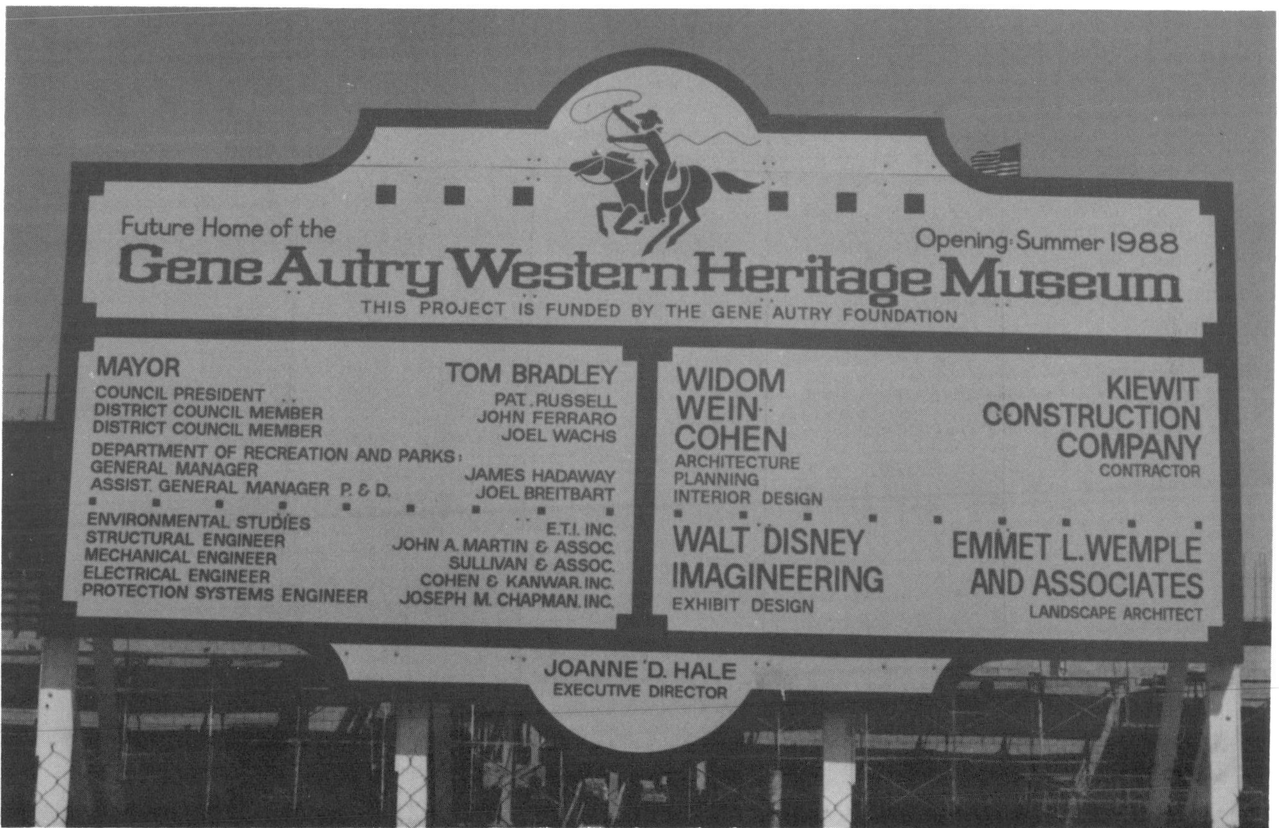

Gene Autry: *You know, folks, building the Gene Autry Western Heritage Museum has been an exciting project for me, and I hope each of you will visit when you're in Los Angeles. This world-class museum with its historical artifacts is my legacy to you and to your children of what the history of the West was really like.*

With those words Gene Autry introduced his Western Heritage Museum to viewers of "Melody Ranch Theater" on the Nashville Network. The museum has been an Autry dream for many years. Gene has commented, "I have always wanted to exhibit and interpret the heritage of the West, to show how it has influenced America and the world."

The planning stage, alone, was a long-time project. Finding the right location, securing the blessing of the city fathers, negotiating all the legal involvements, finding the right personnel to design, build, and staff the museum, procuring the artifacts—all of these details and a million more had to be resolved as the plans for the museum unfolded.

A fact sheet released in 1986 stated that the museum (when completed in 1988) will be "one of the most comprehensive repositories of American West history in the world. Collections will include historic firearms, common tools, conveyances, equipment, clothing, toys, games, and furnishings of both famous and lesser-known people of the Western landscape. Fine art works by such artists as Frederic Remington and Charles Russell will be included."

The museum's mission is both cultural and educational, with exhibits being only one aspect of its function. James H. Nottage, the museum's curator, has stated, "The purpose is to entertain and educate. . . . We expect to enable the visitor to see his place in history, placing contemporary life and personal experience into historic perspective, and to enhance his ability to understand the present."

Artifacts that relate to the real, everyday lives and occupations of people who helped settle the American West are the primary focus of the museum's collections. The West, in museum terms, is an area broadly interpreted to encompass the breadth of the geographical West from Mississippi to California.

The history of the American West from the early explorations of the Spanish Conquistadors and Lewis and Clark to the present day is the focus of the $25 million Gene Autry Western Heritage Museum scheduled to open in June, 1988. The museum chronicles the cultural and historical legacy of America's Western heritage. Plans are to create a comprehensive repository of Western lore and will include internationally renowned collections, as well as artifacts of both the famous and lesser known inhabitants of the west. The museum is a California nonprofit, public-benefit organization established by the Autry Foundation which will fund the construction. The museum will be located in the Pine Meadows section of Griffith Park immediately adjacent to the Greater Los Angeles Zoo and will be situated on 13 acres. The tri-level structure's architecture will be an expression of the Spanish-Mexican Southwest missions in a contemporary context.

GENE AUTRY
WESTERN
HERITAGE
MUSEUM

As a counterpoint to the "real" West, the museum plans to also depict the West of romance and imagination as created by artists, authors, filmmakers, television, radio, and advertising.

As of this writing (fall, 1987) the museum's 12,000-plus collection is an "amalgamation of Autry's personal treasures and the collection of an additional 12,000 artifacts brought together by donations and purchases." Development of the collection is "ongoing with treasures of local, regional, and national significance sought to add to the museum's already important resources."

The museum is being located in the Pine Meadows section of Griffith Park in Los Angeles. The tri-level,

THE SPIRITS Seven permanent galleries each reflecting the powerful influence of the West on the American conscience provide a "walk through history."

SPIRIT OF DISCOVERY depicts the west as it was seen for the first time by those who came to call it home. Clothing, equipment, and tools used to explore and live in this new land combine with art and graphics to tell the story.

SPIRIT OF OPPORTUNITY will reveal the promise and expectation that beckoned the early western settlers — gold, land, and glory. The experiences of the trappers, traders, merchants, craftsmen, and their families will be documented by personal belongings, clothing, and tools.

SPIRIT OF CONQUEST defines the struggle between man and nature, the hardship and abuses faced by these pioneers in a vast new terrain. Indian conflicts, the buffalo slaughter, and the conquest of the continent by telegraph, stage, and rail are presented with the drama that characterizes this colorful period. A stagecoach, railroad materials, and equipment of the Indian and soldier will be featured.

SPIRIT OF IMAGINATION captures myths and fantasy images of the West interpreted on the silver screen, radio, television, and in advertising that fired the imagination of generations of Americans. It provides a history of Westerns, the great stars and supporting casts.

SPIRIT OF COMMUNITY focuses on the interrelationships within families, social groups, and towns. Toys and games, fire engines and quilting interpret how peoples banded together for protection and socializing. Community and conflict are depicted in gambling, saloons, law, and order objects.

SPIRIT OF THE COWBOY traces his Spanish roots and the history of the man who rode the western plains. The sport of rodeo is interpreted from its origin to present day; a collection of cowboy spurs, clothing, saddles, and branding irons from the 17th Century to the nineteen eighties will provide new insight into his life and times.

SPIRIT OF ROMANCE relates to generations of writers, artists, and performers who have nurtured the color and romance of our Western heritage. The image is expressed in the writings of Owen Wister and Teddy Roosevelt, the art of Charles Russell and Frederic Remington, and the wild west shows of Buffalo Bill Cody.

CHANGING EXHIBITS Two special galleries will host changing exhibits on a wide spectrum of topics that define western history and culture. Significant artifacts and works of art from other museums and private collections will explore the western experience in an ongoing spirit of discovery.

Ground breaking for the Gene Autry Western Heritage Museum was held on November 12, 1986. Many Los Angeles dignitaries and old friends of Gene Autry were in attendance. Pictured here at the ceremony are (left to right) Monte Hale (Monte's wife, Joanne Hale, is the museum's executive director), Pat Buttram, Bob Steele, Gene, and Sunset Carson.

139,436 square foot structure will "express the Spanish-Mexican heritage of the Southwest in a contemporary context." In a news release on November 12, 1986 (ground-breaking day for the museum), the planned architecture of the museum was described as "a synthesis of concepts":

The architecture for the Gene Autry Western Heritage Museum is a synthesis of the traditions of Spain, the missions of Father Junipero Serra, and the early plaza concepts of the West.

"The overall design intent is for the building to become a modern extension of the museum program, the artifacts which it houses, the architectural heritage of the West, and the site itself," explained Chester A. Widom, founding partner of Widom, Wein and Cohen, museum architect.

It was designed to encompass a permanent and changing gallery exhibit space, curatorial areas, and administrative offices, a 250-seat theater, a research library, an education center, and a small cafe. The 139,000 square foot museum has been established by the Autry Foundation, a non-profit charitable organization, to collect, preserve and interpret the history and artifacts of the American West.

The museum's basic plan emerges from two plazas which will serve as orientation points for visitors. The main exterior plaza is highlighted by a landmark contemporary adaptation of a traditional mission bell tower and will be bounded by the gallery, theater, education center, museum store and cafe.

The second interior plaza establishes the central thematic space. A 140-foot long mural of the cultures and people of the West will introduce visitors to the exhibition content they may explore in the various galleries. A botanical garden displaying various environments of the West also will be a feature in the interior plaza area.

The entrance to the museum gallery will be placed symmetrically on the building facade that faces the park through the main plaza. A monumental, free-standing glazed ceramic tile arch, deriving its shape from a circle overlayed on a square, is a key focal point.

"Materials planned for the museum are as historically grounded in early California architecture as the forms to be used," Widom explained.

Hand-worked cement stucco, traditional red tile roofing and glazed ceramic tile trim have been designated as standard elements. The various entrances draw historical reference to the wood and steel forms in the development of the Southern California palette.

The entire aesthetic is symbolic of the "Southern California West, yet is not slavish to the recreation of a specific style," Widom concluded.

The Gene Autry Western Heritage Museum is underway in Los Angeles! This photo was taken in July of 1987. The tall structure on the right will be the bell tower at the main exterior plaza. The zoo parking sign currently directs the public to the nearby Griffith Park Zoo.

The Autry Foundation referred to in the news release is a charitable trust established in 1980 through the estate of Gene's first wife, Ina Mae. The Foundation provides for the construction, operation, and maintenance of the museum. The museum represents a Foundation investment of approximately twenty-five million dollars.

And so the Gene Autry legacy to the world is again enhanced in a manner that will entertain and instruct future generations.

COWBOY

A trust to keep:
A boy to lead
A man to forge
A code to set
A mind to mold,

And all the while
Those cows to move
And heroines to save
And Indians to tame
And villains to undo
And songs to sing beneath the stars.

No wonder you got up so early
And your work was never done.

NR

RIDIN' DOWN THE CANYON

And so it seems appropriate to conclude this volume as Gene ended most of his films—ridin' down the canyon with his sidekick and heroines next to him and a cowboy chorus in the background. You can bet the title song is on their lips.

SELECTED BIBLIOGRAPHY

Autry, Gene, with Mickey Herskowitz. *Back in the Saddle Again.* New York: Doubleday, 1978.

Calio, Jim. "Bio." *People* (May 26, 1980).

"Cowboy in Clover." *Time* (August 18, 1947).

"Cowboy Tycoon." *Newsweek* (January 6, 1964).

"Double Mint Ranch." *Time* (January 15, 1940).

"Gene Autry Special, The." KPLZ Radio, Seattle (January 1, 1981).

Gordon, Alex. "I Toured with Gene Autry." *Classic Images* (March-April 1985).

———. "With Gene Autry as He Hits the Trail to *Melody Ranch Theater." Classic Images* (March 1987).

Hake, Theodore, L., and Robert D. Cauler. *Sixgun Heroes.* Iowa: Wallace-Homestead Book Company, 1976.

Heide, Robert, and John Gilman. *Cowboy Collectibles.* New York: Harper & Row, Publishers, 1982.

Horwitz, James. "In Search of the Original Singing Cowboy." *Rolling Stone* (October 25, 1973).

Johnson, Alva. "Tenor on Horseback." *Saturday Evening Post* (September 2, 1939).

Knauth, Percy. "Gene Autry, Inc." *Life* (June 28, 1948).

Oney, Steve. 'The Last Roundup." *California* (November 1982).

Osborne, Jerry. *55 Years of Recorded Country-Western Music.* Phoenix, Arizona: O'Sullivan, Woodside and Company, 1976.

Rothel David. *The Great Show Business Animals.* San Diego: A.S. Barnes and Company, Inc., 1980.

———. Personal Interview with Gene Autry, audio recorded. Los Angeles (January 6, 1977).

———. *The Singing Cowboys.* San Diego: A.S. Barnes and Company, Inc., 1978.

———. *Those Great Cowboy Sidekicks.* New Jersey and North Carolina: Scarecrow Press and World of Yesterday, 1984.

Variety (Files from 1934 through 1955).

FILMOGRAPHY INDEX

David Rothel

About the Author:

David Rothel's lifelong fascination with show business began with frequent visits to his local movie theater, where he followed the adventures of his favorite Western heroes. He has since gone from youthful observer to performer, producer, director, teacher, and published authority on various aspects of popular entertainment. His first book, *Who Was That Masked Man?: The Story of the Lone Ranger,* received enthusiastic reviews, was a main selection of the Nostalgia Book Club, and has been expanded and revised. Mr. Rothel's second book was *The Singing Cowboys,* an informative, back-in-the-saddle examination of the B musical Western films. Next came *The Great Show Business Animals,* a charming work that reflects Mr. Rothel's ability to capture the spirit and analyze the impact of show business phenomena. *Those Great Cowboy Sidekicks* is an in-depth examination of such fondly remembered comic character actors as George "Gabby" Hayes, Smiley Burnette, and Andy Devine. His most recent publication is *The Roy Rogers Book,* a reference-trivia-scrapbook companion to *The Gene Autry Book.* Mr. Rothel's writing is characterized by thoroughness of research, warmth, wit, and understanding.

Other fine books from

EMPIRE PUBLISHING, INCORPORATED

THE ROY ROGERS BOOK, a reference, trivia, scrapbook by David Rothel, is a companion volume to THE GENE AUTRY BOOK. A best seller at the Roy Rogers-Dale Evans Museum and with Western film fans, the book presents everything you ever wanted to know about "The King of the Cowboys." You'll find a personal interview by the author, a filmography, discography, TV log, memorabilia, fan magazine and news clippings, around 200 photos, and much more. Available in both hardcover ($25) and softcover ($20), this huge 233 page volume is printed on heavy glossy stock. Please add $2.00 for postage and handling.

IRON EYES CODY, THE PROUD AMERICAN by Iron Eyes Cody and Marietta Thompson is the life story of the Keep America Beautiful, tear-in-the-eye proud American, Iron Eyes Cody. Told in words and beautiful pictures, Iron Eyes' story includes his long Hollywood career (with such personalities as Cecil B. DeMille, Gene Autry, Roy Rogers, and Ben Johnson), his world-wide personal appearances, his dedication to civic and community work, and his concern for the environment through his association with the Keep America Beautiful organization. A truly great American, Iron Eyes Cody has lived a fascinating life, and now you can read about it in this beautiful book. In hardcover only, the 142-page volume is printed on heavy glossy stock and is available for only $18.00 plus $2.00 shipping.

COWBOY SHOOTING STARS by John A. Rutherford and Richard B. Smith, III is the ideal booklet for the Western film fan. This softcover, 100-page volume contains a check list of all titles of those thrilling, never-to-be-forgotten B-Western films and their cowboy stars. In addition, you'll find the year each film was released, the production company, and the running time. Here is the perfect way to keep track of the films you have seen and those that you want to see. Profusely illustrated with photos from many of the films, this popular book is just $7.50 plus $1.00 for shipping and handling.

LASH LaRUE, THE KING OF THE BULLWHIP, written by Chuck Thornton and David Rothel includes almost everything you ever wanted to know about the man in black who rode fast and lashed his way across the silver screen. Over 150 photographs, complete filmography, personal comments and interviews highlight this book which is available in softcover for only $15.00 plus $2.00 for shipping and handling.

DON'T LOOK UP -- THE REAL STORY BEHIND THE VIRGINIA UFO SIGHTINGS is a day-by-day account of the strange "goings on" in the western Virginia skies where more than 1,000 UFO sightings were recorded in less than a 12-month period of time. This book can be yours to examine for $12.00 plus $1.00 for postage and handling.

TOM MIX HIGHLIGHTS by Andy Woytowich is a 52-page book with 40 illustrations. Tom Mix's life story is told in brief storybook form. The characters are drawn to a perfect likeness by a lifelong fan of Tom Mix. The cover is in beautiful color. This book is available for only $7.95 plus $1.00 postage and handling.

Empire Publishing, Incorporated has been in business for 15 years and is ready to serve YOU. Orders may be placed by phoning 1-919-427-5850, or you may write to: Empire Publishing, Incorporated, Route 3, Box 83, Highway 220 South, Madison, North Carolina 27025. Book dealer inquiries are welcomed. Please be sure to include the required amount for postage and handling when you place your order.

Coming soon from Empire Publishing:

THE ALLAN "ROCKY" LANE BOOK by Chuck Thornton and David Rothel